A BIRD'S-EYE VIEW OF CAMBERWELL looking north over East Dulwich towards Goose Green and Peckham Rye Station; Lordship Lane is on the extreme left of the picture and Barry Road on the right. *Aerofilms & Aero Pictorial Ltd.*

VICTORIAN SUBURB

VICTORIAN SUBURB

A STUDY OF THE GROWTH OF CAMBERWELL

by

H. J. DYOS

Professor of Urban History
in the University of Leicester

with a Foreword by

SIR JOHN SUMMERSON

LEICESTER
UNIVERSITY PRESS
1986

First published in 1961 by
Leicester University Press

Second impression 1966
Third impression 1973
Fourth impression 1977
Fifth impression 1986

TO MY WIFE

OLIVE

WITH LOVE AND GRATITUDE

ISBN 0 7185 1126 3

Printed and bound in Great Britain by
Antony Rowe Ltd, Chippenham

FOREWORD

BY SIR JOHN SUMMERSON

I WRITE this in a house built in 1849 and through the window the life of a London suburb takes its Sunday-afternoon course. This is not Camberwell but an ordinary part of north London which has had its ups and downs and is now perhaps a little on the up. It is a Victorian suburb and in that it shares some major historic factors with Camberwell. Every word I have read in Dr Dyos' text has illumined either by analogy or contrast the formation of my own local scene. I can claim to know my suburb pretty well. On paper I know all the people who lived in my row and the row opposite a hundred years ago; I know (through means familiar enough to Dr Dyos) their names and occupations, the children and servants they had and something of their wealth. In two cases, and only two, traces of their personalities survive in published works or works of art. They are all dead and turned, I suppose, mostly to clay by now and as a matter of fact they had all left the district before they died. There were not many funerals at our church in those days: people came here young and moved on.

I know far less about the people who live here now—I doubt if I could even make a complete list of their names and I do not think they would like it if I tried to find out any more. The Registrar General and the Inland Revenue know but will not tell—at least, not for a hundred years. But I see these people moving about, I see their conformities and oddities of gait and dress, I never shut my ears to gossip and one way and another I have a fairly lively picture of life in the suburb of to-day. What I find perpetually haunting and fascinating is the bare fact of these people living in an environment which they have not made and which was unknowingly prepared for them by the dead skulls and finger-bones in the cemeteries; and of being, in spite of themselves, formed or inflected by it. Across the road, three children are just now trying to get into one little toy car. They are in and the wheels trundle over York paving which no local authority could afford to buy and lay in these days. Over their heads a beautifully graceful Robinia is coming into leaf—perhaps for the hundred and eleventh time on that spot. The vicar turns the corner (where the garden wall collapsed last year) and walks leisurely and seriously towards his church, remembering perhaps how small his congregation was this morning, how big is his fabric and how cracked. Seeing him, I reflect that his church is large less because of Victorian piety than because a building estate of the 'fifties would never 'go' without a good big church. The church set the tone—a sound middle-class tone. But the striking thing is that the church is still there; its spire and its bell invite; and people go to church—not in great numbers, it is true, certainly not now for the sake of social propriety and only, I surmise, in a few cases because of a convinced acceptance of the thirty-nine articles. They go because they need roots, attachment through symbols, and of these the visible fabric of the church itself is not the least.

This suburb of mine is not a period piece. The old houses hereabouts are part of the gross tissue of London, just as are the pre-war flats which I can see down the road (the marks where the oil-bomb crashed into them in 1941 invisibly mended) or the post-war Council flats beyond them or, indeed, the synagogue which is being built on the site of the old vicarage. It is a most ordinary suburb. But like so many ordinary things it holds a mystery—the mystery of its origins and its first makers and denizens and this is, to some minds, a mystery that rankles and goads. Why did they do it like that, with what ambition and for what rewards? On what precedents and with what illumination of mind—or if with none, why none?

Architectural qualities have something to do with this. My own house is of that peculiarly imbecile kind which is architecturally half a 'villa', the whole villa being an ideal to be attained only when my semi-detached neighbour and I conspire to paint our stucco the same colour in the same year. The totality would have a faintly Italian-rustic air like (but not very like) something in a Claude landscape. The window ornaments however are Grecian. They come from the choragic monument of Thrasyllus at Athens but have been filtered through Stuart and Revett and (I suspect) the *Practical Builder* and probably a good many apprentice tracings into the bargain. Quite a substantial thesis could be written on the social-aesthetic snobberies which all these devices represent and on what the builder of my house (a Devon carpenter who made good in London) thought he was doing when he used them. Doubtless he conceived this to be 'taste' and believed that taste was marketable; or perhaps he really liked his work. I do not dislike it myself. But there is no great question of art here. The problems are the larger ones of human behaviour, of things merely happening within a society growing too fast for its mind and making, hand over fist, without creating. This absence of creation is at once the horror and the fascination of the suburb. It is the 'planless sprawl'—that lazy platitude of town-planning theorists—and as such may be dismissed out of hand without being understood. But it is also something which really happened and is really there and was made by real people and for which there are brutish, involuntary but still human causes if you can discover them. If the study of modern man and his environment is worth anything they are worth discovering.

Suburbia has many aspects and to take one suburb and scrutinize it, take it apart and minutely describe its components, is to learn—and to teach—about suburbia itself. To explain one part is to unlock the whole. This is what Dr Dyos has done in his handling of Camberwell and so far as I know he is the first to do it. It is true that we have had some intelligent books on suburbia in general and on various London areas in the last ten or fifteen years; but in detailed and penetrating analysis of a single nineteenth-century episode I rather think that Dr Dyos leads the way.

Much as I have enjoyed the text of this book I think I have enjoyed the notes as much, because of their illumination of the literature of this extraordinarily complex subject. How grandly this literature begins, with the stately Lysons surveying a suburbia where groves still were groves and the villa still roused an echo of Laurentum! After him come the view-peddlers with their ludicrous genteelisms, and the worthy local gentlemen who spent life-times of scholarly retirement writing about the suburbs of their birth or choice. But most of this is before Victoria and it is with her reign that the difficulties begin. Thereafter the student has to grope and burrow in a mountain of forgotten print or go skirmishing after private papers already perhaps strung up on their way to be pulped. Defunct magazines, the files of local newspapers, Reports of Select Committees, old railway-guides, chance references in memoirs and novels, census returns and long out-dated text books on the law of property—this is the printed treasure of the suburban historian. As for original documents, the business papers of that grand motivator, that confidently bowler-hatted field-marshal, the speculative builder, are the prize trophy and here it seems that Dr Dyos has been singularly fortunate. Here at Camberwell we can see the whole thing happening, understand the mechanics. The 'suburban sprawl' is no longer a figure of speech; it becomes something actual. This is important. The actuality of things forgotten (especially, perhaps, things despised) in the recent past, the truth under the surface of late assumptions, the seeing for the first time as *historic* what has only lately been forgotten as *contemporary*, lies very near the roots of creative thought and the formation of new attitudes.

JOHN SUMMERSON

London, N.W.3.

PREFACE

THE Victorian suburb must not only be one of the most obvious but also one of the darkest corners of English social history. In some respects we are more familiar with the physical and social structure of Roman Britain than we are with the apparatus of suburban society in Victorian England. There are, it is true, innumerable books whose titles would suggest the very reverse. But the authors of these books—mostly Victorians themselves—mainly addressed themselves to the archives in the Public Record Office or the Parish Chest, and as a result scarcely ever emerged from the eighteenth century. Practically every suburb of Victorian London, for instance, has been chronicled in this way, some of them by more than one author, and their special or curious aspects have been described by hundreds more. Those writers who did look more narrowly at the contemporary history of some local community were usually content to remain topographers, or compilers of municipal statistics, or biographers of local worthies. Nor has this tradition wholly disappeared.

The notion that the recent past and everyday life are somehow not history is still prevalent, and it is not surprising therefore that the suburb should not have become an historical entity. Its true beginnings have probably appeared too recent, its landscape too ugly, and its social arrangements too ordinary to capture the serious attention of historians preoccupied with grander themes. It is understandable that to those embarrassed with historical riches the Victorian suburb must look rather small change, but in recent years there have been some welcome signs of fresh—if only incidental—interest being taken in the Victorian suburb. Mr Michael Robbins, for instance, included a brief examination of some of the general influences shaping the modern suburb in his *Middlesex* (1953); Professor W. Ashworth's *The Genesis of Modern British Town Planning* (1954) appraised the rôle of the suburb in the context of the development of a tradition of town planning; and under Dr F. H. W. Sheppard's hand, Volume XXVI of *The Survey of London: The Parish of St Mary Lambeth, Pt. II: Southern Area* (1956) has not only assessed the architecture of a particular suburb of mainly Victorian interest but has suggested the broad outlines of a typical piece of suburban development. Numerous articles and lectures and a handful of doctoral theses provide evidence of the same kind.

It nevertheless remains true that the history of the expansion of suburban England is badly neglected. How, one wonders, did suburbs become such a characteristic feature of modern life? Who built them? Who financed the enterprise? What form did they take in bricks and mortar? Who inhabited them? This book has been written in an attempt to answer such questions as these by exploring the growth of a single metropolitan suburb, Camberwell, during the period of its most rapid growth in the nineteenth century, and principally during its last forty years.

This study has arisen primarily out of some research I was most fortunate to have been able to do between 1949 and 1952, under the genial supervision of Mr H. L. Beales (from whom I learnt more than I then realised), in preparing a thesis on *The Suburban Development of Greater London, South of the Thames, 1836–1914*, which was approved for the degree of Ph.D. by the University of London in 1952. Though this was an essential preliminary to the present study, no recognizable portion of the original thesis has been incorporated in these pages. Here the intention has been to examine in greater detail, and in some new ways, the course and phases of suburban expansion in a more limited and more manageable area. Even so the task has been a formidable one. It would, indeed, have been impossible but for the kindness and generous help of many people in giving me access to documents in their possession and, in some cases, to the loan of them, or in giving me valuable information. My grateful thanks are due to the following: Miss I. Darlington, Librarian and Archivist, Members' Library, County Hall, London, and her assistants; L. J. Hobby, Esq., and Miss J. Gibbs, both formerly of the Minet Library, Camberwell; the Town Clerk, Borough of Camberwell; the Directors of the Temperance Permanent Building Society, Abbey National Building Society, Peckham Permanent Building Society, Lambeth Building Society, Camberwell & South London Building Society, and the Phoenix Assurance Company Ltd.; the Trustees of the

Estate of the late Edward Yates; A. J. Carpenter, Esq., of the Minet Estate Office; The Estates Governors of Dulwich College; The British Land Company Ltd.; Messrs Crosby, Lockwood & Son Ltd., publishers; Messrs Gustavus Thompson, Saxton & Morgan, solicitors; Messrs Strutt & Parker, Lofts & Warner, surveyors; Messrs H. M. Grellier & Son, surveyors; the Clergy and Ministers of Religion of Camberwell; H. J. Andrews, Esq.; Hubert A. Robertson, Esq.; Cecil B. Tubbs, Esq.; Mrs M. Forbes, G. Pirie, Esq., R. Orange, Esq., and the late W. Margrie, Esq.

I am also much indebted to Mr L. Thorpe, who willingly gave so much time in making the scale drawings, and to Pyramid Press Ltd. for making available the block for the street plan. My special thanks are due to the Research Board of the University of Leicester for grants which greatly helped in meeting the costs of research. I am indebted, too, to the Editor of *The Town Planning Review* for permission to reproduce in Chapters I and II parts of an article which appeared in that journal in 1954. I am grateful, too, to some of my academic colleagues for their friendly and helpful comments on an early draft of the book: to Dr H. P. R. Finberg, under whose editorship this study had originally been planned to appear in the series of *Occasional Papers in English Local History* (though it had grown too large to allow this); to Professor A. G. Pool, and to Professor J. Simmons, who was most helpful in the preparation of the book for the press. It is a special pleasure, too, to be able to record my most grateful thanks to Sir John Summerson for his magnanimity in writing the Foreword.

It is also a rare pleasure to be able to acknowledge the public spirit and splendid generosity of the Camberwell Borough Council and the London County Council in making grants towards the cost of publication: my warmest thanks are due to them.

I am conscious above all of the incomparable debt of gratitude I owe to my wife. Her constant unselfishness and patience during some very difficult days were a very great encouragement to me and are the main reasons why the book was ever finished.

H. J. DYOS

Leicester, April 1959.

PREFACE TO FIFTH IMPRESSION

H. J. DYOS died in 1978 but his pioneering study of Camberwell, first published in 1961, is still in demand. Urban historians will be delighted with this fifth reprinting of a work much admired as the first systematic account of the origins of a modern suburb. Although Dyos had been primarily concerned with rescuing the suburb from historical neglect, his analysis contributed greatly to our understanding of how a city grows. There are comparable analyses in other countries, notably Sam Bass Warner's reconstruction of the process of growth in Boston in *Streetcar Suburbs* (1962), whilst Bernard Barrett's investigation of the evolution of Melbourne's industrial area in *The Inner Suburbs* (1971) makes even more extensive comparisons possible. But in Britain it was the Dyos approach that continued to inspire and challenge researchers in other suburban territories. During the 1970s a genre of urban history emerged reflecting the enthusiasm Dyos had for explicating the rationality of the urban process. Outstanding examples were F. M. L. Thompson's major profile of *Hampstead: Building a Borough* (1974) and David Cannadine's work on the Birmingham suburb of Edgbaston in a larger study of *Lords and Landlords: the Aristocracy and the Towns 1774–1967* (1980). Other contributions have come from architectural historians, from the elegant general survey of the suburban environment in Donald Olsen's *The Growth of Victorian London* (1976) to the details of residential estates accumulated by the *Survey of London* volumes on the once suburban citadels of Kensington. The history of estate developments has also become a means of charting the topography of suburban change as the recent parish volumes of the *VCH Middlesex* show. In addition, historical geographers have both widened suburban horizons, taking in the urban fringe, and added to the history of suburban developments in the outer metropolis and provincial towns. The latter are represented by essays witnessing to *The Rise of Suburbia* (1982), edited by F. M. L. Thompson, who looks forward to a new future for this theme in urban history. We shall never know what Dyos intended himself for his promised second volume on the social history of Camberwell. He did take up other themes, however, relating to the urban fabric, including more on speculative housebuilders, in particular the South London builder, Edward Yates, and a selection from these writings is available in a collection edited by David Cannadine and myself as *Exploring the Urban Past* (1982). His volume on Camberwell remains nevertheless an invaluable guide to the exploration of a London district which has much yet to tell about the antecedents of our contemporary suburbanity.

Leicester, March 1986 DAVID A. REEDER

CONTENTS

Chapter V

THE BUSINESS OF BUILDING THE SUBURB

Chapter VI

THE PROVISION OF AMENITIES

Chapter VII

THE CHARACTER OF THE SUBURB

ILLUSTRATIONS

TABLES

CHAPTER I

THE MEANING OF THE SUBURB

The Demographic Trend

TO study the suburb is to examine one of the growing points of Victorian society. The vast increase in the size of the population of the country in the nineteenth century meant that the towns in particular had to grow extremely fast to accommodate the rising numbers, and the rapid economic development of the country which was taking place at the same time accelerated the process still more. Thus, the growth of the population of England and Wales from less than 9 millions in 1801 to practically 18 millions in 1851, and to about 32½ millions in 1901, was bound to mean for many places extremely rapid rates of expansion, and from the beginning of the nineteenth century towns of all sizes recorded rapid rates of growth.[1] In 1801 less than 17 per cent. of the population lived in towns of over 20,000 inhabitants, including London, which accounted for nearly 10 per cent. of the total population. Except for the metropolis (which had a population of about 865,000), no other town contained more than 100,000 persons, and a mere handful came within the bracket 50,000-100,000. By the end of the nineteenth century well over half the population was contained in towns of over 20,000 people, and it was in the largest towns of all that the most rapid developments were occurring, especially in the second half of the century. By 1881 47 towns contained over 50,000 inhabitants and within twenty years this number had grown to 77, of which one-third contained between 100,000 and 250,000 inhabitants. There were by 1901 9 towns which were larger even than this, and among these Greater London ranked as a megalopolis of over 6½ millions.

It was in this group of large towns and cities that the suburban trend, which had been noticeable since the 1860s, was becoming most marked from the 1880s onwards. The outer ring of suburbs of Greater London in particular grew by about 50 per cent. in each of the three intercensal periods between 1861 and 1891 and by 45 per cent. in the decade 1891–1901. The four places which experienced most rapid population growth in the whole country in the decade 1881–91 were all suburbs of London,[2] and in the decade which followed the most rapidly growing places were almost all suburban in character: no less than twelve of the seventeen urban districts which recorded rates of growth of over 30 per cent. in this decade were suburbs of London.[3] It was as though the compulsion in the earlier years of the century to bring the growing numbers into the cities and large towns had been replaced by a tendency to scatter them over more and more distant suburbs.

These figures, it must be remembered, are of ordinal rather than cardinal significance. They do no more than suggest a trend for which statistical verification is virtually unobtainable, for it is not possible to trace the suburban development of the large towns realistically in the census data once the tide of expansion had spilled over purely administrative boundaries. This raises a crucial question: what *is* a suburb? At what point in its development does some place become a true suburb, and at what later stage does it lose its suburban status? This is a difficult question and has no unequivocal answer.

The Suburb Defined

The term itself has a long and versatile history, for it appears to have been adopted from the Old French *suburbe* (itself an adaptation of the Latin *suburbium*), probably in the course of the fourteenth century, when Gallic influences on the English language were increasing as a result of widespread contact with French institutions generally. Wyclif used the word in the form *subarbis* in 1380, and that Chaucer should have introduced the term so naturally and easily into a dialogue in *The Canterbury Tales* in 1386 suggests that it had long acquired a definite meaning:

> "Where dwelle ye? if it to telle be."
> "In the suburbes of a toun," quod he,
> "Lurkynge in hernes and in lanes blynde,
> Where-as thise robbours and thise theves, by kynde,
> Holden hir pryvee, fereful residence;"

From this early date the term (or various corruptions of it) was not only used collectively, both in the singular and in the plural, but as a description of some specific and limited place; and it soon acquired, too, a figurative meaning. By the seventeenth century the description 'suburban' was also in use both to signify the place and the resident. The Victorians had, therefore, little to invent, but their reinstatement of the Roman word in the plural form and with a contemporary pronunciation was nevertheless a distinctive contribution to this vocabulary. The term 'suburbia' was a most apt designation to cover both the fusion of suburbs into an expressionless half-urban steppe and to suggest the rise of a kind of fourth estate.

To identify the suburb on the ground is by contrast not so easy. Some tentative attempts have been made by geographers to do so by mapping urban spheres of influence in terms of various functional indices such as public transport facilities or retail delivery areas.[4] But the results seem to suggest too rigid classifications and are in any case unsatisfactory for historical application because the requisite data are not normally available. To some town planners, on the other hand, the ultimate test of the true suburb seems to be the density of its population. The Ministry of Town and Country Planning's map of population density, which was based on the Census of 1931 and published in 1944, was based on a classification of urban types which ranged from "sparse rural", where 1-50 persons were to be found per square mile, to "dense urban", having over 25,000 persons per square mile; "suburban and industrialized rural" was the legend applicable to areas in which the density ranged from 400 to 6,400 per square mile. The application of such a classification to, say, South London in the course of the nineteenth century is obviously quite unrealistic: Kennington would have become "dense urban" by 1841, Brixton would have been "urban" by 1851, while the inner areas would have begun to sink back into the suburban category a little later on.

Suburbia, it has been suggested with more truth, may be defined as a state of existence within a few minutes' walk of the railway station, the shops, and the fields.[5] This may well serve as a description of a middle-class suburb during the forty years or so before the first world war, but at no time would it have been an accurate description of the working-class dormitory. To define the suburb is, in fact, rather like defining the middle classes who virtually created the first of them in their modern form. Both had their distinctive features, but these had their mutations, and it is hard to tell just when form and function had changed so much as to warrant a new name. In essence, a suburb is a decentralized part of a city with which it is inseparably linked by certain economic and social ties.

Its Economic and Social Functions

In economic terms, its function may be regarded as a decentralization of either consumption or of production, or both: where one or other of these functions predominates it is feasible to speak of a residential or an industrial suburb, but there are many suburbs in which these functions are fairly evenly balanced and comparatively few in which either of them is wholly lacking. Sheer proximity to the suburban retail market was itself often a good enough reason for some industries to move into the suburbs. What was usually a more persuasive argument for the dispersal of some industry to the suburbs, however, was the availability of cheaper premises, and the existence of a large untapped supply of female labour. The location of industry in the suburbs cannot, however, be accounted for solely in these functional terms because businessmen are susceptible to pressures of all kinds, and their presence in the suburbs is often unaccountable.

In sociological terms, the suburb may be regarded as providing the environment for the satisfaction of many of the needs of the family and as containing some facilities for the use of leisure. The creation of suburbs represents, however, more than an unconscious attempt by rapidly growing urban communities to separate their homes from their workplaces. It is the product of a whole social and economic process set in motion by a curious blend of romantic idealism and hard-headed realism. It was romanticism which created in suburbia the apotheosis of the Englishman's castle, and it was the Englishman's practicality which found in the suburbs a solution to the problem of where to house the workers. To most middle-class Victorians, and to a rapidly growing proportion of the working classes, the suburb had a meaning which was little less than idyllic. It was not only the seat of respectability but—as William Cowper once so wittily showed[6]—a world of fantasy in which dreams of self-importance and fulfilment could become tangible in the management of some doll's house estate and in the occupation of a unique social niche.

> Suburban villas, highway-side retreats,
> That dread the encroachment of our growing streets,
> Tight boxes, neatly sash'd, and in a blaze
> With all a July sun's collected rays,
> Delight the citizen, who, gasping there,
> Breathes clouds of dust, and calls it country air.
>
> . . . . .
>
> There, pinion'd in a parlour snug and small,
> Like bottled wasps upon a southern wall,
> The man of business and his friends compress'd,
> Forget their labours, and yet find no rest;

Suburban respectability was largely a matter of the right address and possession of it was the source of an indefinable satisfaction which did not evaporate until the social structure of the suburb was unbalanced by the emigration of its top people and the immigration of a different breed of newcomers from some inner suburb. This social leap-frogging made the suburb one of the transit camps of modern society, but the cult of suburban living was fostered on something more than the quest for social exclusiveness and the opportunity for an elaborate game of make-believe. It derived something also from the repulsiveness of some of the aspects of life as it had to be lived in the centre of the city.

The individual's retreat to the suburbs was often a personal solution to a collective sanitary problem. The mounting pressure on relatively limited living room in some parts of the centre of the town in the eighteenth and nineteenth centuries invariably meant some deterioration in living conditions. The resulting squalor led those who could to recoil to the suburbs where they could breathe purer suburban air and drink cleaner water. That unregulated suburban expansion could ultimately nourish its own slums would no doubt have seemed incomprehensible to pioneering suburbians—a neat seventeenth-century term which deserves more use—to whom the daisy and the buttercup must have seemed trustworthy guarantors of lasting salubrity. As it was, both the attempted control of the slums by metropolitan improvement,[7] and the prudent flight of those who could afford it to the suburbs, reflected the increasing sensitivity of the growing middle classes to their urban environment. What an Improvement Act was to the authorities of an urban parish, an adequate income and flexible office hours were to the prospective resident of a suburban one—ways of escape from the lethal consequences of belonging to a tightly packed and socially heterogeneous community at the heart of the city. These were the potentialities which were given a larger meaning still by the mass suburban deployment of the working classes towards the end of the nineteenth century, when suburban migration was consciously encouraged as a fugitive solution to the housing problem at the centre.

The suburb is essentially in a dependent relationship to the whole organism of the city, and the complete suburban area of a city performs only a part of its total functions. The characteristic features of suburban life are thus dichotomous. The home is divided not only from the workplace, but from the main institutions of culture and entertainment, and the interests and loyalties of those living in the suburbs tend to branch away from those in the centre.

In Victorian London the suburban migration of the middle classes tended in this way to harden political divisions and to weaken the forces which were beginning to create a social policy adequate for its day. The unwavering Toryism of the outer suburbs faded appreciably towards the centre, but C. F. G. Masterman's image in *The Condition of England* (1908) of the solid ranks of middle-class suburban voters arrayed against the virulent forces of the working classes, which were by the end of the nineteenth century storming their citadel, is not an entirely fanciful one. Swung high on railway embankments or carried in tubes deep underground the middle classes made their daily journeys to work across a sort of nether world in which the masses lived. In Masterman's imagery the middle-class suburbian looked with profound distrust on the forces which were visibly fermenting in this uncouth laboratory: "he would never be surprised to find the crowd behind the red flag, surging up his little pleasant pathways, tearing down the railings, trampling the little garden; the 'letting in of the jungle' upon the patch of fertile ground which has been redeemed from the wilderness." It was ironical that this same jungle had once been the habitat of the middle classes themselves and that their retreat from it not only tended to make the social divisions more indelible but, by failing to stabilize the conditions of growth and to maintain reasonable standards, had contributed to the social descent of their old abodes. The isolation of the poor—a theme which ran like a crimson thread through so many Victorian social commentaries—was a corollary of the rise of the middle-class suburbs in which geographical insularity was often a symbol of a more fundamental social and political separation. A division of a different kind is perhaps also to be seen within the home, where the family itself began to lose some of its cohesion under the special pressures of suburban life.

It may be that such divisions tended to stultify the social life of the suburbs and to earn for them in the course of the nineteenth century a reputation for trivial and meretricious values and civic spinelessness. Much of this was probably derived by association from the severely standardized and banal appearance of many middle and lower-middle-class suburbs. A faint aroma of disdain for some aspects of suburban life can occasionally even be detected in the tasteless romantic novels—now forgotten and almost pulped out of existence[8]—which relied for their plots and for their readers on the suburbs of the second half of the nineteenth century. It was mainly in this period, when the suburbs were changing both their shape and their social complexion so fast, that they became in some senses the objects of ridicule and even contempt. George and Weedon Grossmith's brilliant but kindly lampoon of Holloway society in *The Diary of a Nobody* (1892) was probably the most urbane of such criticisms, as H. G. Wells's brief but cutting allusions to the social arrangements of Worcester Park in *Anne Veronica* (1913) were among the most astringent. "I must confess honestly," wrote the knowledgeable Mrs C. S. Peel in her manual of middle-class domesticity, *The New Home* (1898), "that the suburbs of any large town appear to me detestable." They had, she was prepared to allow, some advantages, but these were primarily consolation prizes for "those people who yearn for the pleasures of the country and who find their diversions in golf, tennis, bicycling, boating, or gardening, and whom cruel fate prevents from living in the real country."

Suburbia has naturally had its champions, too, though these have now mostly been forgotten. The late Victorian and Edwardian suburbs, which tend nowadays to be seen through a mellow nostalgic haze, were human habitations, and there were two or three contemporary novelists at least who recognized in them some human dignities. Such were Shan Bullock's *Robert Thorne; the story of a London clerk* (1907) and Keble Howard's *The Smiths of Surbiton* (1906) and its sequel.[9] There was above all George Gissing, who knew well and wrote with more insight on the inner ring of London suburbs in the last twenty years of the nineteenth century than any of his contemporaries; in particular, he drew some lifelike portraits of suburban society in Camberwell in his novel *In the Year of Jubilee* (1894).[10] But all these represented too small a literary output which was not wholly scornful of the suburbs that they did little to prevent the reputation of the suburbs for a kind of cultural poverty from getting the upper hand. Thus, of the suburban continent of South London, Sir Walter Besant wrote in 1899 (admittedly with more feeling than accuracy): "It is a city without a municipality, without a centre, without a civic history; it has no newspapers, magazines or journals; it has no university, it has no colleges, apart from medical; it has no intellectual, artistic, scientific, musical, literary centre—unless the Crystal Palace can be considered as a centre; its residents have no local patriotism or enthusiasm . . . it has no theatres except of a very popular or humble kind; it has no clubs, it has no public buildings, it has no West End."[11] Its central edifice, a Frenchman remarked, was a public-house—the "Elephant and Castle."[12]

The State of Semi-Detachment

The modern suburb is clearly less of a geographical expression than it is an attitude of mind and a species of social as well as of economic behaviour. For this reason Epsom early in the eighteenth century was not only a rural market town and a spa but a suburb of London fifteen miles away: "the greatest of the Men, I mean of this Grave sort," wrote Defoe,[13] "may be supposed to be Men of Business, who are at London upon Business all the Day, and thronging to their lodgings at Night, make the Families, generally speaking, rather provide Suppers than Dinners: for 'tis very frequent for the Trading part of the Company to place their families here, and take their Horses every Morning to London . . . and be at Epsom again at Night." A hundred years later such suburban characteristics were fastening themselves likewise on the fishing village and fashionable seaside resort of Regency Brighton. "Great parcels of stockjobbers stay at Brighton with the women and children," noted William Cobbett. "They skip backwards and forwards on the coaches and actually carry on stockjobbing in Change Alley though they reside in Brighton." What coaches permitted railways encouraged, and by mid-century the London merchant commuted daily from Brighton with as much ease as he had once done from Hampstead or Norwood;[14] when, by the end of the century, the Sussex coast had been brought by railway within an hour-and-a-half of the City, its suburban population rose still more, and Eastbourne, Herne Bay, and Hastings were also numbered among London's suburban dormitories.[15] Presumably, it would be more proper to speak of such places out of the tourist season as being more suburban than during it? It was, indeed, a realistic editor of a residential guide to the London suburbs who wrote in the 1870s: "No mere formal radius of distance has been taken as the adoption of any such hard-and-fast line was found inadvisable."[16]

Appropriately enough, the experience of such far-flung suburbs as these might suggest that an essential characteristic of the suburb was its state of semi-detachment. This was not necessarily so, however, for what really decided the intimacy of the physical connection between city and suburb was the nature of the communications between the two and the speed of development. When roads alone provided the main lines of communication the suburbs were reached along continuous avenues of ribbon development, behind which lay the farms and market-gardens which catered for the urban market. The structure of a typical late-Georgian suburb of London was uncramped and its roads were generally neatly articulated with the street plan of the city by means of the main road to town. If there was little attempt to fill in the areas away from the main roads, so too no sensational leaps had to be made deep into the countryside in order to make sure of a suburban address for as far ahead as one cared to look. Development therefore tended to be orderly and the suburb remained literally in touch with the city. Physical continuity between city and suburb was also enhanced by the horse-drawn omnibus and, later, the horse-drawn tramcar, which tended to fill in the vacant areas which had been formed by earlier ribbon development.

The first railways to penetrate the suburbs did little to change this state of affairs. There were exceptions, but as a rule the earliest railways did not cater specifically for regular suburban journeys but for occasional journeys between towns. The building of suburban lines themselves had, however, a profound effect on the social and physical structure of the suburbs because they enormously increased the potential suburban area and made it easy to contemplate removal farther along the line. Many of the lines built around London were laid across the open fields, and those on the south side of the river in particular described generous arcs far beyond the existing built-up area. In their modest way the mid-Victorian lines which penetrated these more distant areas were as much pioneers of human settlement as the transcontinental lines of North America. Their costly and lofty stations (for which some recognizable place-name was not always easy to find) were often planted in the fields, and each became, with the inevitable Station Hotel, the nucleus of a new railway suburb whose only physical and functional link with town, in the beginning at least, was the railway itself. These lines were frequently so far in advance of their potential traffic that their stations are to be regarded rather as advertisements in brick, glass, and iron, than as provision made by public carriers. Later on, the coming of the motor-car tended to blur still more the purely geographical connotation of the term 'suburban,' and to bring practically all rural England within its orbit.[17]

The term 'suburban' has, however, been elastic in another way. Not only did the suburban grasp on the countryside tighten over the years but it slackened in areas which had once been virgin suburb themselves. At the end of the Middle Ages Fleet Street and the extra-mural parishes, like St Sepulchre's, were designated as suburbs. By the beginning of the eighteenth century the suburban frontier on the south side of the Thames was located, according to the title of a contemporary Act, in the vicinity of the "Borough of Southwark and the respective suburbs thereof"; in the middle of the twentieth century the *County of London Plan* located it beyond an imaginary line formed by the continuous belt of working-class districts from Maze Hill in the east to Battersea in the west. The conventional inner limits of suburbia are, however, almost as unsatisfactory as the outer limits, for the places designated as no longer suburban usually appear on closer examination to be little different in function and character from the acknowledged suburbs. The merging of the old suburbs with the central area occurs imperceptibly and it would be pedantic to try and be too precise about it. Suburbanization has come over rural England like some subtle climatic change, and the condition has passed in some places in a similar way.

A London Suburb: Camberwell

This book is about a Victorian suburb to which all that has so far been said readily applies. Camberwell, that is to say the ancient parish of St Giles (which, with some boundary revision, comprises the present metropolitan borough) was in the nineteenth century an inverted pear-shaped area of about 4,450 acres, some $4\frac{1}{2}$ miles long on its north-south axis and $2\frac{1}{2}$ miles across at its widest point. It is situated between a point about a mile and a half almost due south of London Bridge, and another at the meeting of the boundaries of Lambeth, Croydon, and Penge; or, in more recognizable terms to its familiars, roughly between the Bricklayers' Arms Goods Sidings off the Old Kent Road and the Crystal Palace at Sydenham.

It cannot, unfortunately, be claimed that Camberwell was a typical London suburb, for the suburbs of London are an eccentric family. It is paradoxical that in a city in which local patriotism has been rubbed thin by physical contact between once discrete communities, the peculiarities of place and circumstances of

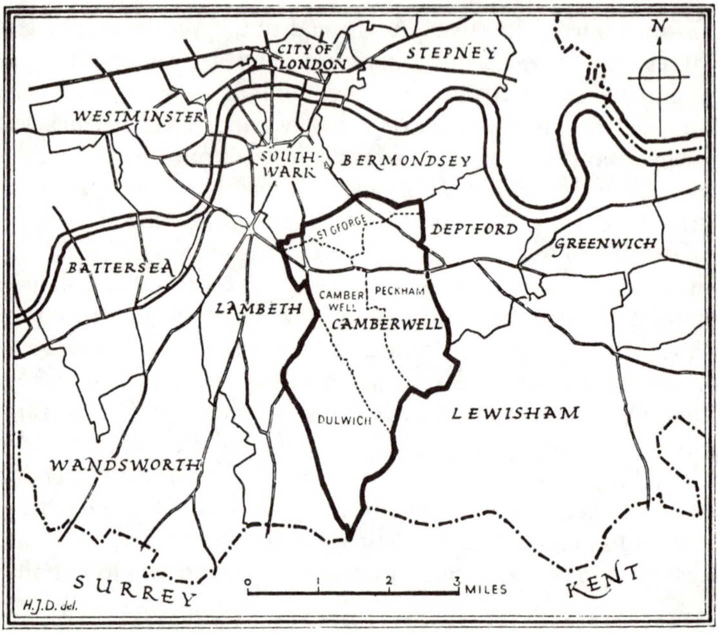

FIG. 1. *The Position of Camberwell*

development should have preserved from this erosion not only some of the physical but also some of the social characteristics of its suburbs. Though this is less true to-day, when local communities tend to become mere microcosms of national life, it at least held good to the end of the nineteenth century. If Victorian suburbs failed to breed local loyalties[18] they nevertheless remained surprisingly peninsular. Their idiosyncrasies were a commonplace to contemporary Londoners, to whom the lofty reaches of Dulwich Village or the spacious avenues of Clapham Park were almost as sharply different physically and socially from the congested streets of Newington and Bermondsey as St James's was distinct from the Seven Dials. And if London itself was still balkanized, Camberwell too contained its own social contradictions: when Ruskin pointed to the Gothic splendours of Champion Hill, the plains of Peckham, and the rural barbarism of Goose Green, he was not merely dwelling on aesthetic extremes.[19]

Although the main assault upon the eligible building plots of Camberwell was a Victorian phenomenon, it was an invasion which had had long years of preparation. To the local incumbent interested in numbering the people, the Parish Register revealed in steadily mounting entries for baptisms and burials since the sixteenth century a clear demographic trend. To market-gardeners on the local loamy soil, this was no doubt convincing in a different way. But what was to these small farmers the warm sun of London's growing food market in the sixteenth and seventeenth centuries had become by the nineteenth the all-consuming star which had begun to devour all their holdings. This effacement of their worlds was woefully protracted, for pigs, cows, and sometimes sheep, could be made to perform the least of their natural functions even in the hideous conditions of a metropolitan slum. Yet by 1811 cowkeepers were in rapid decline in Camberwell, and market-gardeners appeared to tend rather fewer acres than they had done fifteen years before.[20] By this time Camberwell's popularity as a handy and sanitary retreat from the polluting city had become well established: what local legend suggests by the reported residence there of Christopher Wren during the building of St Paul's and of Nell Gwynn during her days of favour was confirmed in less equivocal terms by the leading medical practitioner of his day, John Coakley Lettsom, when he took up residence at Grove Hill in 1779.[21] By the beginning of the nineteenth century, Camberwell—in common with many other districts within ten miles or so of the City of London—had had its landscape dotted by a variety of such villas and ornamental cottages.[22] But what had given to the place by then even more of a suburban stamp were the miniature stucco mansions and terraced villas which had begun to dress the main roads and to congregate here and there in isolated, enclosed estates.

When the Victorian period opened Camberwell had already come within the field of influence of a greater London than could have been dreamt of by the little eighteenth-century village community of probably about two thousand men, women, and children whose apparatus of roads and houses, fields and footpaths, streams and windmills, had been so graphically portrayed by John Rocque in 1762. In Rocque's day the only human settlement worthy of note beyond the rather angular and straggling village of Camberwell itself in the north-west corner of the parish, were the hamlets of Peckham and Dulwich, and some tiny, scattered groups of houses at Peckham Rye, Goose Green, None Head, and Dulwich Wells. By then, with the exception of about 240 acres in the North Field at Peckham and about 130 acres at Dulwich, all uncommonable land in the parish of St Giles had—as elsewhere in a county of irregular field systems where enclosure tended to come early[23]—been enclosed for grass or for plough. The few suburban features which had by then intruded into this wider landscape in the form of scattered houses and ornamental parks had not seriously modified this simple rustic pattern.

Indeed, even when Walter Harrison published his classic *New and Universal History . . . of London and Westminster* a few years later in 1776—a year significantly marked in Camberwell by its first Act for lighting and watching the parish[24]—metropolitan expansion, though inexorable, had still been remote. Yet Harrison could write that "the spirit of building, which has been so prevalent for some years past, appears to have equally affected this part with any round the metropolis; for between Newington Butts and Camberwell several new streets have been formed and a prodigious number of buildings erected. . . ."[25] By 1800, this new suburban temper had begun to call into being the physical framework for a different society for whom existing institutions were inadequate: the south wall of the old church of St Giles, for example, had already been taken back in 1786 to make room for the increased congregation, but by 1825 this accommodation had become inadequate for the new parishioners so the church was again enlarged, and the new "Waterloo Church" of St George's was raised in Wells Street alongside the canal.[26] Gradually, the new suburban society overshadowed the dwindling community which was attached in many different ways to the local soil. This was a process in which old institutions lost their meaning and new ones were given form. A symptom of this was the decline of the local fairs at Camberwell and Peckham, which had outlived their rural functions and survived as mere suburban sprees. Their final disappearance came when enough of the new residents found them irksome and unsavoury anachronisms: the first attempts to suppress them were made in 1823, but although the Peckham Fair was made illegal in 1827, that at Camberwell resisted suppression for another forty years.[27]

The new residents of Camberwell, representatives almost all of them of the prospering middle classes, were growing roots of a different kind, for they were attached instead, as Priscilla Wakefield remarked, to the commercial metropolis, and daily journeyed thither for their employment.[28] They had as yet settled mostly in northern Camberwell, where haphazardly sited buildings were in some parts by this time becoming fairly thick on the ground, and the rural landscape was gradually being denuded of all its leafy features save some bits of sickly grass and bottle-green poplars.[29] It was here that the suburban process was most obviously accelerating in the opening decades of the nineteenth century. It was settlement in this region which caused a quadrupling of the population of the parish between 1801 and 1831, thirty years in which each decennial increment was bigger than the last, and brought the total to about 35,000 by 1837.[30] It was scarcely surprising that few of the many topographers who quizzed this society and its changing environment over these thirty or forty years failed to remark on some aspect of its growth, particularly the elegant houses which preceded later, more plebeian structures, some of which had already begun the conquest of the countryside.[31]

This invasion of the open fields of the parish of Camberwell during the nineteenth century is the subject of all but one of the chapters which follow. Their principal concern is to identify the nature of the process of suburban expansion, to examine the springs of action, and to consider the physical and social product which resulted from it. If it is to avoid the pitfall of extreme parochialism, however, it will be necessary not only to examine Victorian Camberwell as a selected instance of a general phenomenon in the modern history of English cities, but to make use where necessary of broader themes of urban development, and to show the relationship of the part to the whole. The most convenient arrangement for this purpose is not a chronological one. It is necessary to begin, however, with a more detailed examination of the pre-Victorian beginnings of the process whereby the ancient village and parish of Camberwell took on its first suburban characteristics.

CHAPTER II

PRE-VICTORIAN BEGINNINGS

The Rise of South London

SUBURBS began in England, as they did on the Continent, with the extra-mural settlement of persons who stood in every sense on the fringes of urban society. By the sixteenth century the Continental *faubourg* had its counterpart in this country in the 'fore-street,' such as Bankside in Southwark. Here congregated inns, places of amusement, and minor industries, for which there was either no room or no welcome within the strict city limits. By this time the dispersal of industry to the suburbs of London had become quite marked. They contained not only the splinter groups of apprentices and journeymen which had broken away from the craft gilds within the city, but a number of obnoxious trades—such as soap-making, tanning, and oil-boiling—which were ideally sited well away from the living quarters, and several other industries which had migrated to the suburbs to benefit by lower rents.[1] In addition, the suburbs housed foreign immigrants who established industries which competed with the City gilds. The City craftsmen frequently complained of the competitive advantages which their suburban rivals enjoyed, and repeatedly sought a mandate to superintend them.[2] "The freedom of London which was heretofore of very great esteeme," they complained, "is grown to be little worth, by reason of the extraordinary enlargement of the suburbs, where greate numbers of traders and handicraftsmen doe enjoy without charge equall benefit with the freemen and citizens of London."[3]

Not only did a rapid expansion of suburban industry threaten the monopoly of the gilds, but the suburbs of London were in the sixteenth and seventeenth centuries a perennial menace to the maintenance of law and order. In times of riot and rebellion the narrow courts and alleys of Southwark and its neighbourhood had their own mob, recruited from local apprentices.[4] What is more, at a time when disease was endemic it was not easy to prevent waves of sickness which often originated in the suburbs from invading the City itself.[5] It was with the intention of controlling suburban living conditions and the effects these had on life within the City that a Proclamation was issued in 1580 which prohibited the erection of any new dwelling-houses within three miles of the City gates, and tried to establish the rule of one family to each house.[6] But the city's growth could not be kept within such arbitrary limits. Retail shops and lodging houses were already multiplying fast on the South Bank and living room was being created in the suburbs by the conversion of other premises to residential use.[7] Neither specific legislation nor further proclamation could prevent the growth of the suburbs, where 'pennyrents,' 'base tenements,' and 'disorderly houses' continued to spring up unchecked.[8] Until the Restoration serious attempts were made to contain the suburbs by further Proclamations, injunctions, letters, prosecutions, the publication of building schedules, and other means,[9] but public administration of the suburbs was not only bedevilled by the laxity of petty officials but by the huge scale of the tasks themselves. In 1614 the Privy Council pressed the Surrey magistrates to be vigilant against anyone who should "erect newe buildings, divide howses and harbor inmates," and three years later required one of the four aldermen appointed by the Lord Mayor of London to watch for new buildings to keep strict surveillance over Southwark.[10]

As the suburban area widened new legislation had to be given wider application, and in 1657 an Act was passed which was designed to prevent the increase of suburban buildings within ten miles of the City.[11] Between this date and the beginning of the eighteenth century, however, the population of London grew by half as much again, and builders "out of an avaricious temper, without the least regard to these injunctions continued to build as formerly," and the built-up area oozed still farther afield.[12] By this time nearly three thousand houses were standing in part of Southwark alone, and the outlying villages of Peckham, Camberwell, Dulwich, Streatham, Battersea, and Wandsworth were already acquiring their new suburban status.[13] A sure sign that this whole area had begun to take on a different character was the establishment in 1710 of regular mail deliveries within a radius of ten miles from the General Post Office in London.[14]

An even more significant sign of the acquisition of this new status was, however, the social metamorphosis which was occurring at the same time. Hitherto, the suburbs had, as residential areas, largely been reception centres for the urban poor. The Proclamation of 1580 spoke of "great Multitudes of People... Whereof a great part were very poor" and a foreign visitor in early Stuart times said of the suburbs of London that "the greater part are inhabited by an inept population of the lowest description."[15] To judge by one painstaking street-by-street record of the suburbs around 1720, however, a rather more diversified society was coming into being than appears to have been quartered in the suburbs in Tudor times.[16] It is more than probable that the suburbs were never occupied by completely homogeneous social classes, but by the beginning of the eighteenth century the poor were living cheek-by-jowl with the rich to an extraordinary degree. Although poor streets were the majority in Southwark, for example, these were occasionally interspersed by a few houses and streets in which the wealthy lived: St Margaret's Hill (nowadays Borough High Street) was thus entirely upper-class, though the surrounding areas housed craftsmen, labourers, and others.[17] Relatively few merchants and tradesmen had, even in 1720, come south of the river to live, but the numbers had increased in the previous forty years, and were due to increase so much in the comparable period to follow that the social composition of the suburbs became radically changed.[18] The middle classes were migrating to the suburbs.

The Foundations of a Middle-Class Suburb

Of this movement Camberwell was entirely typical. By 1800, it contained, in Dr Lettsom's words, "few poor inhabitants and not many overgrown fortunes."[19] It had become popular among Lettsom's contemporaries because it adequately fulfilled the current suburban requirements: it was healthy, and it was accessible. Before the impermeable umbrella of Victorian brick and macadam had been thrown over the bulk of the parish and piped water supplies and main drainage had been brought to every street, the influence of the subsoil, elevation, and water-supply upon the character of its development had been profound.[20]

The growth of London had long been governed by the distribution of superficial water-bearing strata—tracts of gravel and sand where natural brooks and springs arose.[21] The valley gravel came nearest to the river on its southern side in northern Camberwell. In terms of water supply the area just north of the road between Camberwell and Peckham was, therefore, the most convenient suburb available to City businessmen in this part of London. Here, in contrast to the varying attenuations of sewage which passed for drinking water in the shallow wells on the alluvium farther north, were adequate supplies of uncontaminated water. Here, too, house drainage was not the constant struggle with water-logged basements, which it was in those days on the alluvial soils; and the process of extending the built-up area over this low-lying but healthy tract was also aided by the deposits of a dark brown loam which fed the neighbourhood's voracious brickfields. Where the gravel gave way to clay immediately south of the road from Camberwell to Peckham the ground began its perceptible and erratic climb towards the distant Surrey hills: the southernmost tip of the parish three miles away stood three hundred feet above the mean sea-level of Camberwell Green. The elevation of these southern wooded slopes of the parish fully compensated for the disadvantages of the stubborn clay in which, but for the sandy outcrops of Woolwich and Reading Beds in parts of Peckham and Dulwich, they were encased.

To choose Camberwell as the site for a suburban residence from which to make daily journeys to town was, however, unthinkable for any but the most leisurely travellers before the last quarter of the eighteenth century. The two main roads virtually passed it by, though the Kent Road did skirt the north-eastern borders. For Camberwell to develop as a suburb better communications with the metropolis were indispensable, and these came as the logical consequence of the building of bridges over the Thames, at Westminster, Blackfriars, and Vauxhall.

The substitution of a bridge for the age-old Lambeth Ferry at Westminster in 1750 had little immediate effect on the course of suburban development on the south bank, for although two direct connections were thus made between Westminster and the Kent Road and Southwark without entering the City, the roads themselves, raised on shallow causeways, lay across the marshy tract of St George's Fields, which was far less suitable for human habitation than many districts already open to development on the north bank of the river. The completion of the bridge at Blackfriars in 1769, however, had repercussions of a different order because although it gave access to the same potential suburbs it did so for a much more numerous and tightly enclosed community: the comparative advantages of St George's Fields and of Walworth were much greater for inhabitants of the City than they were for those of Westminster.[22] These were still further increased by the effective extension of the bridge for a mile south of the river by the cutting of a road to a circus from which could radiate more roads. From this carfax at St George's Circus sprang, therefore, a network of turnpike roads which pierced the open countryside and, in one direction, presently brought the tide of suburban development to the northern reaches of Camberwell on the edge of Newington.[23] From this point, in 1782, this system was effectively extended to Camberwell itself by the turnpiking of the road from Newington to Camberwell Green, and from there in one direction to Peckham and beyond, and in another to the fringes of Dulwich. A third avenue of suburban opportunity was created by the opening of Vauxhall Bridge in 1816, and this led within two years—unlike one or two abortive attempts earlier—to the cutting of the Camberwell New Road, in place of the tortuous Cut Throat Lane, direct from Kennington to Camberwell Green.[24]

These roads set new limits to the range of suburban migration, and brought the beckoning, airy slopes at the foot of the Surrey hills years nearer the reach of many suburban aspirants. At a time when even journeys in town were laborious and expensive, Camberwell now had the virtue of accessibility.[25] The journey to the City was short and direct, and stage-coach fares were therefore markedly lower and services more numerous at that time than to any other fashionable suburb south of the river—with the exception, before about 1815, of Putney and Richmond.[26]

The roads on which this traffic ran were clearly the principal means of peopling the new suburb and of supplying it with its daily needs. But this task was shared to a considerable extent with a waterway, the Grand Surrey Canal, which was cut between 1801 and 1811 from Rotherhithe to a point near Camberwell Road, with a branch to Peckham, as an initial stage in a much larger canal network.[27] One intention was to use the low-lying grounds in the vicinity of the canal for cultivating market-garden produce for London, and to provide cheap access to markets,[28] but the canal soon became not only a main traffic artery for transporting bulky goods like road metal, coal, and building timber, but its towpath became a convenient halfpenny hatch for pedestrians, its water was scooped out or piped away for industrial and even domestic use, or for watering the dusty streets, and its banks in time quartered scores of factories, workshops, and wharves, or were levelled and pegged out as building plots.[29]

Ownership and Improvement of Suburban Estates

The suburban framework for Victorian Camberwell was, it is clear, being erected not only before the railways arrived but well before the end of the preceding century; and it may be added that the techniques for its accomplishment were being evolved over quite as long a period. Landowners, both corporate and individual, were gradually becoming more sensitive during this period to the peculiar attractions of building leases, and to the blandishments of a variety of speculators. In time, the business and art of estate improvement was as sedulously cultivated by informed landowners whose estates were marginal to both town and country as by any spirited landowner to be found in either of those relatively uncomplicated spheres. But the first steps in the practical lessons of suburban estate development were harder for landowners to take than they were for their lessees. The annual value of a range of fields which might have been leased from time out of mind by some rule-of-thumb, wanted more careful reckoning as the built-up area trickled nearer some landed estate. Lessees of land which they had taken for terms of fifty or sixty years and more with a minimum of restrictive covenants could regard this approach with equanimity. But what was to them the prospect of some gratuitous gain was to the landowner an opportunity lost. Before building leases could become as familiar instruments of estate improvement as parliamentary enclosure had already become in the countryside, therefore, landowners had much to learn from the experience of seeing opportunities of highly profitable building speculation thrown away in unimaginatively-drawn repairing leases.

For some landowners, however, these speculative opportunities, however golden, were not easy to seize because of legal restrictions. They were either constrained by some strict settlement or by the unadventurous letter of charitable endowment, and such landowners could not as a result lease or otherwise dispose of their lands for building with complete freedom. Private Bill procedure was a costly and protracted business, but as it was the only way for such landowners to remove the dead hand which prevented them from responding to the opportunities created by a lively estate market, it was an effort worth making. So believed the Governors of Dulwich College, for example, when they obtained an Act for granting building leases in 1808;[30] as did, too, the Vicar of Camberwell, who was enabled by Act in 1813 to lease all but five of the $33\frac{1}{2}$ acres of glebe land, a liberty which he quickly took by making agreements for leases for terms of ninety-nine years with several builders in 1819, 1820, and 1821.[31]

This preliminary consideration of pre-Victorian estate development makes it necessary to notice at this point, if only in general terms, the contemporary structure of landownership. The landowners of Camberwell were at this time a numerous and assorted body. Originally the land had formed the basis of nine manors of uncertain extent—Camberwell Buckingham, Camberwell Fryern, Peckham, Dowdales, Bretinghurst, Basing, Coldherbergh, Milkwell, and Dulwich—but with one exception the ownership of these lands had by the 1830s been divided among many medium-sized and small freeholders. It is not possible to say precisely how the land was divided and to attribute each parcel of ground to a succession of specific owners throughout the nineteenth century, but the survey which was made in 1837 for the purpose of tithe redemption gives a clear enough general picture of the distribution of the land; and this is presented in the following table.

The table covers 83.2 per cent. of all the land in Camberwell, and the remainder, some 730 acres, consisted of developed land,

Table 1

THE STRUCTURE OF LANDOWNERSHIP IN CAMBERWELL, 1837

(To the nearest acre)

Size of Tithable Estates	*Landowners*		*Landholdings*	
	Nos.	*Per cent.*	*Nos.*	*Per cent.*
Under 1 acre	61	35.3	29	0.8
1– 4 acres	57	33.0	124	3.4
5– 9 "	19	11.0	132	3.7
10– 24 "	16	9.2	277	7.7
25–100 "	13	7.5	648	17.9
Over 100 "	7	4.0	2,402	66.5
	173	100.0	3,612	100.0

Source: Tithe Apportionment, St Giles', Camberwell, 1837.

roads, and waste: over half the land was used in 1837 as pasture, about a fifth as arable and market-garden, and nearly a quarter formed the built-up area.

The major portion of the tithable land in the parish was owned by a handful of men—seven landowners held between them one-third, twenty owned well over four-fifths of it. The largest estate of all, comprising the whole manor of Dulwich or about one-third of the entire parish, belonged to the Governors of Dulwich College, but there were a score of other extensive estates measuring between 30 and 350 acres approximately. On the other hand, over two-thirds of the landowners held no more than five acres apiece, though their total holding was appreciably less than 5 per cent. of the whole. The pattern which these various estates made on the ground was an extremely intricate one and some of the largest estates were scattered in small lots in different parts of the parish. The whole trend in the distribution of the ownership of the land during the nineteenth century was, however, towards a further multiplication of owners and a still more minute division of their holdings. This occurred mainly when large estates were disposed of piecemeal for building development, and others were divided up when the freehold ground rents which had been created were auctioned off. To trace the innumerable operations of the land market which lay behind these physical changes and by this means to account in detail for the changing face of the whole of Camberwell would be a herculean and unnecessary labour. The nature of the process can be discerned by a study of relatively few estates, and this provides the theme for Chapter IV. For the moment, however, it is necessary to identify two of the largest and one of the smallest estates as illustrations of pre-Victorian developments.

A Case of Uncontrolled Development

The first of these was that part of the Bowyer estate—some 444 acres—which came by a tortuous descent and finally by marriage into the hands of Sir William Smijth in 1810. This was the culmination of centuries of patient enlargement of a family estate by purchase and marriage, a process which had touched at many points the interests of other local families of long standing, such as the Scotts and the Windhams, and which had been governed by strict settlement. The estate once included the manors of Camberwell, Fryern, Milkwell, and Coldharbour, the advowson of the vicarage, the impropriate Rectory, and some other lands, and was parcelled out in some thirty to forty separate holdings throughout the parish. Just before the estate came into the Smijth family it had been diminished by the sale of several pieces to Robert Edmonds, a market-gardener of New Cross, and his son: these, it is worth noting, added considerably to the already substantial estate which had been founded by the father out of the profits of selling vegetables in the London markets and by a win in a lottery.[32] The main portion of the Bowyer-Smijth estate (it became so called when the Rev. Sir Edward Smijth, the tenth baronet, enlarged his surname by royal licence in 1839) soon became heavily mortgaged, and was entirely sold, in separate lots, by about 1860: when the two pieces of land were sold to Edmonds in 1804 for £10,312 they had been mortgaged for £3,500 to Henry Hoare, the banker, and by 1843 the estate had been encumbered by at least one more mortgage of £22,000.[33]

The Bowyer-Smijth estate is a classic instance of the landlord's failure to gauge the speed at which London was expanding south of the river from the 1780s onwards. Its annals tell a tale of lost opportunities of fixing sensible ground rents and of imposing proper stipulations when the land was let on both repairing and building leases. The growing debts of the estate at a time of extremely rapid building development may indeed be a measure of this inexpert response to changing conditions. Building leases —that is, tenancies on the condition among other things that a stipulated sum or a specified type and minimum amount of building be provided by the lessee within a given term—had been granted on the estate as early as 1763. Building development was then slow, and it is perhaps not surprising that landlords should sometimes have been caught napping. Only one of the early building leases on the estate had a term as short as 31 years, and the rest were for 61 and 91 years. These were no longer than the average repairing lease, but this is not surprising as flexibility in estate management was less necessary when the land market was stable: when a landowner could not anticipate getting a better return from his land in the foreseeable future he would naturally tend to agree on terms, even for a repairing lease, which protected him from unnecessary changes in tenancies.

At a time when the suburban development of Camberwell was slow and there existed no other special inducements to shorten leases, landowners were therefore content to lease for building for as short a term as they could get (since in this way they could profitably rack rent the improved property earlier), and for any other purpose for as far ahead as they could look. Similarly, the covenants they could write into building leases and the amount of builders' capital they could steer into the improvement of their estates depended, as much as anything, upon their bargaining skill. But when few speculative builders could be induced to venture their capital—or other people's— as far afield as Camberwell, landowners were probably glad to compound for the investment of quite modest sums by smaller men. Thus, Pièarce Condon's lease for seventy-one years from 1763 of a small strip of land off the north-east corner of Camberwell Green at £4 a year, included the covenant to spend £200 within two years in building one or more brick dwelling-houses; and John Castle's lease of a plot of similar size in the High Street for sixty-one years from 1775 at £13 a year contained a similar commitment.

Before the end of the eighteenth century, however, the scale of capital investment in domestic building and with it the character of building leases on the Bowyer-Smijth estate was changing. Between 1785 and 1793, seven years of plenty for London builders, eight long leases were granted which required the outlay by the several lessees of either £500 or £600 in the erection of one or more houses. But during the next thirty years or so new lessees had to invest much more, usually between £1,000 and £5,000, though even these larger sums cannot be considered extortionate as the actual outlays were much heavier than this.

The modest ground rents which had been fixed by the landlord on the assumption that lessees' outlays on building would not greatly exceed the sums covenanted to be spent soon bore little relationship to the gross rack rentals of the improved properties. For example, John Rolls, a cowkeeper, had leased in 1786 for a term of 81 years at £60 a year the twenty-two acre Albany Road estate, which covered about a third of the length of Albany Road and formed a junction with the Old Kent Road near the spot known as St Thomas à Waterings. When Rolls leased it, this estate comprised three cowhouses, two stables and some other farm buildings, and five fields; and he undertook "to expend within two years the sum of £600 at least in building one good Brick Dwelling House or more on the premises." By 1830, the estate had been transformed by the building of as many as 147 houses, several workshops, and a vinegar factory. Another lessee James Cross, had in 1793 taken the eleven acre Gravel Pit Field on the south side of Southampton Street for a term of 61 years at £50 a year. His agreement was to build one brick tenement to cost at least £500, within the next three years, but he was not to dig for gravel, brick earth, or other materials under a penalty of £5 per load. Nevertheless, the ground was soon covered by some 198 houses, a brewery, a public-house, and a number of shops. Another lease, which committed Messrs Garland and Fieldwick, masons and builders of no mean order, to building eight or nine houses at £550 apiece—a total outlay of some £5,000 within five years of 1825—on some fields straddling Camberwell New Road, was used to build four times this number. A similar piece of development was of the Shoulder-of-Mutton Field, which was bounded on the south by the Old Kent

Road and on its other two sides by converging open ditches or sewers. This lease was for 61 years from 1820 at the usual peppercorn or nominal rent for the first year and £80 a year thereafter, and committed the lessee, William Law, to an outlay of £4,000 within six years in building dwelling-houses. Within ten, the field had become, though not fully developed, an estate of about 85 houses.

Easily the most dramatic and probably one of the most interesting changes of all occurred on the Bowyer-Smijth estate in an area of nearly forty-five acres lying at right-angles to and fronting the turnpike from Walworth on its western side, just inside the parish boundary.* This estate was leased in 1781, a year before the turnpike was extended from Newington to Camberwell Green, for a term of 85 years at £143 a year. The lessee was a William Austin, though by 1819 the estate had been demised to three persons, Ray, Farmer, and Bates. When leased to Austin the area comprised five fields of meadow or pasture ground, and the stage then reached in the suburban development of the area did not justify any special covenants in the lease beyond those normally included in an ordinary lease for agricultural purposes. These were that all trees were the landlord's and open land was to be kept under grass during the last ten years of the lease. The penalty for ignoring the last requirement was a fine of £50 per acre; but an even heavier fine of £500 per acre was liable to be incurred if the soil was taken for brickmaking. The penalty was probably considered heavy enough to prevent housing development, but by 1830 the estate was half-covered by some 580 houses, several shops, cowsheds, piggeries, a couple of public-houses, some workshops, and a glue factory. These were sited in such a way as to suggest that the land had not only been let on loosely-drawn leases by the ground landlord, but had been sub-let on equally badly drafted sub-leases, probably at rents which required very intensive development to justify them.

* Broadly speaking, this was what came to be known in later years as the Sultan Street area, enclosed between Camberwell Road, Wyndham Road, Farmers Road, Tamerton Street, and Bethwin Road; the area beyond Pitman Street was at that time in the parish of St Mary, Lambeth. When leased to Austin the place-names were Pail Fields, Mill Fields, Watch-house Field, and Dunghill Fields.

That leases could create such handsomely improved ground rents must be interpreted as meaning that the local demand for relatively low-cost housing was expanding much more rapidly than the landowner realized. The suburb was growing fast, and the probable scale of investment in houses depended on too many variables to give the landlord grounds for confident prediction of the speed of events. Nor could he tell how things would go by looking at events elsewhere. For London as a whole the inflation at the end of the Napoleonic War and the demand for living accommodation by demobilized soldiers and others who flocked in made it the centre of post-war opportunity, and builders' expectations of profit from supplying the needed houses had soared. This summer of prosperity in the housing industry came to an end when the general economic climate changed in 1825, and from this time to about 1832 both new housing and new building of all kinds contracted sharply.[34] Events in Camberwell, however, did not follow this trend, for the scale of investment which must have been made in building terraced villas and other small houses after 1825 was increasing, not declining.

The explanation must be that Camberwell's popularity was growing with a new class of suburban migrants for whom an individually sited mansion on some much more sparsely settled suburban frontier was out of the question. There was no sharp line of demarcation between these different densities of development, but they were plain enough on the ground. On the Bowyer-Smijth estate down to the end of the 1830s the chief areas of more intensive development were to the north of the Camberwell-Peckham road. South of the line the pace of change slackened and ambitious schemes of development were liable to go off at half-cock: south of Goose Green stretched the largest single piece of the Bowyer-Smijth estate, a series of fields totalling about 96 acres, which, though planned for development as early as 1836, were not opened up for another thirty years.

Some Successful Estate Management

The second of the three estates whose pre-Victorian history is to be considered at this stage was typical of the slower pace of development to be found before the 1830s in most of the area south of the Peckham Road. This was the estate of the de Crespigny family, who, like the Minets who had settled in another part of Camberwell, were Huguenot refugees from France at the end of the seventeenth century. The original estate, a single area of about 80 acres on rising ground between Denmark Hill and Grove Lane, was formed out of land bought by the family from time to time down to 1783. This was nearly doubled in extent in 1808 by the purchase of a number of scattered pieces of land lying to the east of Rye Lane at Peckham. The Peckham part of the estate was mainly let for agricultural purposes before the 1830s, but the original area at Denmark Hill formed part of the fashionable quarter surrounding The Grove which had been developing since the last quarter of the eighteenth century.

The striking difference between this development and that on the Bowyer-Smijth estate farther north was that none of the lessees on the de Crespigny estate had taken the same advantage of the loosely-drafted lease as, for example, John Rolls or the successors to William Austin had done. It is true that three or four of the twenty-two lessees of de Crespigny land—the largest single leasehold was probably over twenty acres—were deliberately prevented by the landowner before the end of the eighteenth century from building more than a very few houses, and that some others had covenanted not to build public-houses, to dig for sand or brick earth, or to carry on any offensive trade, but the majority of them appear to have had a free hand to develop their holdings as opportunity permitted.[35] That hardly any development did occur was not a symptom of the lessees' unresponsiveness to a buoyant property market but of the height which the tide of suburban development had still to rise before it lapped those particular shores.

It is clear from all this that these suburban landowners needed both keen foresight and considerable bargaining skill if they were to enjoy in their own lifetimes the appreciating land values of their estates. It is true that the average ground rental on the Bowyer-Smijth estate rose from about £3 per acre in the 1780s to over £20 by the 1820s, but it seems probable that when compared with the rise in the real value of their lands this was but a sluggish adjustment to rapidly changing conditions.

Some landowners, however, were not so rapidly overtaken by the increasing pace of suburban development, and where the granting of building leases would not have been propitious they occasionally renewed leases for agricultural purposes on terms which reserve their rights of re-entry if conditions changed, so as to draw up building leases. The third estate to be considered at this point was a good illustration of this. This was one of the estates belonging to the City of London which provided part of the income needed for the upkeep of old London Bridge. The estate consisted of ten acres of meadow on the south side of the Old Kent Road, and had been managed by the Bridge House Estates Commissioners since at least the sixteenth century.[36] The cowkeeper John Rolls, himself a freeholder and a lessee of other land extending in a continuous belt across this part of the parish, had first rented the estate in 1775 for £40 a year, apparently as a tenant-at-will, but within two years the lessors contemplated laying out its field for building, and had the younger Dance, their clerk of works, prepare a plan for this purpose. To Rolls, the estate was indispensable to his farm layout, and to avoid its loss he himself proposed spending £100 within three years on repairs to the existing property—a sum about equal, it was reckoned, to the value of the buildings—if he could have a repairing lease for twenty-one years. To the sub-committee which had examined Dance's plan and Rolls' offer, the latter was in 1777 the better prospect. But they recommended that the terms of the lease should stipulate that if brick earth were afterwards discovered, or if at any time it should "be thought more advantageous to let the Ground for building," a proportion of Rolls' outlay should be refunded and new agreements made.[37] Rolls had been rash in committing himself to such a large premium, for the sub-committee was "rather doubtful whether [the estate] would answer to build Houses," and he soon found himself before the committee for failing to keep his agreement. He had been unsuccessful in letting the house, which was ruinous, and stoutly defended his intention of spending the agreed sum, but contrived at the same time to obtain from the committee what amounted to a building lease for a term of 61 years at the same rental, with the covenant to spend £500 within three years in building a substantial brick house under the direction of Mr Dance. In the end the lease was drawn up, at Dance's suggestion, for the expenditure of £400 only, and when the lease expired in 1841 this had been the approximate limit of his improvement.

The Great Wen

It is clear from all this that the speed of suburban expansion in these pre-Victorian years was already startling. London had been swelling visibly since the sixteenth century. The process was arrested for a time by the confiscation of the lands of the score or so of religious houses which had existed in pre-Reformation London, and many of these had become so many building estates by about 1560. The swelling continued apace over the next hundred years despite every ingenious effort to contain it, and the catastrophe of the Great Fire in 1666 accelerated the growth of the suburbs still more: "what are the suburbs now become," asked Rolle in his tract on the *Burning of London*, "but as it were the inside of the late famous city carried and placed without the walls?"[38] Such growth was as disturbing as it was spectacular. It troubled government under Crown and Commonwealth alike and seems to have alarmed all but those whose interests rose by it. Nicholas Barbon, the most celebrated apologist for the growth of Restoration London, viewed these suburban developments with complete equanimity; in *An Apology for the Builder* (1685) he argued vigorously for the commercial advantages of an expanding metropolis, and excused it too on the grounds that it was simply for "the natural increase of Mankind."

The more widely held view of London's growth, however, was of a "Head swelling to too great a disproportion that it is att once become unwieldy and destructive to itselfe, and hath also left the other parts of the Kingdome languishing and deprived of its nutriment."[39] Dean Tucker, too, found such growth a public mischief in the 1770s, and put an old word to a new use in describing it: "If therefore the Increase of Building, begun at such an early Period, was looked upon to be no better than a Wen, or Excrescence, in the Body Politic, what must we think of those numberless Streets and Squares which had been added since!"[40] To William Cobbett forty years later the suburban spreadeagling of the town was more offensive still, for the suburbs were in his view the habitat of a *rentier* class which preyed upon the rest of society. Half the way from Walworth to Croydon, a distance of some nine miles, he noted recently built "stock-jobbers' houses" lining the road, and expostulated violently about such appendages to The Wen—a term which had now become a proper noun.[41] To the growth of London Cobbett characteristically ascribed any number of political ills,[42] while to his contemporary, John Loudon McAdam, the size and continuing growth of London were unmistakably evil.[43]

The suburbs of London, it is plain, had been growing for a long time when the Victorian period opened. Yet the changes which had so far occurred were no more than a prelude to still more rapid change in the years to come, years in which the city and its old environs exploded into a new Greater London. Camberwell was for the moment one of a number of villages in the vicinity of London which had had long independent existences. Within the previous sixty years the old structure of village society had begun to be altered by the coming of new people whose lives were related to the city rather than to the countryside. It was still possible in 1837, however, to be aware of Camberwell, both as a village and as a parish, as a place apart from London itself. Within the reign of a single sovereign this was irrevocably changed. By 1901 Camberwell had not only experienced in some part or other all the vicissitudes of suburban growth and decline, but had begun to merge in function and in form with other suburbs on every side and to become in consequence part of the great continent of suburbia.

CHAPTER III

THE CONDITIONS OF DEVELOPMENT

The Pace of Change

THE speed and authority with which the raw new streets of unassuming houses strode into the countryside in the years which followed were quite irresistible. Victorian Camberwell, like many other London suburbs, was the arena for changes which rubbed out almost overnight the familiar landmarks of the townsman's evening stroll into the fields, and puzzled and shocked the suburbians themselves, who could measure the retreat of the open country in terms of furlongs per year.[1]

> The fields are broken up, and in their place,
> Form'd into narrow strag'ling streets, are seen
> Cold, scanty dwellings of a starvling race,
> And all around is silent, dim, and mean,
> And gone for e'er the flowr's, the fields, and meadows green.

Such was the common lament. Coupled with it was the inevitable question which occurred to anyone who looked back on the events of his own lifetime through the middle decades of the nineteenth century: "Is this monster city again to double and treble itself?"In such a period London had enlarged its borders by some five times and its population by some two or three. Londoners juggled lugubriously with the statistics: theirs was a city, one of them reflected in the 1880s, which covered a hundred square miles and contained 2,000 miles of streets, a city which measured ten miles across, and whose sewers discharged $5\frac{1}{2}$ tons per week.[2] It was therefore no accident that the metaphors generally used to describe the stealthy rapidity with which London was growing should have been military ones. "The main army is preceded by an advance of villas . . . seizing a few picked positions," reported one correspondent. "Then come the more solid ranks of the semi-detached . . . along the high roads and in the neighbourhood of railway stations."[3] To Wilkie Collins, "Alexander's armies were great makers of conquests, and Napoleon's armies were great makers of conquests, but the modern Guerrilla regiments of the hod, the trowel, and the brick-kiln, are the greatest conquerors of all; for they hold the longest the soil that they have once possessed . . . with the conqueror's device inscribed on it—'THIS GROUND TO BE LET ON BUILDING LEASES!' "[4]

The regularity with which the city grew fresh limbs was to some of his contemporaries nothing more remarkable than a kind of biological change, but to most people the suburban expansion of Victorian London was the subject of everlasting wonder, chagrin, and complaint.[5] "What is then the picture?" asked one dismayed onlooker. "The old familiar field is cut up; the favourite blackberry hedge is cut down; the path along the mill-stream is closed; the well-remembered windmill has given place to a railway-station; the footway across the waving corn is no more; the stream in which he bathed is bordered by terraces and villas; the turnpike is gone; the little country alehouse at the corner has been covered by a Building Society with poverty-stricken houses; the green lane has probably become 'Victoria Street, leading to Albert Square'." "On both sides of the railway loop [between Loughborough Junction and Peckham], which a year ago was the pride of the locality for pretty scenery," complained another observer as the tempo of change quickened still more, "small houses . . . are rising almost as rapidly as summer mushrooms . . . Nunhead is fast becoming a brick-and-mortar wilderness. . . There is no prophet with vision clear enough to say to what limits the metropolis will extend in 1881."[6] In another part of the parish, Peckham Park* was developing so fast at this time that the place was "fast *losing* its suburban character . . . and promises shortly to form a little town in itself."[7] Within twelve months the correspondent of *The Builder* reported that in this locality a thousand houses had been built across the large market-gardens around Meeting House Lane, and Goldsmith House was soon to come down to make way for more: "in no district is this state of building activity more conspicuous than in several places south of the Thames," he reported; "amongst others the rural portions of Camberwell, Peckham, Hatcham and other districts

* The Duke of Marlborough's old estate between High Street, Peckham, and the Old Kent Road, bounded on the north-east by Asylum Road and on the north-west by Commercial Road.

are rapidly being converted into urban localities."[8] To a contributor to the *Saturday Review* in 1875 Camberwell had in fact completely transformed itself in the previous fifty years: then, it had been in the country, "but a child born there last week would assuredly be a Londoner, if not a cockney."[9]

What was it, it must first be asked, that determined the speed of this development? A brief answer to this question is that there were five important influences.[10] The first was demographic, for the growth of population in London itself was bound to impart to the growth of its suburbs an almost irresistible momentum. In addition to its natural increase, London was annually adding tens of thousands to its population by immigration from the countryside and overseas, and this led automatically to a geographical extension of the built-up area. Secondly, the pace of suburban development was governed by the increasing ability and willingness of more and more people to lengthen their journeys to work, and by the increasing tendency for business firms to move into the suburbs. Thirdly, the rate of suburban expansion was powerfully influenced by the availability of capital with which to finance the process. The fourth element in this expansion was the widespread acceptance of the convention of the single family dwelling and of the quest for social exclusiveness. Lastly, the tempo of events was governed by the force of local circumstances affecting the tenure of land and the development of estates. It is now necessary to examine these influences more closely.

Growth of the Population

The first and most fundamental stimulus to suburban development, which Camberwell felt in common with other London suburbs, was the remarkable fertility and growing expectation of life of the Victorians themselves, and their tendency to flock increasingly into London. During the eighteenth and the first half of the nineteenth centuries, London was growing not only faster than the population as a whole, but much faster than both moderate-sized and large towns; and, if, during the last quarter of the century, she gave the appearance of having fallen behind the rate of expansion of most provincial cities this must be because London had already spilled over her boundaries and the increases in her population were otherwise attributed. At the end of the nineteenth century Greater London was growing at the rate of an extra 100,000 inhabitants per year.[11] As capital and metropolis, London was a magnet whose field of attraction, though weaker at its limits, included the whole of the British Isles, and to it were also drawn large numbers of foreign immigrants. It is important to bear in mind that Camberwell was in consequence a segment of a city which grew from about 865,000 in 1801 to over $4\frac{1}{2}$ millions in 1901, and which contained at least one-sixth of the population of the whole country.

The growth of this massive concentration of human beings—the greatest which the world had yet seen—was the central fact in the demographic development and social change of any one of its parts. It was a process which might be considered in three overlapping phases. The first of these was the intensive settlement of the districts which made up the core of the city, and by 1861 these had been completely congested. From this date the population of Central London was thinned out by the wholesale demolition of dwelling-houses and the erection of more non-residential buildings. By the decade 1881–91 eleven out of thirty historic districts of London were consequently showing regular decreases in population, and any further increase in London's population had thereafter to take place in the surrounding districts.[12] This filling-up of the remaining districts of the Registration Division of London—the present London County Council area—comprised the second phase of the growth of modern London. For a relatively brief span of years almost all the districts which received Central London's overflowing population could be identified within this area, but by the 1890s it began in its turn to lose by migration more than it received, and although it continued to grow its rate of growth was cut by nearly a third.[13] The final phase covered the penetration of the suburbs of Greater London, an area identical with the Metropolitan Police District.

Camberwell, which occupied some 4,450 acres within the Registration Division of London, exemplified the second phase of this unique expansion.[14] Measured in the skeletonous terms of the censuses, it grew from 39,868 persons in 1841 to 259,339 in

1901: during the whole Victorian period, therefore, the population of this suburb expanded over seven times, a rate of expansion which was exceeded south of the river only by the superficially larger outlying dormitories of Wandsworth and Lewisham, in which suburban development had hardly begun in 1837. To measure this growth by a different standard over the nineteenth century as a whole, it could be said that in multiplying her population over sixty-five times Camberwell grew more in relation to its original size than any other district of London.[15] By the end of the century, this population was practically at its peak and, after climbing fractionally above this down to 1921, fell steadily thereafter.[16] The following table sets out the numerical data in more detail.

TABLE 2

THE GROWTH OF POPULATION, 1841–1911

(Intercensal percentage increases are given in brackets)

Census	*Registration Sub-districts*				*Totals*
	St George	*Camberwell*	*Peckham*	*Dulwich*	
1841	11,225	14,176	12,563	1,904	39,868
					(40.4)
1851	15,849	17,742	19,444	1,632	54,667
	(41.2)	(25.2)	(54.8)	(−14.3)	(37.1)
1861	20,333	21,297	28,135	1,723	71,488
	(28.3)	(20.1)	(44.7)	(5.6)	(30.8)
1871	33,851	31,254	42,160	4,041	111,306
	(66.5)	(46.9)	(49.8)	(134.6)	(55.7)
1881	50,810	59,104	71,089	5,590	186,593
	(50.1)	(89.1)	(68.7)	(38.3)	(67.6)
1891	63,366	81,686	83,483	6,809	235,344
	(24.7)	(38.2)	(17.4)	(21.8)	(26.1)
1901	65,589	90,465	93,033	10,247	259,339
	(3.5)	(9.7)	(11.4)	(50.5)	(10.2)
1911	63,837	97,042	89,563	10,961	261,403
	(−2.7)	(7.2)	(−3.7)	(6.5)	(0.8)

It is clear from the table that the rate at which the population was growing had, however, begun to decline in all parts of the parish by the 1880s. From a gain of some 15,000 persons in the decade between 1841 and 1851 the accretion had steadily increased over the next thirty years to reach its maximum between

1871 and 1881, when Camberwell's population increased by over 75,000 persons, or nearly 68 per cent.

Movement Into and Out of the Suburb

Although this demographic tide was slow to ebb—the decennial increases down to 1901 were each greater absolutely than those for the few decades before 1871—an undertow of emigration which was not perceptible on the surface was soon drawing away more migrants from Camberwell than were coming to it. Of the 75,000 persons by which the suburb had grown during its years of maximum development in the 1870s, about 52,000 represented the balance of migration into and out of the district, and 23,000 were the result of natural increase.[17] But the stream of migrants which had been chiefly responsible for the growth of the suburb since the beginning of the century, and which was now in full flood, soon declined, and it had dried up altogether by the end of the century. Of the increase of about 49,000 persons recorded between 1881 and 1891, only about 17,000 could be accounted for by net immigration, but in the last ten years of the century the increase of about 24,000 persons was wholly accounted for by natural increase, and would have been higher had not more people—over a thousand—left the suburb than came into it. By 1911, the balance of migration had detached a further 25,000 from Camberwell, and this attrition continued, despite the comparatively low average population density, in the post-war years.

Camberwell remained throughout its years of expansion a suburban vestibule. Its London doorstep was packed tight with a barely moving throng of suburbians, for most of whom the economic and social barriers to suburban removal remained unyielding. They could not afford to move deeper into the suburbs. If the Sub-district of St George was the doorstep of the parish that of Dulwich was the spacious back-garden. This was the most thinly populated and rustic part of the whole parish. To the middle-class inhabitants of this area the financial restraints which sheer distance from town placed on the outward movement of the working classes of St George were an effective social insulation. The Registrar-General's Camberwell was, however, a statistical abstraction which hid these realities in broader generalizations. His four Sub-districts of St George, Peckham, Camberwell, and Dulwich, were designed mainly for administrative convenience, and their data scarcely hinted at these suburban trends. In the Sub-district of St George lived a population which was about twice as numerous, acre for acre, as any other in the rest of the District throughout the nineteenth century. Crudely assessed—without making allowance for open spaces or inland water[18]—this density rose from 25 persons per acre in 1841 to 148 in 1901. On the other hand, in the Sub-district of Dulwich, the population density rose over the same period from a mere one to seven persons per acre. And between these two statistical and geographical extremes ranged the suburban corridors of the Sub-districts of Camberwell and Peckham, both of them taking in districts which had reached markedly different stages of development; in these, the average density rose from 10 to 73 per acre. Apart from Dulwich, whose population was prevented from rising above about 10,000 by the strict qualitative control exercised over the area by its principal landowner, the Estates Governors of Dulwich College, the speed at which this part of the suburb grew was too rapid to be reflected in marked variations in tempo between the remaining Sub-districts, though in all three maximum intercensal growth was recorded in the 1870s. These comparisons are clear in the following table.

TABLE 3

POPULATION DENSITY, 1841–1911

(Persons per acre to nearest whole number)

Census	*Registration Sub-districts*			
	St George (447 acres)	*Camberwell* (1,381 acres)	*Peckham* (1,169 acres)	*Dulwich* (1,453 acres)
1841	25	10	11	1
1851	36	13	17	1
1861	46	15	24	1
1871	76	23	36	3
1881	114	43	61	4
1891	142	59	71	5
1901	148	66	80	7
1911	143	70	77	8

Sources of Immigration

Like any other suburb during its years of expansion, Camberwell grew by absorbing migrants from elsewhere. Where did these come from? Did they, like the vociferous cockneys whom Ruskin observed bearing down like Vandals on the Crystal Palace, all come from inner London, or were they drifting in from the surrounding countryside?

To say whence they came in terms of last addresses is out of the question, but it is possible to suggest the main sources from which this stream of migrants sprang during the period of greatest growth, on the assumption that what was true of the whole was also roughly true of its part. Of the vast numbers of newcomers who swarmed on Victorian London from all parts of the kingdom and abroad—a quarter of a million of them in the 1840s but practically double this number in the 1870s—a growing proportion had destinations south of the river: between 1841 and 1851 about a quarter of all immigrants to London became South Londoners, but within the next thirty years this proportion had risen to well over a third.[19] Apart from the 1840s, when over 11 per cent. of such migrants to South London had come from Ireland alone, nine out of ten of them had come, though not necessarily directly, from all parts of the United Kingdom; but of these two or three had merely crossed the river from North London.[20] Briefly, the sources of this migration to South London between 1841 and 1881 were: nearly 40 per cent. came from the adjacent areas of metropolitan Middlesex and extra-metropolitan Surrey and Kent, about 28 per cent. from the neighbouring south-eastern counties of Sussex, Hampshire, Berkshire, Essex, Suffolk, and Norfolk; and most of the rest were drawn from an area south of a line between the Severn and the Wash, though an increasing proportion was arriving from the industrial north towards the end of the century. In South London, as in North, these newcomers never represented more than between 12 and 16 per cent. of the total population in any single decade,[21] but the cumulative effect of these prodigious transfers of population was to create urban communities in which not more than half their members had been born within South London at all.

These were the demographic influences which appear to have touched Camberwell as much as any of her metropolitan neighbours.[22] What came into the Registrar-General's viewfinder at each ten-year interval was, of course, merely the frozen climax to a decade of movement.[23] The majority of Camberwell's population, we can conclude from these infrequent snapshots, were born Londoners—some 65 per cent. of them in 1861 and 76 per cent. in 1911—but to log their removals, even in very general terms, cannot be done with accuracy. The impression made on contemporaries, however, was that migration from one street to another, or from one district to the next, was on a scale which the tantalizing data of the Censuses never uncovered.[24] "North of Peckham Road," wrote Charles Booth, "is a large district becoming steadily poorer as the fairly comfortable move South and immigrants from Walworth arrive."[25] Such social transformations were the visible products of innumerable uncharted migrations of families on the move to tap fresh credit, or to find cheaper rooms, or simply to 'get a bit decent'." They were also symptoms of rising land values, which were having the effect of squeezing out residential accommodation in the centre of the city. Since the beginning of the century government and commerce had been easily outbidding the rents which most families could afford to pay for living room there, and when the available sites for premises of any kind were seriously reduced by demolitions for railways, new streets, and other civic improvements, these rents were inevitably raised to still more prohibitive levels.[26]

Suburbs within walking distance of the river, especially if they had already developed slums for other reasons, or like Camberwell had continued to give outdoor poor relief while some other parishes relied solely on the Workhouse, tended to become reception areas for part of the population which had been displaced by these means. In this way, the Golden Lane and Petticoat Lane Improvement Schemes meant considerable deterioration in housing conditions in parts of Camberwell and Peckham.[27] In the last twenty years of the nineteenth century paupers in Camberwell trebled in number, and new levels of overcrowding were being reached. "The poor squeezed out of other parts come here," the Chairman of the Vestry explained, "and Camberwell suffers."[28] It was not, however, the poor alone who made this exodus from Central London. To one local newspaper reporter, at least, these evictions from the centre to make way for "palatial residences, monster hotels . . . business premises . . . a new street, or other metropolitan improvement" produced the involuntary migration not only of families which stocked suburban tenements, but of others whose unclipped flight took them to the lordly mansions of Dulwich, or whose retreat was to the modest homes of Camberwell.[29] It is clear from this that suburban migration had no simple geographical pattern nor precise social content. Unrecorded though most of it was, even in statistical abstractions, it was the sum of this unknown medley of removals which was the means of populating the entire suburb.

The Journey to Work

The second stimulus to the suburban development of Camberwell came, as it did elsewhere, from improved transport facilities. The creation of an adequate system of suburban communications was important in two ways. Its fundamental rôle was to increase the ability and willingness of more and more people to undertake longer journeys to work. It also provided some of the essential services needed for building and maintaining the suburb, and for making it, by means of local services, a viable economic and social entity. It is important to bear in mind at this point that there were in a functional sense two Londons. There was the London which was a gigantic industrial and commercial organism of intricate and interdependent parts; and there was the London which was no more than the aggregate of local communities, each of which was in some respects almost self-contained, preserving some of its individual characteristics and serving many of its own needs. The functions of suburban transport were thus both metropolitan and local, and it is these which must now be considered as formative influences in suburban development.

It is true that the lengthening of the journey to work was in one sense partly the reflex of rising real incomes, shorter working hours, and, above all, greater regularity and security of employment—trends which were becoming general for increasing numbers of potential suburbians during the second half of the nineteenth century. For many workers, however, this improvement in their welfare was not a necessary preliminary to suburban existence at all. Their daily shuttling to and fro was possible on foot because employment opportunities within the parish or near it became increasingly numerous and varied as businessmen of all kinds came to recognize the advantages of suburban locations. Comparatively low suburban rents for industrial premises and a growing market for local labour thus led not only to rising employment in the local retail trades of Camberwell and its suburban neighbours but to an expanding demand for labour of all kinds in local factories, workshops, wharves, and yards.

It is problematical how far this industrial decentralization was itself a stimulus to suburban growth, for though the new jobs created by expanding firms were likely to tempt workers into the suburbs to live, the suburban dispersal of industry was unlikely to have occurred on a large scale before the market for local labour had been developed sufficiently to meet the demands which businessmen expected to make upon it. In the context of Camberwell's development, this stage was unlikely to have been reached before the last quarter of the nineteenth century. There was here a relationship, however, in which cause and effect would have been indistinguishable at times even to the most highly sophisticated businessmen of the day, and it is not possible with the slender evidence at hand to do more than observe the relationship. It is more than probable, for example, that one contribution of the Grand Surrey Canal to the suburban development of Camberwell was to confer special advantages on the factories, timber yards, coal wharves, and miscellaneous businesses which congregated on its banks, and that their need for workers led to the populating of the neighbourhood. The same may be true of the tramway sheds, omnibus yards, and railway goods sidings of North Camberwell and Peckham, of the South Metropolitan Gas Company's works on the Old Kent Road, and of the cemeteries at Nunhead and Honor Oak which had their local corps of gravediggers. But what can be said of the growing number of industries, large and small, which were moving into converted dwelling-houses or premises of their own making north of the Peckham Road? No clear answer can be given.

Victorian Camberwell had no distinctive industrial character of the kind that silk-weaving had once given to Spitalfields or chair-making to Bethnal Green. Its industrial character was on the contrary strikingly heterogeneous. Although there were to be numbered among its population by the end of the nineteenth century a significant proportion of London's hatmakers, printing trade employees, and clerks—Camberwell contained in 1901 more clerks than any other part of London, some 22,000 of them, or about 12 per cent. of the total—there is no way of discovering how many of these were employed locally. The total numbers involved in any particular trade were in any case usually comparatively small, while the proportions of its workers engaged in all other branches of industry were unremarkable.[30] Few industrial premises—apart from a noticeable concentration of breweries—figured among the entries in local trade directories before the 1880s, and the miscellaneous enterprises which were then brought into being did not give to Camberwell any very marked industrial characteristics. None of them was particularly large. There were makers of tarpaulins, linoleum, Venetian blinds, leather goods, sacks, bottles, vinegar, sauces, mineral waters, and so on, but more important than any of these were the numerous ancillary trades to the building industry, house-building itself, road services, some market-gardening, and a catholic array of dealers, bespoke tailors and shoemakers, and retailers of all kinds.[31]

That there was no single source of large-scale industrial employment locally did not mean, therefore, that the proportion of the working population of Camberwell in local employment was necessarily small in aggregate. Indeed, it is probable that the majority of workers living in the parish at the end of the nineteenth century made no demands at all on public transport to make their journeys to work. Of the 159,844 South London members of trade unions who in 1897 were questioned through their branches about their daily journeys to work, only 36,557, or less than a quarter, travelled daily.[32] Although it cannot be inferred from this that reliance on public transport services for reaching work was of the same order in the different suburbs of

South London, it does suggest the probability that more people either had local jobs or reached their work elsewhere on foot or bicycle than used bus, tram, or train.[33]

For these suburbians, at any rate, the development of adequate facilities for suburban travel was apparently irrelevant; but to a growing minority of workers in the City and the East and West Ends, and of performers of innumerable, unclassified journeys in the opposite direction, such facilities were the calculable elements among the variable costs of the suburban life. There can be no doubt that to many of the former at least the lack of suburban communications would have closed the door on suburban existence altogether, and would also have retarded the growth of local trades which sprang into being to cater for suburban needs. But it is seldom possible to identify with certainty the precise contribution of such transport facilities to the development of particular neighbourhoods because there is no way of discriminating accurately between contemporaneous influences on suburban development which were not recorded at the time in some reliable statistical form. What alone is reasonably certain is that few daily travellers—whether they were holders of First Class season-tickets or of twopenny workmen's tickets—can have been totally indifferent to the length and the cost of the journey to work. And the account which follows of the suburban public transport services affecting Camberwell is therefore a compound of these two elements.

Turnpike and Parish Roads

Until the 1860s the daily journey to work was necessarily governed by the available roads and the public transport which used them. Suburban road transport, it has already become clear, had had a long history when the Victorian era opened. Ancient highway, country lane, and turnpike had, in both a figurative and literal sense, already laid down the template of Victorian suburban expansion. This was obviously true of Camberwell for, apart from the untidy weave of streets created by scores of uncoordinated builders and land companies, neither arterial nor main road was added to its communications in the course of the nineteenth century. There was, of course, some widening here and straightening there, and the corruption of ageless trackways into an unrecognizably suburban idiom. But new routes between city and suburb, though occasionally proposed, were never cut: like that of London as a whole, the road system of Camberwell remained basically the same throughout the Victorian era.[34]

When approached from the London side, the parish appeared to be enclosed between the Old Kent Road in the east and Camberwell High Road in the west—lines of departure from the metropolis which began, the one at London Bridge, and the other at Blackfriars. The suburb could alternatively be entered from a point farther west, Westminster Bridge, whence the route ran through Kennington and along the Camberwell New Road to Camberwell Green, where it joined the High Road. From here it was extended eastwards by the road to Peckham, and beyond this to join the Old Kent Road at Hatcham. The triangle enclosed by these three roads was truncated in the north by Albany Road, and cut up by the Grand Surrey Canal and its branch. South of this triangular wedge were only three principal avenues of further penetration: the first, which led by way of Herne Hill, skirted the western boundary of the parish, and led to Dulwich Village; the second branched off Denmark Hill at the "Fox-under-the-hill"—an inn which stood on Denmark Hill until demolished during the construction of the South London Line in 1865—and led first to Goose Green and then to Dulwich Common; and the third stretched southwards from Peckham High Street to Peckham Rye.

The function of these roads as channels for daily journeys to work depended most, of course, on the public transport services which used them, but it was also affected by the character of the road authority. Although the mileage of turnpike roads within the parish was soon exceeded by that of the parish roads—in 1857 the Vestry superintended 32 miles of roads as against less than 6 miles still controlled by the turnpike trusts[35]—the turnpikes remained in monopolistic control not only of all roads into the suburb, but of the principal internal roads too. This situation, however, soon changed. Except for the Dulwich College toll-road, the Camberwell turnpikes were parts of larger road systems which had by the 1850s got so seriously into debt as a result of railway competition that it could only be a matter of time before sheer financial debility weakened their hold even on the comparatively profitable town roads. But before this happened the turnpike trusts were a powerful influence on the course of suburban development. According to Sir Joseph Paxton (to whom a road toll must have been a particularly vexatious hindrance to popular enjoyment of his Crystal Palace), South London was "laid out in the worst possible manner . . . in order to converge the roads upon certain turnpikes which you must come through on that side [of the river]."[36]

With falling receipts elsewhere it was natural that turnpike trustees should have looked to their metropolitan revenues to keep solvent, and new gates were thrown across many side-streets in the effort to canalize traffic which was always seeking toll-free routes. "Let the traveller drive through the Walworth Gate southward," invited one champion of toll reform, "and note how every road, every alley, every passage has its 'bar'. One part of the parish of Camberwell—where the more humble classes of the community dwell—is completely isolated, and the back districts are cut off from all intercommunication by the Turnpike and Ticket System."[37] Around Southampton Street and in Dulwich, it was claimed, the toll had positively deterred development.[38] Such assertions are hard to test, but it is worth remembering that a turnpike system which was rapidly becoming archaic provided a natural vent for more complaint than it really deserved. New tolls and new gates in Peckham, so wrote one indignant correspondent to *The Times* in 1850, had resulted in a penny rise in the omnibus fare to town, but it was more commonly agreed that the toll was seldom an element of crucial importance in fixing the price of suburban travel.[39]

The gradual recognition that toll-roads were nevertheless inconvenient anomalies in South London suburbs—as they had long before been recognized to be north of the Thames—came in 1865, when scores of turnpike gates were swept away, and responsibility for upkeep of the roads was made the responsibility of the new Highway Districts.[40] This financial burden inevitably varied from one suburb to the next according to its complement of highway, but in most of them rateable values were rising quite dramatically so the new commitment was not onerous: the 6 miles or so of turnpike which the Camberwell Vestry took over in 1865 was only a fraction of the 45 miles of streets it was administering by 1870, and a smaller one still of the 112 miles for which it was responsible thirty years later.[41] With three or four uses for every ratepayers' pound, however, postponement of expenditure on street improvement could easily be justified. It is significant, therefore, that the major improvement of these years, which was the widening of Camberwell Church Street and Peckham Road, was financed by the Metropolitan Board of Works, and that the widening of Rye Lane, Peckham, which was an equally urgent piece of street improvement, was left undone. Camberwell's main roads were of more than parochial importance, however, and that more was not done to modernize them in order to carry an annually increasing traffic was much less a matter of straitened Vestry finances than it was of confused objectives, limited finance, and vague administration at the centre.[42]

Coaches and Omnibuses

If the roads themselves changed little in the course of the nineteenth century, the public transport services which they carried certainly did. Regular coach services between Camberwell, Peckham, Dulwich, and the City and Westminster had been steadily increasing for at least sixty years before the 1830s; but impressive as this growth appeared in terms of arrivals and departures of Camberwell coaches, the facilities were modest when measured against the size of the community these coaches served. By 1834 some seventeen coaches were to be found daily on the roads between the City and Camberwell, and they completed between them some ninety separate journeys,[43] but although Camberwell was by then far better served than any other suburb south of the river, the total capacity of all these coaches could not have exceeded a thousand seats, and the number available at the usual hours of travelling for business must have been very much smaller. Though only a tiny fraction of the working population of Camberwell could have travelled by such means, it was clear from the general dissatisfaction with these services that coachmasters were failing to keep pace with a rapidly rising demand in the suburbs for more road services.

The omnibus, a Parisian creation imported by George Shillibeer in 1829, had however already demonstrated its special suitability for short stage services at relatively low cost elsewhere in London, and scores of jobmasters and coachmasters were putting omnibuses on the road.[44] After 1835 the three principal coach proprietors in Camberwell—Tanner, Prince, and Glover—turned to omnibus operation, and they were quickly joined by a dozen others;[45] but, even allowing for an impressive elasticity in the working hours of their clients, suburban omnibuses still appear to have catered less for the regular journey to work than for the casual visit to town. For the next decade or more no bus left Gracechurch Street for Camberwell or Peckham before 9.0 a.m., and the earliest service into the City was therefore about 9.30 a.m.[46] That omnibus services at this time were spaced out fairly evenly over the whole day and that their published times of departure were generally for outward journeys and not for inward ones were symptoms of an early stage in suburban development: the solicitous practice of calling for one's customers with the morning bus was poles apart from the anonymity and indifference of the rush-hour. Omnibus operation as a personal service was, however, in rapid decline during the 1840s, and by 1852 buses were leaving Gracechurch Street for Camberwell every ten minutes. Within another five years, Camberwell-bound buses were crossing London, Blackfriars, Waterloo, and Westminster Bridges every five minutes, and the frequency of these services was such as to make reference to a timetable or to the distinctive liveries of rival operators practically superfluous.[47]

One reason for the increase in these services was the intensive competition which had grown up between omnibus proprietors. Their number was, however, sharply reduced by the amalgamation of most existing omnibus businesses into the London General Omnibus Company Ltd. in 1856 and the organization of almost all the remainder into working associations.[48] The two principal operators who served Camberwell were the London General and Thomas Tilling, a man who had begun a jobbing business with a single horse in Walworth in 1845, but who by

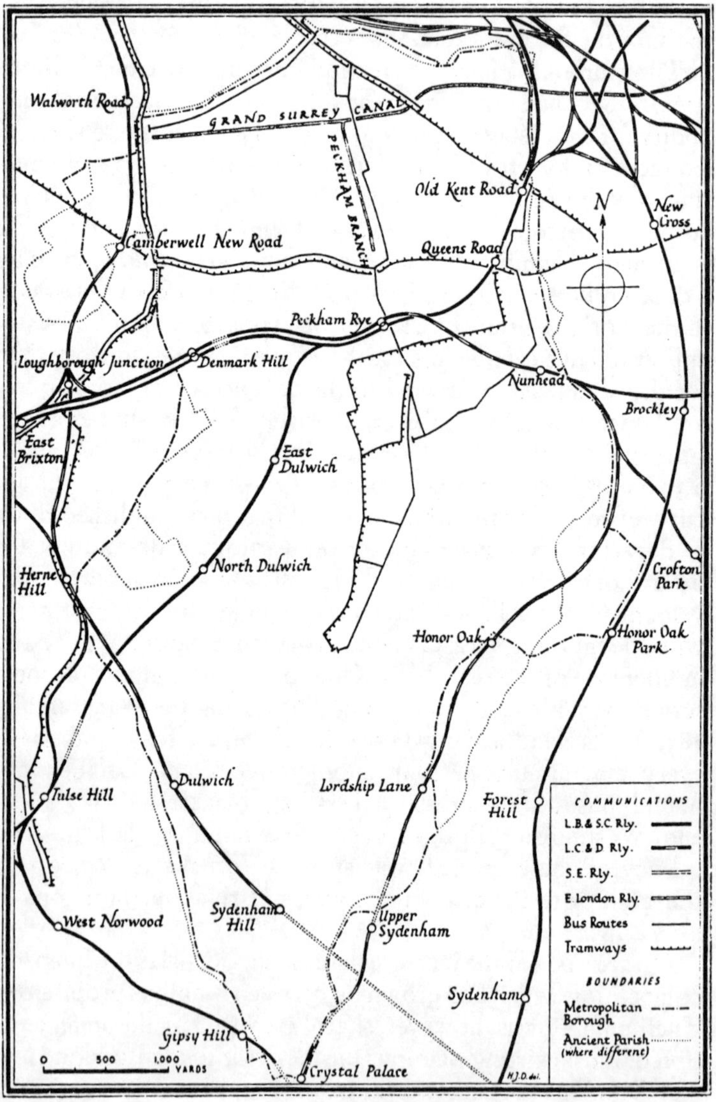

FIG. 2. *Public Transport Services*

1851 had bought the stock and goodwill of a single omnibus and started a service of four buses a day between Rye Lane and Oxford Circus at a fare of 1s. 6d. Within twenty years Tilling's stable had grown to nearly four hundred horses and within thirty-five years to fifteen hundred, a figure which suggests his fleet of omnibuses may by then have grown to well over a hundred.[49]

To the residents of Camberwell in the years from 1835 to 1862 the omnibus was literally the common carrier, for no other public transport was available for passengers. Camberwell was little more than a mile and a half from the City at its closest point, and it must have made its contribution to the 200,000 walkers who were reckoned to file daily into the City along the principal roads in the 1850s.[50] This kind of journey to work had been more usual before the omnibuses appeared, as is clear from the opening of numerous short-cuts—'halfpenny hatches'—between the main roads, and there were certainly substantial numbers of regular walkers to work sixty years later; though the proportion was falling.[51] By the 1860s the omnibus had brought regular suburban travel within financial reach of the better paid clerk and artisan, for though fares had not yet reached their lowest level they had been halved in thirty years: the single fare between the "Lord Nelson", Old Kent Road, and the Bank had fallen by then to threepence; between Camberwell Green and Gracechurch Street to fourpence; and between Peckham or Dulwich and Gracechurch Street to sixpence.[52] What is more, the earliest buses were by then running at times which made it possible to be at work at the latest by 8.30 a.m. To cater for a mass demand was, however, to abandon completely the localities in which customers could be counted in half-dozens rather than in hundreds and many ambitiously sited new estates remained perpetually busless as a result.[53]

Railways

The saviour of these suburban pioneers was the railway. For the residents of Camberwell before the 1860s the railway had been at the most a profitable investment and a godsend for distant travel—that is, beyond London—but it was not the means of getting to work. The locomotive was in truth practically middle-aged before it appeared in Camberwell. As with communication by road, Camberwell had had none of the vicarious benefits of straddling trunk routes to the south coast. The line to Southampton passed miles to the west, while those to Brighton and to Dover ran just out of convenient reach to the east; and even the line which, in 1852, had pursued the Crystal Palace to its new site at Sydenham at the southernmost tip of the parish, gave Camberwell proper no railway access to London, for it passed instead through Streatham and Norwood. There was nothing surprising in this because Camberwell did not lie on the shortest lines to these various points, nor was she much worse served than many other suburbs at that date.

Suburban railways had so far been something of a financial adventure because the return had been problematical and few companies had been prepared to act as suburban pioneers. Gradually, however, the deserted stations which merely punctuated the route to more distant destinations attracted their first suburban customers, and by the 1860s suburban railways could be regarded as sound propositions. Not surprisingly, a high proportion of the tangled lines proposed to Parliament in the little mania of railway promotion in London in the 1860s were suburban in character, and it was in the years 1862 to 1868 that Camberwell became one of a new ring of railway suburbs.

The first line to appear inside the parish was not strictly intended to be a suburban one at all, but simply the metropolitan extension of the expanding network of the newly-named London, Chatham & Dover Railway. This was the culminating move in a deep strategy aimed at breaching the South Eastern Railway's monopoly of Continental traffic by providing a more direct route to Dover. To this end the Chatham Company had already leased part of the Victoria terminus of the West End of London & Crystal Palace Railway, but the retaliatory move of the South Eastern in carrying its line from London Bridge to Charing Cross was answered by the Chatham Company's obtaining powers in 1860 for building another terminus in the City. The Chatham Company had in this way planned to install itself in two London termini, one in the City and the other in the West End. The City line was opened between Herne Hill and Elephant

& Castle in October 1862, and had arrived at Blackfriars on the south side of the river by June 1864; the river itself was spanned when the line was opened to Ludgate Hill in December 1864, and the City penetrated deeper still when the line was extended to Farringdon Street in January 1866, to Holborn Viaduct in March 1874, and finally to St Paul's in May 1886. The connection with the West End at Victoria was completed in July 1863.

Although competition for the Dover traffic was the principal reason for this sudden rash of London termini—the South Eastern also had three of its own—their construction must also be reckoned as extravagant gestures in the courtship of potential City and suburban travellers. The right rail connection with town was as much the practical requirement of the 'desirable neighbourhood' as the correct social atmosphere was its romantic ideal. To this extent, therefore, the advertisements on the fascia boards at local stations and on the hoardings of speculative builders and house-agents were preaching to the converted. What the house-hunter in these new suburbs was not to know, however, was that this prodigal expenditure on City termini would not only be a crucial factor in placing the Chatham Company in Chancery for five years—1866 to 1871—but in preventing the expansion and improvement of their lines, and in causing an increase in fares.[54] What was probably also a consequence of this prodigality was the abandonment of an intended loop line from Walworth Road Station to connect at Peckham Rye with the High Level Crystal Palace line, which is referred to presently. It is true that the City Line of the Chatham Company was quadrupled between Loughborough Junction and Blackfriars within a year of its opening, but even this was apparently insufficient to prevent frequent congestion of trains and chronically late arrivals for businessmen coming up from the suburbs.[55] To the season-ticket holders of Camberwell, however, this particular route to their employments was of slight importance when it was first opened, for it provided only three stations within the parish—Camberwell New Road, Dulwich, and Sydenham Hill—none of which was for some years at the heart of suburban development.

Next in both chronology and importance was the line opened by the Crystal Palace & South London Junction Railway in

August 1865. This was operated by the London, Chatham & Dover Railway and ran between Peckham Rye (or, more accurately, Cow Lane Junction) and a new high level station at Crystal Palace. But if the Metropolitan Extensions of the Chatham Company had been built principally with trunk traffic in mind, this new junction railway had been conceived as an approach to a turnstile. Since June 1854 the gleaming bulk of Paxton's wonder had lured a constant traffic of Londoners along the lines of the Brighton Company from London Bridge, and this traffic had been swollen by another stream from Victoria since 1860. The Chatham Company's line now permitted for the population of Peckham what an omnibus from Camberwell Gate had already done for that of Camberwell—given them access to a new source of entertainment. But the suburban migration of the Crystal Palace had not merely enlarged the scope of London's entertainments, nor simply shrunk the Sydenham Heights, as Ruskin thought, into three long lumps of clay. It had above all marked these slopes down for building leases. The rôle of the new railway in creating this suburb at the Palace gates was, however, for many years quite insignificant. Nor was its contribution to the development of the potential suburbs *en route* at all impressive before the 1880s. Its conventional apparatus of stations set in the fields did little to attract suburbians who could still find virgin suburb much closer to the city, while the tardy journeys they would have faced on the slowest line in South London were bound to be positively repellent. And when the Walworth Road loop line, which estate agents had been declaring with confidence in 1867 was essential to the success of the new line to the Crystal Palace had to be abandoned, estate development was retarded for ten or fifteen years.[56]

City and suburban railway traffic had so far been a by-product of other ventures, but the building of the South London Line between Victoria and London Bridge in the years between 1862 and 1867 was an overture to the suburbians themselves. Two companies, the London, Brighton & South Coast Railway, and the London, Chatham & Dover Railway, had schemes for this route, and the construction and working of it was a carefully contrived compromise between their competing interests.[57] In August 1866 the line was opened between London Bridge and

East Brixton, including four new stations in Camberwell—Old Kent Road, Queens Road, Peckham Rye, and Denmark Hill—and the opening in the following May of the final section between East Brixton and Battersea Park completed the whole project to connect London Bridge and Victoria through the expanding suburbs. A spur between East Brixton and Loughborough Junction had already been built in 1863, and another was added between the latter and Denmark Hill in 1872: these considerably increased the flexibility with which the new lines could be used for they permitted entry to the City itself over the lines of the Metropolitan Extensions to Ludgate Hill, Farringdon Street, and St Paul's. The final instalment of railway to be made in Camberwell was the South London & Sutton Junction Railway which was built on to the South London Line at Peckham and ran south-west to Tulse Hill and beyond. When it was opened in October 1868 it included two further stations within the parish, at Champion Hill (known as East Dulwich after 1888) and North Dulwich.

What was the effect of these suburban lines on the journey to work? It must be admitted that it is probably as difficult to generalize retrospectively about this as it was for the railway companies themselves to predict the volume of traffic. Only two of the new stations were north of the Peckham Road and the remainder were on the suburban frontier farther south. Although the initial effect of these lines was often to cut the time spent on the shorter journeys to work by as much as a half they did not lower fares, but rather tended to raise them. It took, for example, about a quarter-of-an-hour to get from Denmark Hill or Peckham Rye to London Bridge on the South London Line, while the journey by bus to Gracechurch Street—at the same sixpenny fare—took about double the time; from Old Kent Road by rail to London Bridge cost fourpence, but by bus from the "Lord Nelson" to the Bank was only threepence. Longer rail journeys nevertheless cost proportionately less while the time saved was even greater. On neither the buses nor the trains were fares yet cheap enough for families whose budgets hardly permitted daily journeys to work by public transport at all. The First Class season-ticket holder who travelled upwards of twenty miles could usually afford it out of the savings he made by living in the country rather than in the town,[58] but this was not the case on much lower standards of living and tighter family budgets.

Tramways

Before 1870 neither omnibus nor train had opened up the suburbs to the working classes because to pay a shilling a day for fares alone was an impossibility on an income of a pound a week or less. A shilling a week was, however, a different matter, and this was the measure of the contribution of the tram and the workman's ticket to the suburban development of London in the last thirty years or so of the nineteenth century.

Had G. F. Train, the tramway pioneer, been more successful with the services he had operated in Victoria Street and between Westminster Bridge and Kennington Gate in 1861 and 1862,[59] it is possible that Camberwell also would have had a tramway ten years before it actually did. Train had written to the Vestry in October 1860 to get permission to operate a tramway, but the Vestry decided to watch the outcome of the unfortunate Victoria Street experiment.[60] Train's failure left the omnibus associations in sole control of public street transport for nearly a decade.[61] This phase came to an abrupt end in South London in 1869 when Camberwell was involved in the development of a comprehensive network of tram-lines.

Once authority for a horse tramway had been given to the Pimlico, Peckham and Greenwich Street Tramways Company in that year a complete system of tram-lines was begun, with the idea of linking the main roads of North Camberwell with Blackfriars and Westminster Bridges and Vauxhall Cross, and by January 1872 the whole system was in operation.[62] The only addition made to it before the end of the century was the rather ridiculous appendage of the London, Camberwell & Dulwich Tramway Company, which took trams south of the Peckham Road. The company was founded under a different name in 1882 and three years later had three miles of track open between Lordship Lane and Peckham Rye. Unfortunately the promoters had not only made an untimely start when capital was scarce, and had rashly proposed to penetrate streets in which the convenience of a local tramway was evidently thought less desirable than the maintenance of property values, but they had failed to agree with the Vestry on the widening of Rye Lane. As a result, no tram-car used these lines before 1895 or 1896, and by 1901 even the desultory profitless services which were run at weekends over some of these lines came to an end. Its futility as a local tramway had already become a local joke, and the company which had been capitalized at nearly £95,000 was in 1904 swallowed up by the L.C.C. for a mere £6,500 or so, and two years later scrapped.[63] The successful tramway invasion of East Dulwich and Peckham did not come before 1906–8, when the L.C.C. system was extended by an electrified route from Herne Hill to Goose Green and thence in one direction to Rye Hill Park and in another to Dulwich Library and Forest Hill. In Victorian Camberwell, however, the tram still belonged to the region north of the Peckham Road, and south of it lay districts which relied principally on the single-horse bus and, above all, on the railway.[64]

The "Workmen's"

The tramways were the final links attaching Camberwell to the vast, haphazard, intricate structure of London's communications. The whole system worked like some self-regulating clearing house which permitted an almost infinite variety of journeys. It was a system nevertheless whose latent capacity for mass travel was in the 1870s still far greater than its actual contribution to it. Little used suburban railway stations or half-empty omnibuses were the most obvious symptoms of this, but even where there was no obvious working below capacity the whole apparatus of metropolitan communications was capable of carrying more people farther and cheaper than it had so far done.

The conviction that this was so arose mainly from the realization that as well as exacerbating the housing problem of Central London by their wholesale demolitions the railways also provided a possible solution of it. Although they were by no means the first agents of slum clearance, their rôle as destroyers of working-class homes in Victorian London soon attracted as much publicity as the engineering feats which brought about their destruction. What is more, politically influential people reluctantly came to recognize that far from migrating to the suburbs, as they had been expected to do, the displaced persons of the railway age poured instead into the nearby streets where overcrowding was almost always dangerously high already. But if railways contributed to the creation of new levels of overcrowding in Victorian London they also suggested a way out of the difficulties. For what sprang out of a sense of rough justice to the lips of working men themselves, who had been turned out of doors by the demolitions, had also occurred on grounds of sanitary expediency to an early generation of town planners: cheap railway fares to and from the suburbs for the working classes. To Parliament, which was reluctant to meddle in economic matters, and to railway directors, who scanned the probable costs, this was a much more palatable prescription for these ills than the alternative of re-housing the dispossessed. If not a complete answer to the problem of where to house the workers this was at least some alleviation of the pressure for space in the central areas.

For the suburbs which were affected the decision to run workmen's trains was a pregnant one. The social structure of the suburbs had hitherto been controlled by their geographical and financial isolation. In lowering the cost of daily suburban travel to a level which the bulk of those in regular employment could afford, however, the workmen's ticket created a vast new travelling public on a different reach of the social scale. By this means the subtle social transformation of London's suburbs which had been going on since the eighteenth century with the migration thither of the middle classes, was now dramatically accelerated as the working classes arrived in force to take possession of them, and to drive the middle classes farther afield.

Long before 1883, when the issue of workmen's tickets was made compulsory under certain conditions, such facilities had been created on some of the trains serving Camberwell. The first workmen's trains on the London, Chatham & Dover Company's line to Ludgate Hill were started early in 1865. The company was not at first obliged by law to run such trains, but its Act for new lines in 1864 prescribed a minimum service between Peckham Junction and Ludgate Hill of one train in the morning before 7 a.m. and another to return in the evening after 6 p.m.:

tickets were to be issued to *bona fide* working men only, the fare was to be a penny in each direction, and the train was to stop at all stations. The Brighton Company was not at this time legally obliged to run any workmen's trains, apart from those on the East London Railway (which it leased) between New Cross and Liverpool Street. New Cross was, however, within easy walking distance of Hatcham and Peckham, and the workmen's services which were available after 1876 into Liverpool Street were probably used to some extent by working men from this neighbourhood. In 1883 the potential scope of such services—some 25,000 workmen's tickets were being issued daily throughout London by 1882—was greatly increased by the passage of the Cheap Trains Act, which repealed the passenger duty on all penny-a-mile fares and at the same time compelled all railway companies to introduce workmen's fares as and when required by the Board of Trade. Meanwhile, similar facilities had become available in Camberwell on early morning trams, as required by the original Acts which had brought the tramways into being.[65]

The State of Communications in 1895

The mechanism for the journey to work between Camberwell and Central London had by now taken on a form which altered little over the last twenty years of the nineteenth century. Apart from some comparatively minor extensions or restrictions of existing services, all that significantly changed during this time was the expanding scale on which these travelling facilities were used. But if Camberwell's connections with Central London can almost be said to have taken on by then their definitive form this cannot be described as comprehensive, for transport facilities varied greatly from one part of the suburb to another. This patchiness had a direct connection with the state of the development of the districts concerned, and it is now necessary to examine this variableness in order to measure its effect. The direction and volume of the public transport facilities as existing in 1895 are therefore given on the accompanying map (Fig. 3).[66]

It is clear from the map that the horse omnibus—suburban pioneer though it had been and all-powerful though it still was in

London as a whole—was by 1895 the least important means of travel from suburb to city. Most bus services to town still pursued the main roads, but the all-conquering tram had edged it from some of these altogether, and forced it to pick its way through minor streets or to probe the new half-built areas in

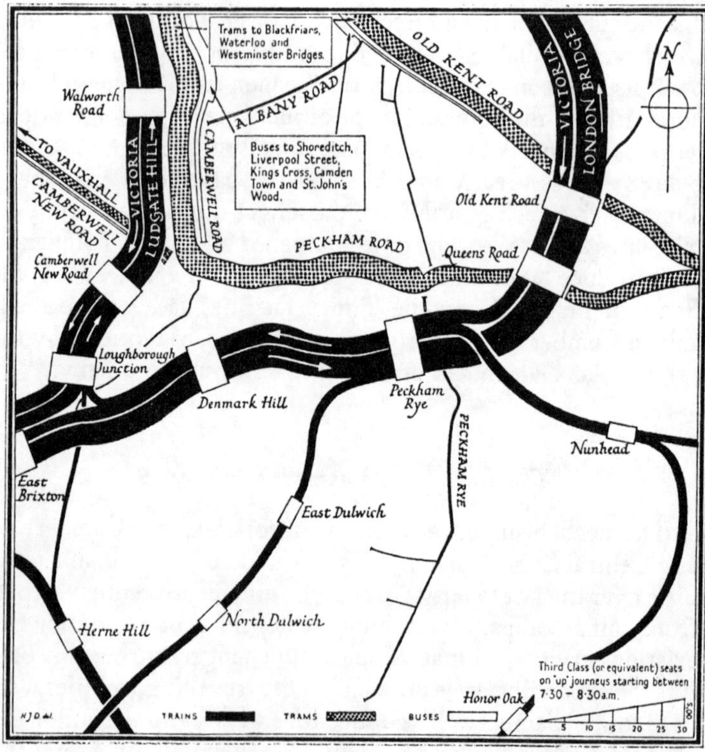

FIG. 3. *The Flow of Suburban Traffic in 1895*

search of a new travelling public. Where traffic would support a twelve-minute service of horse-buses, so it was reckoned, a tramway would pay,[67] but by the 1890s the traffic on the most important of Camberwell's main roads would have required horse-bus services of a minute or less. The tram had therefore taken undisputed possession of long stretches of main road—Queens Road, and the Old Kent Road between the canal and New

Cross Gate—and wherever the horse-bus lingered to challenge its supremacy the tram, though still horse-powered, carried on an average two or three times the number of passengers who used the buses, and on one stretch of road, Church Street, tram passengers outnumbered bus passengers by nearly fifteen to one.[68] The principal services, all provided by the London Tramway Company,[69] had termini at or near the Thames bridges—Blackfriars, Waterloo, Westminster, and Vauxhall—and to each of them but the last, trams were available at intervals of three to twelve minutes anywhere on the Old Kent Road, Peckham Road, and Camberwell Road from about 7 a.m. to almost midnight; a comparable service to Vauxhall had its starting-point at Camberwell Green.

The principal railway to serve the northern part of Camberwell was the South London Line of the L.B. & S.C. Railway. Originally intended for a much lighter traffic—its first permanent way was a very light affair[70]—this line carried some of the heaviest suburban traffic in South London by the 1890s, with trains leaving Peckham Rye for London Bridge during 'rush hours' every five or six minutes, and for Victoria every ten. Peckham Rye was, however, a junction, and consequently had much better services than could be had anywhere else. The tapering down of services beyond this point was very marked. Workmen's tickets were available at all stations—for twopence return on the line between Victoria and Ludgate Hill, for threepence on the South London Line, and for fourpence elsewhere.[71]

The journey to work from Camberwell at the end of the nineteenth century was evidently a varying experience. The massive concentration of most public transport facilities in the area north of the South London Line contrasted markedly with the thin provision which was made on the other side of it. If cheap fares had helped to fill up the inner suburbs—the density of population was almost a function of their cheapness around some railway stations in South London—the lack of adequate transport had left others half empty.[72] In these districts angry residents fulminated in crowded public meetings against railway companies which valued Continental traffic above suburban, and failed to recognize the expanding needs of the new districts.[73] And in them, too, rashly speculating builders saw the paint on their houses peel before they could dispose of the improved ground rents or find their first tenants. These were no more than the characteristics of the suburban frontier where the lack of adequate communications was usually the most notable feature.

Capital for House-Building

Victorian Camberwell, we have seen, was no island. Its attachment to the metropolitan mainland brought it within range of the general influences governing the growth of London at large. These were chiefly demographic, but there were also economic and psychological factors at work which contributed to the speed at which the fields were laced with streets and houses. The supply of living accommodation was not an automatic reflex of the demand for it, nor was this determined solely by the pressure of population. There was no simple equation in this matter.[74] The profitability of house-building, and therefore of the supply of new houses, depended among other things on the alternative earnings of the capital used in it. This meant that the provision of suburban homes could either be retarded for lack of capital which had been put to more profitable employment elsewhere; or it could be expanded far beyond current needs when idle capital was put to what was considered safe use. The alternative uses for such capital were usually commercial, and house-building in the suburbs therefore tended to have a kind of tidal rhythm imposed upon it by the rise and fall in the demand for all kinds of business premises.

The finance of suburban house-building was governed still more fundamentally, however, by forces which were operating at even longer range. The London capital market in the second half of the nineteenth century was a cosmopolitan institution, and this meant that the counter-attractions of investment overseas powerfully affected the flow of capital into relatively unprofitable enterprises—like house-building—at home.[75] The cycles of building activity which were set in motion in these ways were clearly discernible—despite the flattening effect of local influences—even in the experience of individual suburbs which were in process of expansion. In Camberwell, these fluctuations in house-building synchronized closely with the general trend:

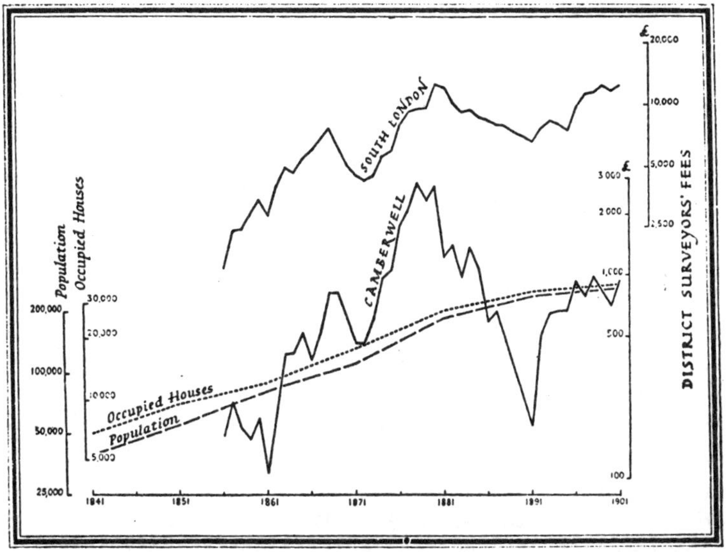

FIG. 4. *Fluctuations in House-Building (logarithmic scale)*

peaks of building activity were reached in 1868–9, 1878–80 (when the total volume of construction per annum was about three times greater than at either of the other two peak periods), and 1898; and house-building was at its lowest ebb in the intervening years 1871–2 and 1891. The accompanying graph gives some idea of the magnitude of these fluctuations.[76] Although the supply of new houses in Camberwell obviously varied very considerably from one phase of the building cycle to another—in reaching the highest peak in 1878 the output rose over six times in as many years, and fell to a fifteenth of this by 1891—there seems to be no evidence that there was during the lulls in activity an actual shortage of houses. For London as a whole, empty houses were seldom less than 4 per cent. of the total during the last quarter of the nineteenth century, and in Camberwell the proportion was much higher:[77] this suggests that the fickleness of capital in alternating between employment at home and abroad did not mean that too few houses were built when capital left the country, but suggests on the contrary that too many were built when it was free again to be put to use at home.

The housing industry was bound to be hypersensitive to these influences because it was an industry whose products had unusual durability, and it was also one in which hundreds of small builders reacted independently of each other to the same market influences. Easy money and a rising market for houses therefore led almost automatically to over-building from time to time, and this was particularly evident in the early 1880s, when the suburbs were glutted with new but tenantless houses: "An array of unoccupied houses meets the eye in all directions," observed the Chairman of the largest land society in London in 1885, "and even, where some few of the newest buildings have recently succeeded in finding tenants, at greatly reduced rentals."[78] In East Dulwich, where speculating builders had put up nearly 5,000 houses in the previous ten years, about 40 per cent. stood empty in 1881, according to an amateur census enumerator who reported the situation in unusual detail to a public meeting in the district in support of suburban railways.[79] In 1907 a similar state of affairs had developed on the Waverley Park Estate at Nunhead, where Edward Yates, one of the very largest builders in South London, had since the 1880s built 742 houses; here, the number of empty houses had grown larger and larger over recent years, and by 1907 310 stood empty.[80]

The Separate Family Dwelling

Manipulated though it was by these financial strings, the growth of the Victorian suburb was not determined wholly by them. What partly governed the prodigal rate at which London's suburbs swallowed the surrounding fields was the type of housing which was developed. The separate family dwelling, however desirable it may have been for domestic happiness—Edwin Chadwick once showed that the need for it was greatest among the poor[81]—was easily the most extensive means of suburban development that could have been devised. The alternative, intensive development by block dwellings, was either unacceptable to the average suburban tenant or house-owner, or never became practicable on purely financial grounds. To remove to a suburb was not merely to change one's address but, according to locality, to place oneself on a particular range of the social scale. Architectural taste, like manners, travels downwards, and it must have seemed unthinkable that one's house should not bear some resemblance, however remote, to the façade and the layout of more exclusive properties. "In one part," it has been written of the mid-Victorian suburb, "the better order of houses imitated as pompously as they could the architectural grandeur of the mansions owned by the large incomes; in another, the worst order of houses respectably, but narrowly, escaped a general resemblance to the brick boxes of the small incomes."[82]

For this and similar reasons it might be argued that members of such an imitative society had a conscious preference for the single family dwelling, but it could also be shown that there were strong economic factors working in the same direction. Where the cost of the land has been a small proportion of the total outlay on housing development it has always been easier and cheaper to provide single dwellings rather than flats. And an important feature of London's development has been that the relatively low cost of available suburban land has precluded the necessity of intensive housing development of the kind needed for high-cost flats or compulsory re-housing in the centre of London. What ensured this supply of relatively cheap building land in the suburbs was the fact that, unlike the land speculation encouraged by credit association systems on the Continent, speculation in London was in building; as a result, the height of houses became practically a function of site values, which tapered off gradually towards the perimeter of the built-up area.[83]

The Force of Local Influences

To these various general influences on the speed at which the suburb grew was added at every point the force of local circumstance.[84] What demographic change itself, the development of suitable suburban transport services, the availability of capital, and the cultivation of a preference for *bijou* architecture did in effect was to fix an approximate calendar of events; but what gave to the process its exact chronology was a concatenation of circumstances which varied from place to place.

Some of these influences, as we have already seen, were physical: subsoil and elevation, for example, were both sanitary and social factors in suburban development from an early date, for naturally well-drained estates on raised ground—such as those, for example, on Champion Hill—changed hands at premiums which came to be reflected in the value of the property erected on them and in the social status of their first occupants. Nor was this much less true when the widespread introduction of water-borne sewage disposal after the 1860s made the cesspool, if not the open sewer, archaic. Low-lying estates were a tricky speculation at any time, for not only was elaborate land drainage expensive, but house-hunters remained dubious of builders' talents for it. The topography and the timing of estate development also depended on a whole range of personal factors, such as the attitudes and financial circumstances of individual and corporate landowners. This is clear in one sense from the casual nibbling at their estates by the de Crespigny family, and in another from the carefully controlled development of the vast Dulwich College estate. Or the pace of development was implicitly determined by the covenants and stipulations, especially as to the capital value of the building programme, which lessees were required—or were not required—to fulfil: the extremes of behaviour in this respect were probably best expressed on the one hand by the meticulous estate management of the Dulwich College Estate Governors, whose leases translated into practical terms their precise social requirements of an exclusive, spacious suburb of expensive homes and prosperous tenants, and, on the other hand, by the unsophisticated letting of the Bowyer-Smijth estates, which allowed at least one of them to experience the full declension of meadow to slum in a single generation.

Brief as it is, it is clear from this glance at some of the special elements in the development of particular estates that both the timing and the density of their development depended to a considerable degree upon the unique circumstances prevailing in the locality. The detailed modulation of individual estates depended in turn, however, on the manner in which they were developed. And it is consequently now necessary to consider how this was done, and to reflect on what might be considered the obstetrics of suburban development.

CHAPTER IV

THE FORMATION OF BUILDING ESTATES

The Makers of the Victorian Suburb

THE making of a Victorian suburb was a process which appeared to those outside the business to have an awful efficiency. Acres of ploughland and meadow and orchard were pricked out in unending terraces with almost superhuman speed. To the bystander the great swathes of new suburb appeared sometimes to swarm with nothing but speculating builders, whose business careers were a history of bad workmanship and bad debts. Yet to take a casual look at what now remains of the Victorian suburb one would think that it had been created by a relatively small band of people. The endless repetition of basically similar streets of small houses gives the impression that the land was carved up in large tracts and handed over to substantial contractors working by methods of mass production. Such appearances are deceptive. The more one looks the more one is struck by two things: first, that the average Victorian suburb was the product of the unconcerted labour of many men; secondly, that hardly any of its type can truly be said to have been *created* at all. The evidence for the first of these impressions is in the innumerable tiny variations in the style of construction of the houses, even when these are terraced, the numerous breaks in the lines of the eaves, the restless changes in the treatment of windows, doors, bays, and so on. That the Victorian suburb was no consciously made artifact is evident enough from a walk along its disjointed streets and from the attempt to find reasonable explanations of the directions some of them took. And when one turns from scrutinizing such inconsistencies on the streets themselves to tracing them on a large-scale map such impressions become convictions.

The truth is that the process of making a Victorian suburb was largely an unconscious one, and it might almost be said that the great majority of them simply came about as the result of the influences which were the subject of the last chapter. These were so diverse and uncontrollable that it is not surprising to find how rare it was for a single individual or a small number of them to govern the whole development of a particular suburb. To have done so would have required not only a remarkable concentration of ownership of land and capital, and a despotic control of local affairs, but would have had to extend as well over some of the more general factors governing the growth of towns and their suburbs. In fact, the typical Victorian suburb was neither a conscious creation nor the work of a homogeneous band. The makers of the Victorian suburb were a mixed and very numerous company, in which must be numbered not only those who were recognizably in the suburb-building business, but many others whose contribution to the structure of the suburb appeared remote or insignificant. Thus, among the makers of Victorian Camberwell must be listed not only landowners, land companies, and builders, but the financiers of their enterprise, the providers of essential services, the caterers for leisure, the custodians of building standards, and the suburban communities themselves. Any such list would be a long one. Building societies, solicitors, estate agents, shopkeepers, music-hall performers, publicans, priests, schoolmasters, ratepayers, lodgers, vestrymen, district surveyors, and so on, all influenced the shape and the character of the suburb.

Not all their respective rôles can be examined here, but in the pages which follow an attempt is made to evaluate the parts played by those principally concerned in landscaping the suburb and peopling its streets, and to examine the way in which this was done. It is necessary to begin in the present chapter by clarifying the alternative methods by which the whole process of development could be set in motion, and then to examine this in the light of some representative pieces of development. The following chapter is given to an examination of the various business operations involved in making a suburb. It is also concerned with the activities of the speculative builder which are considered by reference to the business records of one of the largest of his kind to be found in Camberwell during the last thirty years of the century.

Estate Improvement by Building Development

The first overt step towards the formation of a building estate was generally taken by the landowner. From the 1840s the number of landowners who could legally consider the granting of building leases was being increased by changes in the law relating to settled estates and to charity and ecclesiastical land;[1] and the law relating to building development was also being clarified by both general Acts and by a string of judicial decisions.[2] In the course of the nineteenth century, too, more and more manuals and handbooks were being written by surveyors and barristers to indicate the pitfalls and the opportunities of suburban estate development. In these the process was often made to look as straightforward as the little jingle which served as a slogan for it:

> The richest crop for any field
> Is a crop of bricks for it to yield.
> The richest crop that it can grow,
> Is a crop of houses in a row.

These anonymous lines appeared in Tarbuck's *Handbook of House Property* (1875), one of many such primers.[3] But the path of estate improvement was bound to remain devious for there were almost always several alternative procedures.

The landowner might, for instance, turn builder himself and employ his own labour to work directly under his orders. He might alternatively engage a builder under contract to perform the whole of these tasks for him. This course involved decisions later on about the terms on which the finished houses should be disposed of, either by sale or by a short lease. As this was perhaps the riskiest imaginable course of action for a freeholder, it was not a very common method of estate development, and there was no known instance of it in Victorian Camberwell. The landowner might decide, while keeping as tight a control as he wished over the nature of the development, to lease his land to an individual, a firm, or a building association, who could either do all the work or sub-contract it to others, or do part of it and then assign all interest in the property to someone else. The contracts necessary to carry this out would be based upon a building agreement made between the landowner and a contractor for the granting of leases for completed houses at a certain house rent or for an overall ground rent. The latter arrangement permitted the builder to create a leasehold (or 'improved') ground rent which he or his assigns received from the occupiers of the houses.

The landowner might lastly consider the possibility of selling the land outright in one of three ways. The first course open to him was to convey the land in fee for building in return for a perpetual rent-charge. Secondly, he might sell to an estate development company which would employ contractors and builders to lay the roads, install drainage, and build the houses. Lastly, he might sell the land directly to individual builders, either piecemeal or in a single lot. If he decided to sell part of the land outright, he might still contemplate the desirability of imposing certain restrictive covenants on the building in order to secure uniformity or to maintain minimum architectural and sanitary standards. The practical alternatives were, in short, to sell or to develop by building lease.[4]

To retain the freehold interest in his land but to increase its rental by building development was generally a more attractive course of action to the owner of a moderately sized or extensive estate than to sell it outright because the ultimate gain was likely to exceed by a handsome margin the proceeds of selling his land and investing the purchase money in other securities. He could by this means both enlarge his unearned income from ground rents without adding to his own outlay, and at the same time watch his land grow more and more valuable as the reversion of the lease approached and finally give him or his heirs the opportunity of rack-renting the improved property at perhaps five or even ten times the equivalent of the original ground rent.[5] Freehold ground rents of nearly £2,000 a year on the Selwyn estate near East Dulwich station, for example, were reckoned in 1889 to be worth at least £21,000 a year in rack rents at current prices when reversions occurred after terms of from 54 to 87 years.[6] Some freehold ground rents worth £640 a year which were put up for sale on the Denmark Park estate in 1879 were calculated to have an ultimate rack rental of over £4,000.[7]

The usual way of developing an estate by building lease was for the landowner to enter into a contract directly with a number of builders—a term of some elasticity, as we shall see—to erect houses of a stipulated value and to pay a ground rent to cover the entire area taken for building. Such a practice never really hardened into an invariable formula but it had wide application, both to the deployment of opulent mansions in a garden suburb and to the squeezing of a scrabble of working-class houses onto a bit of waste. What varied in the development of this heirarchy of suburban estates was not so much the basic procedures as the terms of development and the personnel involved.

The Short Building Lease

It is necessary before looking at some of these estates individually to examine briefly the nature of the leasehold interest in building land and its effect on building development. The chief characteristic of the short building lease—that is, leases for terms up to 99 years—was the terminable interest of the lessee. In London the duration of such leases had been gradually lengthening since their introduction on the basis of 31 years or so early in the seventeenth century, and towards the end of the Victorian period the usual term in South London had lengthened to around eighty years.[8] At the end of the term of the lease the lessee or his assigns undertook to allow the landlord to re-enter into full possession of the land with all its improvements, and to deliver it up in good condition and repair. When Sir Claude Champion de Crespigny was adjudged bankrupt in 1881, his estates heavily mortgaged and his gross income from them having been reduced since 1868 from £8,000 a year to under £3,000, it was pointed out that some leases had just fallen in which would increase his income by another £800, and a further improvement was expected to follow in 1890. "It must be a great consolation to the owners of leasehold houses at Camberwell to know that their expenditure will set a ruined landlord on his legs again," was the comment of the radical *Echo*.[9] It was both this feature of leasehold tenure and the encouragement it appeared to give to shoddy building which earned for the arrangement such a bad name in Victorian London, where leasehold and speculating builder and building society were frequently used as terms of abuse about suburban housing.[10]

Much of this vituperation was misdirected, for not all leasehold property which had been built as a speculation was faulty, nor was all freehold property impeccable. The house-jobbers and house-farmers, middlemen between landlord and tenant, dealt also in freehold property. A large part of the protest about leaseholds was in truth a complaint about landlordism in general. This was bound to be prevalent in a city in which comparatively few people lived in their own freehold homes. Freehold may have comprised about a third of residential property in London in the last quarter of the nineteenth century, but the proportion of homes which were occupied by their owners was much smaller than this.[11] On the Selwyn estate at East Dulwich, for example, which was developed by building lease between 1870 and 1878, only 11 per cent. of the 650 houses and shops were occupied by the head lessees in 1889: the absentee leaseholders—'the landlord' to the occupiers—were mostly private individuals (75 per cent.) living throughout South London, or builders (9 per cent.), or insurance companies, land and building societies, and investment associations (5 per cent.).[12] To the unfortunate lessee of property when its building lease fell in the leasehold system usually stood for a heavy bill for dilapidations and a reversion to the rack rent, or full rentable value of the property. But there was at least one substantial advantage to the community at large. Notwithstanding the slightly higher rate of interest which normally had to be paid on capital borrowed on leasehold rather than freehold estates, leasehold rentals were probably lower than they might otherwise have been because the supply of houses was increased by the operations of many small builders for whom the avoidance of a large capital outlay on the land made all the difference to their output. The leasehold system almost certainly meant that houses were built more rapidly than they would have been under a purely freehold system.[13]

This had not, however, always been an unmitigated advantage. The leasehold system made it all the easier for small speculating builders to set up business. The activities of the worst of them were hard to control, and the bad practice of drafting vague building agreements brought into being some suburban slums almost as black as those in Westminster or Seven Dials. The failure of the landlord to prescribe and enforce adequate restrictions on the lessee was not, however, a permanent feature of leasehold development. Some later leasehold development was conducted irreproachably. On the Dulwich College estate, for example, all building was supervised by Charles Barry, the architect to the estate, and lessees' obligations were precisely drafted and scrupulously applied. Edward Yates, one of the largest builders in the parish from the 1880s, was also punctilious in the management of his estates, not only where he was the freeholder and direct landlord to his tenants, as on his estate at Nunhead, but also where he was himself a lessee. There were always some freeholders, however, who were content to leave all supervision to the district surveyor. The first district surveyor in Camberwell was appointed in 1845. His activities were governed by the London Building Acts, and beyond the enforcement of some minimum standards of building practice in new construction and repair work, and the condemnation of dangerous structures, he was able to do little to prevent the appearance of slums. The continuing operation of loosely-drawn leases of a generation or two before and the still greater persistence of the houses and cottages which had been built under their authority were of far greater influence.

The Development of a Small Building Estate

The most complete evidence which is available of the process of estate development by means of building leases in Camberwell concerns the two Bridge House estates on either side of the Old Kent Road. These lands had belonged to the Corporation of London since at least the seventeenth century, and with others elsewhere in London provided an income for the maintenance of London Bridge. We have already observed one of them as the scene of some pre-Victorian building development, and it is the subsequent development of this estate which is to be examined now.

The ten acres of meadow which later became the Trafalgar Avenue estate had first been considered for building development as early as 1777, but plans were shelved till the expiry of the long lease which had at that time been granted to John Rolls, the

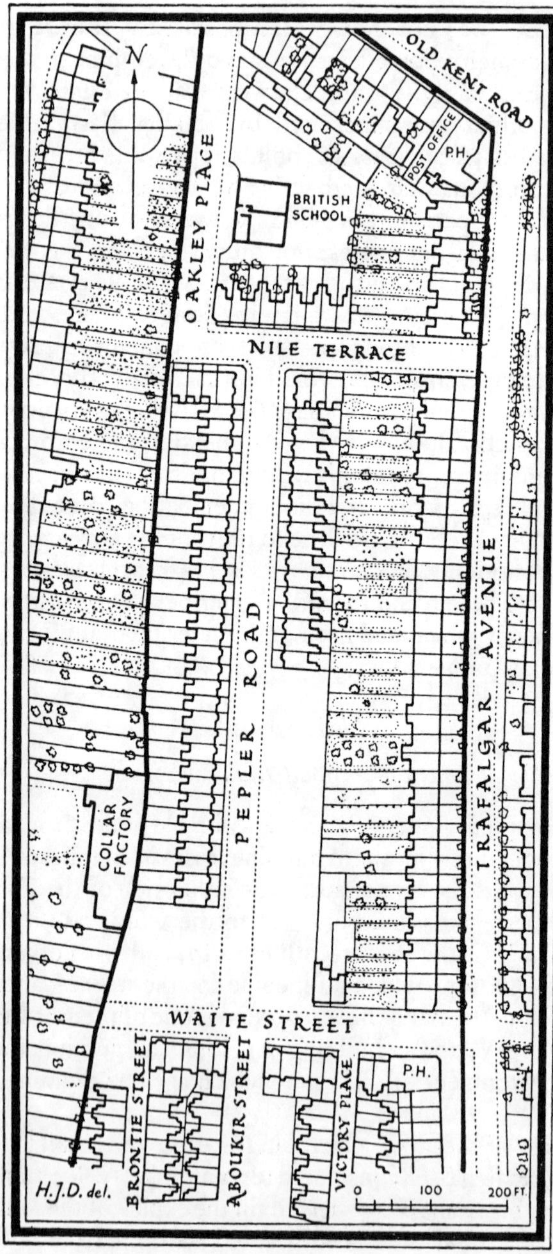

FIG. 5. *Trafalgar Avenue estate, 1871*

cowkeeper. Before the lease fell in, in 1841, the sub-committee for letting the Bridge House estates had carefully considered the future development of the land and had instructed the Clerk of Works to prepare a ground plan and elevation of houses which might be built on it, and to recommend a method of letting it;[14] two years later the plans were agreed.[15] The disposal on lease of the ground adjoining the Old Kent Road presented few difficulties. The house which Rolls had built in 1780 had become the "Lord Nelson" public-house, and it appears that in 1840 its tenant undertook under a 61-year lease to provide entirely new premises.[16] Oakley Terrace, which adjoined it with a frontage to the Old Kent Road, was run up mainly by a Lambeth builder, John Gurney, by 1844;[17] and on the west side of the footpath to Peckham which ran southwards from the "Lord Nelson", a robust terrace of seven brick and stucco villas had been built to some rigid specifications by Benjamin Southall between 1842 and 1846.[18] A lease had also been granted, in 1844, to the Old Kent Road and New Peckham British Schools, whose schoolrooms were built behind Oakley Terrace.[19]

The development of the remainder of the estate was a more complicated affair. The first advertisement of the land for building purposes at the end of 1843 evoked no response whatever, and despite some improvement of the sewerage arrangements, the provision of a metalled road instead of the Peckham footpath, the lengthening of the proposed tenure from 61 to 80 years, and still more press advertisement, no acceptable proposals for taking the ground on building lease came in for over seven years.[20] The land had meanwhile been occupied by Rolls' former tenant, and in 1848 it became for a short time the home ground of the St George's Cricket Club.[21] By 1851, however, the estate had become ripe for building, and a couple of proposals were submitted, one from a City builder and the other from two local builders who had formed a partnership. Building agreements were made with both of them for 80-year leases at ground rents which were based on a rate of 4s. 6d. per foot of frontage.[22] The building specification was as rigorous as before, with the additional stipulation (based perhaps on experience elsewhere) that no place-bricks or rubble were to be used, nor earth or rubbish of any kind to be mixed in the mortar: any failure to keep the terms of the building agreement was to involve a penalty of £1,000.[23] By the following year these houses had been built. They were arranged in two terraces of five and eight houses—both were on three floors, but one had an Italianate and the other a late-Georgian flavour—and they formed a continuous rank on the next available plot to Southall's on Trafalgar Avenue, but separated from it by an opening for a new road onto the land behind.

There was now no doubt about the eligibility of the land for building purposes, and the covering of the remainder of the estate proceeded more rapidly. A plot of ground, which would front the north side of the proposed new street which was being considered to form a right-angled connection between the Old Kent Road and Trafalgar Avenue, was leased early in 1852 to Benjamin Southall at a rate of 2s. 6d. a foot frontage, and on this was built within twelve months a plain brick terrace of nine two-storeyed houses.[24] At the same time the sub-committee was approached by C. R. Dennison of Asylum Road, who proposed taking a 400-foot frontage at 4s. 6d. a foot, and this was accepted for the remaining length of Trafalgar Avenue to a point opposite Glengall Terrace: within six months leases were being granted on the first of these houses to be completed.[25] Proposals were also being received for building agreements of various kinds for parts of the vacant ground at the back of Trafalgar Avenue.[26]

The moment was now opportune for completing the layout of adequate sewers on the estate, and for the formation of a gravelled road parallel with Trafalgar Avenue down the centre of the estate.[27] Though the urgency of providing a new sewer was increasing with the completion of every new house, the local landowners could not agree on the sharing of the cost and four years passed with nothing done. One was willing to contribute a tenth of the £300 needed, another would pay nothing because his was only a life interest, though his tenants were ready to spend £60; the Metropolitan Commissioners of Sewers refused to accept any responsibility.[28] By the summer of 1856 the delay had become intolerable, and Dennison, the principal lessee, wrote to complain that he had spent altogether £10,000 on the estate but that prospective tenants of the ten large houses which he had ready for letting at £40 each were put off by the uncovered ditch at the rear. But by now the Local Management

Board for Camberwell had come into being and it was prepared to remove all open sewers and provide covered ones if the City Corporation would pay £250 towards the cost, and this appears to have been done.[29]

The delay in developing the vacant ground at the back of the houses on Trafalgar Avenue also caused other complaints, particularly of the invasion of "a questionable class of persons" from Neate Street. Such reconnoitring was supposed to be connected with a series of burglaries, and a close-boarded fence was erected against the intruders.[30] The land was let instead, with obvious discretion, to the London Rifle Brigade.[31] If the estate was to prosper not only had the wrong people to be kept out but the right people had to be let in: a swivel bridge to replace a footbridge over the Surrey Canal at the bottom of Trafalgar Avenue was one way of doing this, and the Corporation therefore headed the subscription list with a hundred guineas.[32]

Though the section of Trafalgar Avenue above Glengall Terrace had been practically completed by 1855 the ground at the back was left untouched for another ten years. At least one bid to use part of it was made during this time, but the subcommittee hoped to lease it in not more than two large pieces. Advertisement of it early in 1865 brought two more likely proposals, one of which was from Dennison who proposed a ground rent of £300 a year, and this was accepted.[33] Work now started on the new roads,[34] but at this point Dennison died, and his interest was taken up after some months and the collapse of one other building agreement, by a Mr Charles Kynock.[35] Kynock's part in the development was both unsatisfactory and fleeting, and within six weeks he had turned his interest over to a Mr Joseph Lewis, who had been heavily involved in building development in the City.[36] Within three weeks the new lessee's street layout was approved by the Metropolitan Board of Works, after amendment, and within three months all his plans had passed the City architect.[37] Within two months he had built the public-house and thirteen shops which completed that part of Trafalgar Avenue.[38] Lewis appears to have used a single builder, J. G. Brightmore of Stratford, to do most of the work, and by 1875 it had been completed. Leases were granted from time to time in denominations which were convenient for disposal to investors in freehold ground rents—in groups mainly of between two and twenty houses.[39]

The estate was now fully built over. The density of building had, in general, been such that there was hardly any scope for more intensive development as the site appreciated in value. Oakley Place alone gave this opportunity, for as the function of the British School there was supplanted by the London School Board schools it was closed, and the land used instead in the 1880s for a terrace of six grey brick villas in the architectural idiom of their day.[40] Thirteen replicas of these, which were the speculation of the same man (who had lived in the same street) also slotted into place opposite. These were, however, just off the estate, having been built on the gardens of the houses in Cobourg Road, which a Wesleyan Methodist Church had already invaded in 1873. Also on the perimeter of the estate was St Mark's Church (an early, rather dull piece of Norman Shaw, dated 1880) which, like the Methodist church, was built on the gardens of houses farther down Cobourg Road.

Small though it was, the Trafalgar Avenue estate was typical of much of the development of Victorian Camberwell. It had two obvious features. The first was the contrast between the long preliminary period in which the demand for building land was growing up around it, and the sudden explosiveness of the final stage in which the land was smothered with houses. The second was the way in which so many people's interests became focused upon it as it developed. This convergence of many interests in the land and its improvement was, however, governed throughout by a wary landowner. What happened elsewhere when the landowner lost interest in the reversionary value of his estate, or failed to impose his own standards on its development is the subject of later sections of this chapter. Next, however, it is necessary to examine the fortunes of the really large estate during its developmental stage.

Building Development on a Large Scale

The de Crespigny estates at Camberwell and Peckham, though developed under comparable legal forms, were a contrast in both their execution and their general character. The Camberwell estate, which was an area of about eighty acres on rising ground between Denmark Hill and Grove Lane, bore nowhere the harsh imprint of the builder of cheap, expressionless houses. There had been a shadow of this, it is true, with the leasing in 1821 of a small parcel of ground behind the "Fox-under-the-hill" on Denmark Hill. This was the subject of a lease for 98 years at a ground rent of £175. 6s., with the covenant to build twenty-three houses and was the beginning of Grove Place and de Crespigny Terrace, whose development continued into the 1850s.[41] But apart from this—and the unlooked-for nibbling out of Champion Grove in the 1830s—most development on the de Crespigny land was of a different order. Lessees were principally men of property, the land was leased in large plots of up to eight acres for terms of eighty years and more, and the leases generally included covenants and stipulations which effectively governed the character of the development. Lessees were required, for example, "to spend at least £1,000 in erecting a messuage or forfeit £500," "not to build more than six dwelling-houses," "not to allow a tavern or public-house to be built," "not to erect any dwelling-house on the land behind," "not to build any bow window or projection," "not to carry on any offensive trade," and so on. The stipulated value of the houses varied mostly between £700 and £1,000 and their number under a single lease between one and five.

Exacting contractual obligations like these brought into being on Champion Hill by the 1840s a suburban *élite* whose jealousy for its social standards became in time a powerful instrument for maintaining them. The early formation of a residents' association here to superintend the lighting and maintenance of its own gravelled road was less of a defence against the Vestry than a mark of social detachment, and the gates which this plutocracy put up with a trace of symbolism at the entrances to its domain were made solid enough to keep a rabble out.[42] Despite the intrusion of Denmark Hill station into the very middle of the estate in 1865, the subsequent development of its other parts was a repetition of this theme in a minor key. Champion Park, a cut of about three hundred yards between Denmark Hill and Grove Lane, and some stretches of ground on Denmark

Hill itself, had already been edged by sizeable villas before this happened, but the completion of Windsor Road on the other side of the station at this time was entirely in keeping with the rest. The houses were each worth about £600 and had been built by the local builder, Edwin Heritage, and William Elsdon of Wandsworth Road (to whom he appears to have assigned his interest) under well-drawn individual building leases of 89 years dating from 1865. Ground rents of £10 on each house were payable by the builder until he had found a purchaser and had assigned the lease to him—as with No. 13, for example, which was sold to a Lombard Street tailor in 1868 and No. 11 which was sold to a fish salesman of Lower Thames Street in 1882.

The de Crespigny estates at Peckham were developed rather later and more intensively than those at Camberwell. One of them consisted of the house and grounds known as Heaton's Folly on the east side of Rye Lane; the other an area between Rye Lane and the Nunhead footpath from Queen's Road. The former was first leased for building in 1833 for 89 years at £460 a year. The lessee was to spend £6,000 in building a row of at least eight houses worth £300 each. The de Crespigny family recovered the estate for £4,000 in 1841 on the death of the lessee, and except for the addition of a Baptist chapel on Rye Lane about 1865,[43] the twelve houses which had been standing in Hanover Park and Rye Lane when the de Crespignys recovered the estate represented the only development for over thirty years. About 1870 building re-started and numerous builders, mostly local men, began to develop on 89-year leases the whole of the ground bounded by the railway, Rye Lane, Hanover Park, and Clayton Road. Most of the enclosed roads—Clayton, McKerrel, Moncrieff, Cerise, and Raul Roads, and Hanover Park—were made and populated during the 1870s, when about 150 houses went up, but the whole process was not completed before the end of the 1880s.

The history of the other estate farther down Rye Lane, which was built up between 1864 and 1886, was similar to this.[44] The second parties to the head leases were not only local speculating builders—and one speculating plumber[45]—but a number of City businessmen who either sold out when the building was finished or found builders as sub-lessees, who in turn built the houses and held on to them as an investment. The 'interests' in a particular property thus quickly became complex, especially when in addition mortgagees became property holders by default—as, for example, when the Planet Building Society took over twenty-three houses in Heaton Road in 1869 when a local builder became bankrupt.

The contrasting character and mode of development of both the de Crespigny estates were reflected on a much grander scale in the contemporary evolution of the Dulwich College estate. This corresponded to the Manor of Dulwich, an area of nearly 1,500 acres, which was gradually developed by building lease following the Act of 1808 which had first granted such powers to the College Governors. By the 1850s a beginning had been made in carving out on its southern slopes a number of large building estates. The 55 acres of Lapse Wood, Ambrook Hill Wood, Peckarman's Woods, and the Low Cross Woods, for example, were taken by a certain Francis Fuller in 1854 for 84 years at a ground rent of over £2,000 a year for the purpose of building 2 family hotels, 3 taverns, 188 dwelling-houses and a church with a parsonage. Another man of property, R. H. Marshall of Norwood, took fourteen acres on Gipsy Hill in 1859 for a similar term, and undertook to erect houses of a minimum value of £1,000 apiece. Numerous building agreements involving heavy outlays of capital on substantial villas were made over the next fifty years, principally for the development of land which formed the perimeter of the estate, but it would appear that in one case only was the building of houses over £600 in value the work of professional builders, among whom more valuable property was thought to be a risky speculation. The developers of large building plots like these were either men of means or estate companies which had been formed for a particular development. An example of these was the Red Post Hill Land Company Ltd. which, from its City office, undertook in 1894 the building on Sunray Avenue of about fifty semi-detached and detached houses of a value of £700 and £900 each.

A much larger undertaking was the Tulse Hill and Dulwich Estates Company Ltd. which was formed in 1885 with a capital of £150,000 to acquire and develop the Tulse Hill Park estate in Norwood and the Dulwich Manor House estate. The case of the latter is interesting as an illustration of the shifting basis of the contractual obligations involved.

The Dulwich Manor House estate comprised Alleyn's manor house and the surrounding land, in all about twenty-one acres, and had been held on a 21-year lease in 1859 by Mr F. Doulton, M.P., who paid £150 a year for it.[46] Subsequently, the Governors had agreed with him on a ground rent of £450 a year in return for a programme of development which included widening the existing road and making a new one, spending £3,000 or more a year in building houses, two-thirds of which were to be worth at least £1,000 each, and the other third £800 each.[47] A formal building agreement was made in May 1861, when the terms of the lease were fixed at 84 years and the number of houses at 46. Although some houses were built in Alleyn Road and Alleyn Park between 1862 and 1866, Doulton had run into financial difficulties and the land was auctioned in 1869. The buyer was a John Westwood, who presently agreed with the Governors to continue the development under lease for 84 years. This agreement had lowered the stipulated value of the houses to be built to the range £450–£1,000, and the annual ground rent on each completed house appears to have been brought as low as £1. The manor house had at this point been demolished[48] and the whole estate was ultimately assigned by Westwood through two or three intermediaries to a Mr Edward van Vliet, a successful builder and owner of some three hundred substantial houses at Norwood. Van Vliet it was who appears to have contrived the Tulse Hill and Dulwich Estates Company, sold to it his interest in the estate, and joined its board of directors. He then undertook the development of the estate at an improved annual ground rent (which was payable to the company) of £1,855 in a full year. The company's outgoings were expected to total £550 a year, made up of £400 which was payable to the representatives of Westwood and a ground rent to the College Governors of £150 on 150 houses at £1 each, so the net improved ground rent which it could expect to receive was about £1,305 a year. Van Vliet eventually had his plans approved and leases were granted from Midsummer 1888 at a ground rent of £1 per house.[49]

Piecemeal Development

It seems clear that even on the estates of the greatest suburban landowners there were always difficulties in the way of planned and orderly development. The more divided the ownership of land in a given area, however, the more likely did it become that the general layout of its streets would be intricate and ill-contrived. In general, the jigsaw of landed titles which had been produced by generations of dealings in the land market was reflected with remarkable fidelity by the superstructure of the suburb. What tended to increase the complexity of the resulting street pattern still more was, on the one hand, the piecemeal disposal of quite large estates, and, on the other hand, the dissection of the gardens of large houses whose original owners had not only watched with pecuniary interest the rise in local land values but had whiffed the scent of social change. Unlike the bold planning of some larger estates, these developments were less prescient than opportunist, but their total effects on the face of the suburb were far from trivial. For the moment we are concerned with piecemeal development. It is helpful here to look at two areas which were to some extent the obverse of each other in this respect. For sometimes a speculator seized his opportunities to good effect at a crucial point in the development of a particular area, and by bringing under one hand several neighbouring pieces of ground unified its development reasonably well. Sometimes, however, an estate which had been held in one piece was broken up and developed piece by piece, usually with disastrous results on the layout of the area.

An example of the contrast between these two courses of development was the Glebe estate and the surrounding lands. The glebe land belonging to the Vicar of Camberwell was disposed of in a way which, if it did not result in planned connections with contiguous estates, did give a unity to the estate itself. The first development was of North Terrace on Church Street in the 1820s.[50] In 1847 the rectangular piece of ground jutting northwards from the main body of the glebe was sold in order to cover the expenses of the legal processes and the preliminary work in laying out the estate.[51] This piece appears to have been bought by the only other landowner in the area, Mr W. J. Hudson, a resident of nearby Addington Square, who also took a

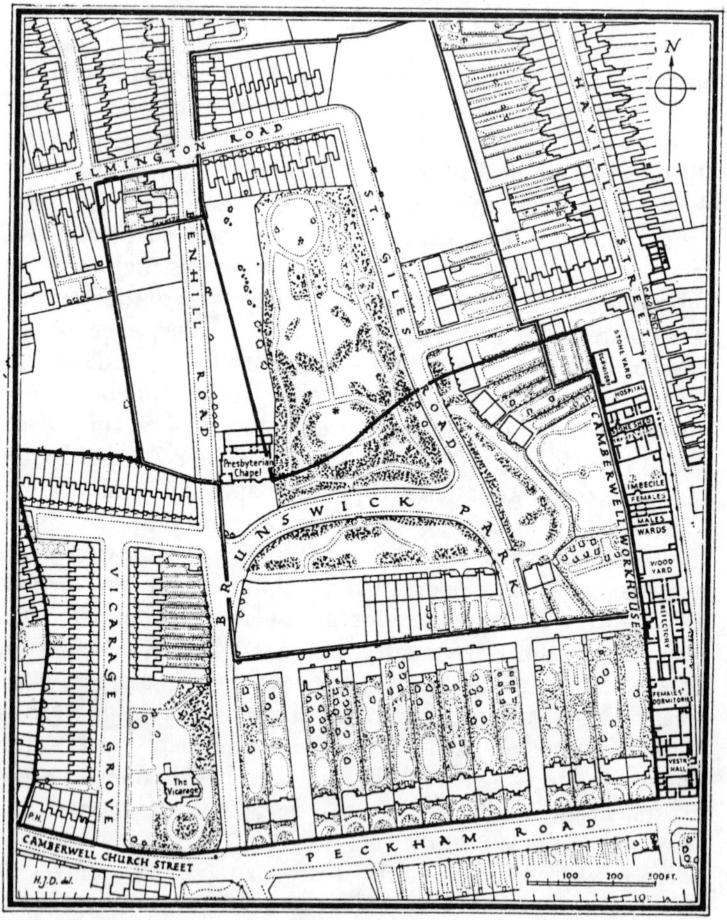

FIG. 6. *Glebe estate, 1871*

The double line marks the perimeter of the overlapping estate projected by W. J. Hudson in 1847.

lease at the same time of the rest of this section of the glebe land —some seven acres of meadow—lying behind North Terrace. With the land of which he had held the fee simple since 1842, Hudson was now in a position to plan the arrangement of the whole of this part of the estate. Some of it had in fact already been laid out for building (as the sale of part of the glebe suggested), but Hudson changed the direction of the roads, provided the general framework of what became Brunswick Park, and entered into an agreement in July 1850 with a builder, Borsley, to have fifty houses erected at the rate of four a year. Only six houses were actually built, in the south-east corner of the square, and, as time had been made the essence of the contract between Hudson and Borsley, Hudson re-entered into possession of the land in 1854.[52] This piece of ground now remained intact, however, during the rest of its formative development. Though Hudson himself was later deprived of it by a Chancery decision in a suit on behalf of his infant children, both the freehold and leasehold parts of the estate were acquired together in 1863 by an estate company, the Freehold and General Investment Company Ltd., which auctioned off both building land and houses in 1866 and 1867.[53] The plots themselves changed hands throughout the period of building, which was mainly done by a City surveyor, Henry Connew of Gracechurch Street, but also by several small local builders and by another estate company, The Crown Land and Building Company, which completed some of the carcasses[54] and severally leased the properties. Though protracted by these dealings, the general pattern of development was not much modified by them, and the final layout of the estate was not unlike Hudson's scheme of 1847. The roads connecting Brunswick Park with other streets were likewise sensible and direct.

The internal convenience and general accessibility which these roads gave to residents of the Brunswick estate are an interesting contrast both with the area towards Camberwell Green—a tangle of streets produced by careless leasing—and with the two missing pieces in the development as so far described. The first of these was about five acres of the glebe fronting Church Street which had not been included in the Act of 1813 authorizing the Vicar to grant building leases. The Ecclesiastical Leasing Act of 1842,[55] however, made its development possible, and the site of Old Vicarage House was leased to Thomas Stirling, builder, who in 1845 began to build Stirling Terrace and the "Stirling Castle" public-house. The rest of this land was used for the new

Vicarage in 1852, and behind it was developed between 1863 and 1868 the Vicarage Grove estate. The original lessee was the North London builder who had built the new Vicarage and he was to put up fifty houses within four years; but in 1865 he assigned his interest to John Roycroft, a local builder, who did the work.[56] The layout of Vicarage Grove itself was an obvious choice. Its axis was naturally governed by the rectangular form of the estate and by its attachment to the rest of the glebe land in Brunswick Park. This was an affiliation which emphasized the more forcibly, however, the physical detachment of Vicarage Grove from the estate then being developed on its western flank, from which it was separated for many years by a brick wall at the point where a junction with Belham Street would have been entirely feasible. The second of the pieces of development so far unaccounted for was the part of the original Edmonds estate lying between the northern edge of the Vicarage Grove estate and Elmington Road. This was developed under building lease by a Kennington builder, S. Sansom,[57] in 1879 and 1880, and called Sansom Street. It was developed too late to connect with Vicarage Grove, but had an opening instead into Harvey Road, which had been completed about twenty years before.

The second area of piecemeal development to be considered lay between Peckham Grove and Cator Street. Here the gradual disposal of a large estate, which had at the end of the eighteenth century been in the hands of the Shard family,[58] was accompanied by the progressive debasement of standards of development. By 1834 the land had come into the possession of Charrington, the London coal merchant, who sold it to Richard Nicholl of Barnet. Nicholl's interest in the land was short-lived, for he died in 1838 and left it to his family. During the ensuing period the pattern of development appears to have been taking shape: Grosvenor Road and Peckham Grove, which gave access to this area, were cut and building begun; and contemporary maps suggest that a gridular arrangement of streets had been conceived for the development of the whole area lying between Peckham Grove and Sumner Road. Though most of this larger area was developed in this way the nineteen acres which lay between Peckham Grove and Cator Street had a different experience. They were sold by Nicholl's legatees to James Smith, landlord of the "Rosemary

Branch" tavern, which stood on the south-western tip of the area, and in 1864 Smith sold about seven acres of it to form a small building estate consisting of Blake's Road and Hornby Road, which was built up during the next fifteen years.[59] The remaining land was kept for some years as a cricket field and place of amusement attached to the tavern, but it too was auctioned at Garraway's in 1867. It then changed hands at a rapidly advancing price at least three times in the next five years, before being bought in 1875 by a local magistrate, Richard Strong. The new owner had already had some success in estate development at Denmark Hill, and within two or three years—by an incomparable feat of ingenuity—five new roads with names out of Scott's novels had been made and some 240 houses built on them. The executor of this was a local man, Mr Adams Murphy of Camberwell, who appears to have been architect, surveyor, and estate agent combined.[60]

The cramped configuration and general inaccessibility of these streets was partly the result of putting so many houses on them, but in essence the estate was a casualty of divided ownership. These streets were in marked contrast to the uninhibited lines of Grosvenor Place and Peckham Grove which had first brought the tide of development to Nicholl's land over thirty years before. By the time these streets were laid out the surrounding districts had all been developed and the residuary landowner simply did what was expedient.

Building Estates on Back Gardens

The first phase in the development of the Victorian suburb lasted for as long as land was relatively cheap and suburbians wealthy. Then, building plots of an acre or so were no more than modest and those of fifteen or twenty were not exceptional. At such a time, when little standardized building was being done in the relatively remote suburbs, the most eligible sites for these elaborate establishments were naturally along the main roads. It was here that the old order was being changed by the builders of small houses after intervals of forty or fifty years, or more. This was a metamorphosis which was as much social as structural and the speed at which it occurred therefore varied from place to place.

The first signs of change could be discerned among the large houses along the Peckham Road, and by the 1850s and 1860s the ground plan on its southern side in particular was changing fast. By then it was no longer necessary to climb to an attic window to view the advancing cliffs of the new suburbia for they were visible from the ground floor. Perhaps the old epoch had already closed, for the function of some of these mansions had changed years before: Pelican House, the former home of Miles Stringer, a local celebrity, had in 1825 become a school, and Peckham House, the seat of the wealthy Spittas, had been converted into a private lunatic asylum; the Manor House itself, The Basings, followed the same course in 1854 by being converted into a school.[61]

The southern thrust of Lyndhurst Road in the 1840s and the carving out of Talfourd Road and Denman Road by the British Land Company between 1857 and 1862, and the building of long terraces of houses costing around £350 each were thus a conspicuous confirmation of a trend.[62] They gave to the district a new look which was both a challenge to the opportunism of the owners of existing houses which had cost three or four times that sum, and a hint of the changing social climate. Typical of such development was the Bushy Hill estate, a rectangular area of about twenty acres with a narrow frontage to the south side of Peckham Road almost opposite Camden Church and adjoining the Talfourd Road estate of the British Land Company. When the house had been occupied about 1820 by Admiral Sir John Knight it was rated at £160 a year—the same figure as for the de Crespigny estate at Champion Hill—but within fifty years this property had little more than scrap value. The whole estate was auctioned in 1866, when the top end was bought for building purposes, and again the following year, when the remainder was disposed of.[63] Within five years about twenty houses were put up by two or three small speculating builders, but the development was greatly accelerated in 1877 when the estate changed hands again. The old mansion was now demolished and the land laid out for about two hundred villas by Adams Murphy, the local architect.[64] The layout was predetermined by the estate's elongated shape, for its form was basically an alley whose width barely allowed back gardens to the terraced villas on the western side of the road at its top end, and whose length of half-a-mile was unpunctuated by any side roads into either Talfourd Road, which was already built up, or into Crofton Road, which was not developed till the following year.

A decade later this kind of development had spread south to East Dulwich. Here, for example, was an estate of about eight acres on the southern edge of Goose Green which had been bought and partially developed with large houses by Thomas Baily, farmer and stockholder in the East India Company, between 1804 and 1837. By the 1870s the estate was being encircled by modest villa development to the south, and its own frontage to Crystal Palace Road had been lined by some groups of semi-detached and terraced villas. This naturally put a premium upon the serpentine walks and shrubberies of the few houses whose grounds covered the bulk of the original estate, and the sale of the largest of them, Norland House, in 1877 was a preliminary to more intensive use of the ground. Notwithstanding the opinion of a local journalist that the sale would involve no changes in the locality, the estate was auctioned again three years later at the top of the market as a freehold building estate, whose possible layout was expertly indicated on the auction particulars.[65] A terraced street, named Worlingham Road, swept through these triangular-shaped grounds along the suggested route between 1881 and 1887 and Norland House itself, dismembered of its grounds, survived the operation to house from 1881 a small congregation of the Church of Scotland[66] (*see* Figs. 7 and 8).

Still farther afield the same process was beginning to gather momentum as the large houses of an earlier generation were literally engulfed in a new villadom. Though the beginnings of this conversion could have been discerned as early as the 1840s—Champion Lodge, the seat of the de Crespignys on Denmark Hill, was pulled down in 1841 in order that its grounds could be let on building lease [67]—the tumbling of these bastions of the first suburb occurred only very occasionally for at least another forty years. By the 1890s, however, the freeholds of some of the mansions on Herne Hill and in parts of Dulwich were being snapped up by speculators and rows of small houses raised in

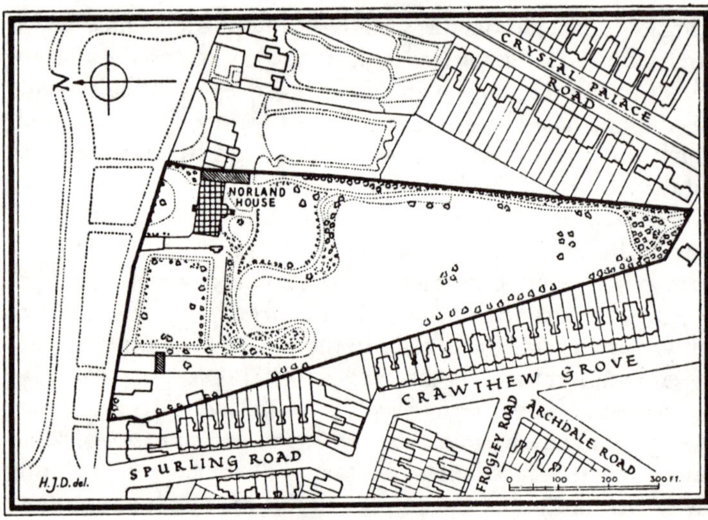

FIG. 7. *Worlingham Road estate, 1880*

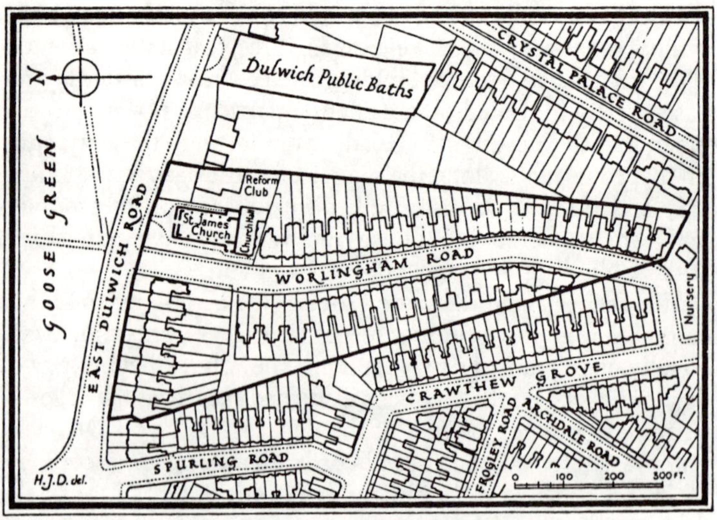

FIG. 8. *Worlingham Road estate, 1895*

their place.[68] Sometimes the texture of the street plan alone remained as a kind of archaeological evidence of a suburban society which had vanished when the brick boxes of the invaders were dumped on its flowerbeds.

The Making of a Suburban Slum

There were occasions when this trend of more intensive development of suburban land got out of control, and back gardens —even quite small ones—became garden suburbs of an unusual kind. The terraced contents of such an area were not so much arranged in streets as in frontages. Frontages which had insinuated themselves into the back gardens of houses which had an address on some authentic thoroughfare, or which had found a use for ground which the larger houses had prodigally enclosed behind them. One such area was the confusion of alleys and courts which was enclosed by Lomond Grove, Camberwell Green, and Camberwell Road. By the 1880s this had become a garden suburb in which the lawns had already served as building plots and the gravel paths as streets, though no street-names were to be found. Waterloo Square was a foursome of three-roomed houses around a common yard which was reached under an archway between Nos. 116 and 118 Lomond Grove. Green's Square was a two-sided arrangement of small cottages at the end of an alley, Green's Row, which had begun as a turning off Camberwell Road. Guildford Place, which was on one side a terrace of ten houses—all of which could boast two bedrooms upstairs—and on the other a plot of building land which might yet take ten more, was in essence the dead-end of a more remote passage still. Osborn's Cottages and Osborn's Buildings were bungaloid terraces at the bottom of the gardens in the rear of some shops on Lomond Grove.[69]

An even blacker spot was the box of streets between Crown Street, Wyndham Road, Pitman Street, and Bethwin Road. By the 1840s, what had been originally forty-five acres of meadow (when the area was leased for 85 years in 1781) had shrunk to a mere quadrangle enclosed on two sides by a heap of hundreds of brick or weather-boarded two-storeyed cottages, on another by

FIG. 9. *Sultan Street and its environs, 1871*

a row of small villas, and on the fourth side by the long back gardens of the tall terrace facing Camberwell Road. The original lessee seems either to have sub-leased or, more probably, completely assigned his interest to individuals who in turn disposed of their interests in a similar way. There were created in this way at least twenty-five recognizable interests in the estate by the time the original lease still had over thirty years to run. There was no reason why the new interests which thus came into being should have been governed by any other conditions than the extremely loose terms originally made for the leasing of the estate in 1781, and individual lessees were therefore able to develop their parts of the estate in their own way.

In these circumstances neither the physical superstructure nor the social content of this area was likely to be homogeneous. The elegant and uncluttered façade of Windmill Place on Camberwell Road was in sharp contrast to the shed-like array of Hawkin's Cottages which squatted in the back gardens of some houses in Wyndham Road, or to Bennett's Court, or Baker's Yard, or Mayhew's Buildings, each of which used a single building plot for half-a-dozen houses or more. The differences in social class in the area were at first wide. The Census of 1851 recorded in one street a small manufacturer, a solicitor, a master mariner, an engineer, some government clerks, and several house proprietors; in another, labourers, charwomen, servants, porters, and dustmen. There were, however, other streets in which lines of social demarcation could not be drawn with precision, for they contained all grades of working-class families, complete with lodgers, as well as small employers who kept a servant or two. Here and there, however, the clannishness of some immigrant Irish was producing homogeneity of another kind. Such were houses in which seven or eight different surnames and up to twenty inhabitants were to be counted under one roof. The adults were all young, mostly employed as labourers and washerwomen, and, to judge by the ages of the native-born children, most of them had arrived within the previous decade. This tendency towards overcrowding, the intermixture of cowsheds and piggeries with dwelling-houses, and the opening of glue and linoleum factories, a brewery, and the establishment of haddock-smoking and tallow-melting yards soon combined to give to the whole area both the odours and the society of the authentic slum. The sickly smell of costermongers' refuse combined with these to make an atmosphere which seemed in the nostrils of one regular visitor to the district to be a concoction of haddocks and oranges, of mortar and soot, of hearthstones and winkles, of rotten rags and herrings.[70]

When the deterioration of a district was well-rooted in legal prescription, as this one was, the process tended to be cumulative. What accentuated this trend still more was the physical isolation of the district from less shabby neighbours by the barrier of the railway viaduct which arose on the back gardens of the houses in Camberwell Road when the Chatham Railway thrust its way to the City just before the original lease of the estate was due to expire in 1866. The sealing off in this way of a small network of streets close to a main road was a fairly prolific source of slum conditions, which the building of some new property did little to allay.[71] When the only vacant ground at the back of Crown Street (which had reverted to the Smijth family with the rest of the estate) was leased afresh in 1867 the ultimate character of the new building had, therefore, already been decided. The new lessee was the speculating builder John Roycroft, who, after having done some preliminary work in laying out the estate and forming Hollington Street and Sultan Street, appears to have sub-leased it immediately to one or more other builders. These actually built the 168 barrack-like six-roomed houses in yellow brick, each on three floors, which soon dressed these streets.

Though the subsequent vicissitudes of this property left little documentary trace, the scraps of evidence which do remain suggest what probably happened to the ownership and occupancy of most of these houses. Roycroft conveyed one of the plots in 1867 to a Simon Scrase, builder, of Lorrimore Street, Walworth, at an annual ground rent of sixteen guineas. Scrase quickly ran up on this ground Nos. 1–11 (odd) Hollington Street, and then sold the improved ground rents in February 1868 to a John Andrews of Ealing for £1,090; Andrews in turn sold his interest to a Samuel Chittick of Old Kent Road in 1878 for £1,150; Chittick raised a mortgage of £1,000 on this property early in 1879 from the Woolwich Equitable Building Society, but defaulted on the repayments, and the society therefore sold the houses in 1885 for £750 to a Thomas Brown, mason, who was allowed to leave £700 of the purchase money on mortgage; Brown subsequently came to extend his property holdings to include Nos. 1–23 (odd) Hollington Street and removed, by 1891, to a better address in Vicarage Grove.[72] All this time tenants came and went, though the types remained constant, and by 1889, when Charles Booth's investigators inspected some of these very houses they had become abodes of squalid poverty. Each floor, and sometimes each room, was separately occupied, and the whole house might contain as many as eighteen persons. No. 21 Hollington Street, for example, was tersely described in terms which could have been applied to many of the neighbouring houses: "*ground floor*—2 rooms, 5 persons, man, wife, and 3 children—very queer and very poor—wife does not send children to school because they are ragged; *first front*—1 room, 1 person, widow alone—lives on what she can get; *first back*—1 room, 3 persons, man, wife, 1 child—very poor; *top front*—1 room, 5 persons, man, wife, and 3 children—big girl generally idling about; *top back*—1 room, 5 persons, widower and 4 children—drinks what he gets—children at school—room clean and tidy."[73] Such was, in part, the pathology of the suburban slum. This was probably the worst building estate to be found in Victorian Camberwell. It was a malformation which had largely come about through bad legal draughtsmanship.

CHAPTER V

THE BUSINESS OF BUILDING THE SUBURB

Building Societies and Freehold Land Societies

IN the last chapter the emphasis was laid mainly on building estates, and the personnel concerned in their development remained largely incidental to this theme. It is now time to consider these more directly, and it is convenient to begin with the operations of building societies and freehold land societies. These and kindred undertakings were of crucial importance in the Victorian suburb because they were one of the principal means of financing its development by advancing money both to builders and to the occupiers of houses.

Though building societies and freehold land societies had different roots their functions in the Victorian suburb were at times almost indistinguishable from each other. Building societies had been formed since about 1775 for limited objectives, mostly in order to use pooled resources for the building of a specific number of houses for their members, but sometimes in order to complete some project for the community as a whole, such as building a local inn. By 1825 at least 250 building societies of all kinds had come into existence, some only momentarily. They were then chiefly concentrated in the Midlands and the North, but by 1846 the total had reached about 2,000 and they were to be found in almost every important town and in some of the largest villages in all parts of the country.[1] It was about this time that freehold land societies first became important for housing development. There are some grounds for thinking that they had a longer history than building societies, but they did not take on their distinctive character until after 1832, when the reformed county franchise included all persons holding a forty shilling freehold. The number of freehold land societies was boosted during the Anti-Corn Law agitation of the early 1840s, when the acquisition of forty shilling freeholds was first used by the Liberals in the attempt to wrest political power from the dominant landed interest.[2] The cost of such a vote was well over £50, but this was greatly reduced when it was realized that the acquisition of estates on wholesale terms and their subsequent division into forty shilling parts was a more economical procedure: how cheaply votes could be created in this way is clear from the purchase by the Westminster Freehold Land Society of 30 acres of land at East Moulsey in 1850, for 260 voters were added to the electoral roll for West Surrey for £4,700, or just over £18 apiece.[3] The Birmingham Freehold Land Society, which was registered in 1847, was the first to act upon this principle, and others (not Liberals only, but Conservatives, too) rushed to follow this example. Before 1852 the operations of the freehold land societies had undoubtedly changed the political complexion of a number of counties, but after this the electoral gains of each party tended to nullify each other and freehold land societies ceased to be effective tactical weapons in the hands of the political parties and became instead the means of providing cheap freehold building plots in the suburbs.[4]

It is, unfortunately, not easy to relate much of this activity to the growth of a particular suburb such as Camberwell. Many societies existed but few left helpful records. There were by 1854 well over sixty freehold land societies operating in London and its suburbs,[5] but the number of building societies operating in the area—there were probably 2,500 of them in the country at large—was not so easily counted.[6] Some of the latter were closely identified by name or association with the development of different parts of London, even when the terminating principle upon which the earliest societies had been run gave way to a permanent basis from the 1850s onwards. For example, the Lambeth Building Society, formed in 1852, identified itself both with its own locality and with Peckham, New Cross, and Bermondsey;[7] and the Temperance Land and Building Society (later, Temperance Permanent), formed two years later, made the bulk of its advances in Peckham, Camberwell, Walworth, and Brixton.[8] There were also much smaller, more localized societies. One of these was the Camberwell & South London Building Society, established in 1875, which did a small mortgage business in south-east London. The only other society with such a marked affiliation with Camberwell as a whole was the Peckham Permanent Benefit Building Society, formed in 1855. This was the successor to a terminating society known as the Peckham Mutual Investment and Equitable Building Association, which had been formed eleven years before. It was, however, a tiny concern with average annual advances of only £500 or £600 down to 1875.

The smallest of such societies were usually highly selective in making their advances and did so mainly to owner-occupiers. But some other societies had their own estates, or more usually lent freely to speculating builders.[9] Much of London's suburban development was financed in this way, though advances to builders were petering out from the 1870s. A typical example of such borrowing was that of J. C. Ring of King's Road, Peckham, who borrowed from the Temperance. His account for 1868–9 ran: 25 August, £30 advanced; 20 April, application for £900, £830 agreed upon when houses finished, £530 advanced; 19 May, £180 advanced, further application for £900, £830 agreed to, £480 advanced on account; 1 June, £70 advanced on account; 29 June, £35 advanced on account; and so on.[10] Such data as are available on the operations of individual building societies are plainly too random to be at all satisfactory as evidence of the parts they played in the development of a particular suburb. There are, however, better grounds on which to gauge their contribution to the operations of a particular builder, and these will be examined in the final section of this chapter.

Freehold land societies, too, left little historical trace. Apart from stray references to their activities in particular localities in publications like *The Builder* and the *Freehold Land Times*, nothing is known about the activities of the great majority of them. The largest of them all, the National Freehold Land Society, formed in 1849 with the two chief architects of the freehold land movement—Richard Cobden and John Bright—on its board, did not altogether escape record.[11] By the middle 1850s it had handled well over a hundred estates of varying sizes up to 250 acres at a total cost of over half-a-million pounds. It was very active in the suburbs of London, especially south of the Thames, where more than a quarter of all its estates were located by this time, and it was here that it had begun the practice of inviting tenders from builders for erecting houses on its estates.[12] The expansion of all this business was, however, somewhat hampered by the law of mortmain which prevented freehold land societies from holding land even for the purpose of dividing and re-selling it. This had been circumvented by the technicality of directors acting as land agents, but there were snags to this, and when general limited liability became available in 1856 the Society seized the chance of forming a joint stock subsidiary to perform this function. This was the beginning of the largest land company to operate in London generally and in Camberwell during the nineteenth century—the British Land Company Ltd. The purpose of this company was to buy and sell land, and to develop building estates, on which purchasers of the plots could have houses built by means of mortgage loans from the National Freehold Land Society: the parent company was prepared to advance the whole of the price of the land and two-thirds of the value of the proposed building.[13] This was a facility which was naturally very welcome to small speculating builders, and after twelve years' operation of this scheme it seemed to one shareholder in the National as if this kind of accommodation was the special province of the two undertakings: in Camberwell, he complained, he could not have put a pig in the houses which had been financed in this way.[14]

Though the general outlines of its development are known, details of the activities of the British Land Company are unobtainable as the company's records perished during the last war.[15] In addition to numerous small estates, the company bought and re-developed during the 1860s and 1870s some of the land in the region of Cronin Road and East Surrey Grove, and several individual houses and their grounds at Dulwich and Grove Hill, but it also undertook more spectacular development, like the forty-acre Peckham Rye estate between Camberwell Grove and Bellenden Road (1872–4), or the two hundred-acre Friern Manor Farm estate at East Dulwich (1865–78).[16] The company was solely concerned with the preliminaries of estate development and was ready to auction off the land once the estate had been properly laid out, the roads built, and the major services supplied. This process did not normally take long. The first plots on the Peckham Rye estate were being auctioned only three

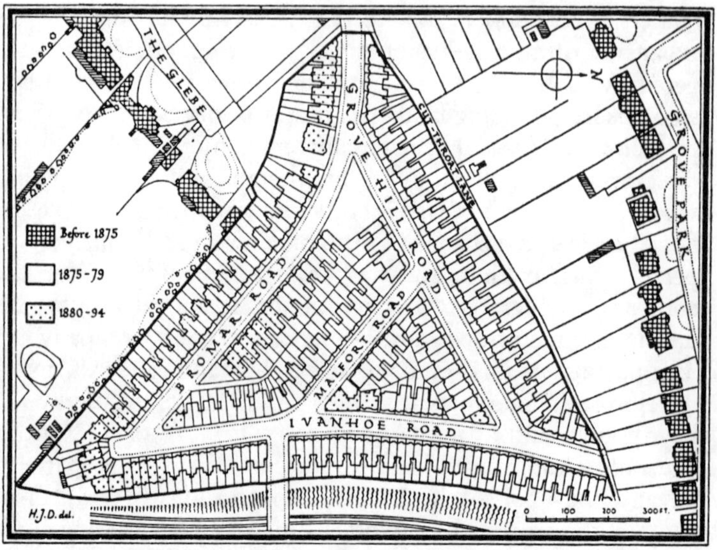

FIG. 10. *Denmark Park estate, 1895*

months after the company had bought the land, and those on the much larger Friern Manor Farm estate at the end of a year. These building plots were principally disposed of at auctions held either at the Auction Mart in Tokenhouse Yard in the City, or at local public-houses, at intervals of three or four months or more according to the condition of the land market, and they came by this means into the possession of the builders themselves. Occasionally the company disposed of the freehold of an estate without having made any preparations for building development. A quarter of the Peckham Rye estate, for example, was left undeveloped in this way between 1872 and 1875. It was then sold in one lot as the Denmark Park estate, whereupon the familiar process of development on building lease was carried on by a score of different builders in the next four or five years.

Though the financial terms on which these estates of the British Land Company were developed cannot be known, there are some details, which can now be examined, for a development which was in many respects similar to that undertaken by the British Land Company, and in which that company was partly concerned.

A Land Company in Operation

The estate to be considered was part of the Bowyer-Smijth estates covering an area of just over 100 acres between Goose Green and "The Plough", Lordship Lane. This was the location of some abortive estate development which has already been noted as having occurred in 1836. The southern half of this estate was put up for auction at Garraway's by the trustees and mortgagees of Sir William Bowyer-Smijth in 1864, but it was not sold until two years later when part of it was bought privately by the British Empire Mutual Life Assurance Company.[17] The purchase price was £14,765, or about £615 per acre, which was rather a high figure for the time.[18] How a Life Office of this kind came to embark on the highly speculative venture of suburban estate development is not at all clear.[19] The solid certainty, to mention no other, of municipal investment—the Camberwell Vestry, for example, had mortgaged the sewers rate for £49,000 at 5 per cent. to three London insurance companies in 1865–6[20] —was perhaps considered unwarrantably cautious when suburban building had been booming for ten years. Insurance companies were not, of course, quite unused to the business of suburban estate development because several of them had already had some years' experience in arranging annuities to cover building society repayments. But whether the original intention in this case had been simply to act as a freehold land company and to lay out the estate for building before wholly disposing of it, or to undertake the complete programme of development, including the financing of the building and making final arrangements for the sale or lease of the completed properties, is not at all clear. It is possible that the sudden change in the general financial climate which occurred so swiftly after the contract for the purchase of the estate had been made with the vendors on 4 May 1866 caused a change of plan. The dramatic collapse of the discount house of Overend, Gurney and Company a week later was a black event for all those businesses which rested on the uncertain foundations of short-term borrowing, and builders of suburban houses were among those who in consequence found credit scarce and dear. It is not improbable, therefore, that the

British Empire Life Office was unexpectedly forced to finance the whole enterprise and not merely its initial stages. The beginning was not auspicious.

The first three years were occupied in laying out the estate. This was, however, no straightforward matter. It seems that before this occurred the British Empire Life Office entered into some form of agreement with the Perpetual Investment and Building Society of New Bridge Street in the City. The loss of the relevant documents has left the relationship between these two bodies in doubt.[21] It is not clear whether the building society became joint owners, mortgagees, or contractors for some of the works, but what is clear is that the costs of preparing the estate for building purposes were shared equally between the insurance company and the building society.[22] The area of their joint operations occupied twenty-four acres between Lordship Lane, South Cross Road (soon to be known as Whateley Street), and the line of what became Barry Road and Heber Street. In August 1866 a professional surveyor was appointed to prepare a ground plan, and this became the basis for the usual application to the Metropolitan Board of Works to approve the direction, levels, widths, and names of the proposed new streets and the diversion of footpaths, and for the submission of drainage plans to the Vestry.[23] By the following May the work had advanced to the stage of making detailed plans and sections and of drawing up the specification for the building of the principal roads: tenders for the work were invited by advertisement, and the first contract placed for a sum of £3,591; within eighteen months two much smaller contracts for roadmaking were given to two other firms. As the roads were made, the surveyor from time to time pegged out building plots, and by the end of 1868 some 595 frontages of 16 feet apiece (except on Lordship Lane where these were widened to 48 feet) had been marked on the ground.[24] The surveyor also importuned the Vauxhall Water Company to agree both to laying its mains on the estate and to supplying all builders' needs entirely gratis.

The estate naturally had common boundaries with others alongside, and agreements had to be made at this stage to share with their owners the costs of making and sewering the roads which divided them. In August 1867 agreement was reached with one neighbouring landowner to connect the estate with his sewer; and the following spring an agreement was made by the British Empire Life Office and the Perpetual Building Society to share equally with the British Land Company the cost of making part of Caldwell Street (presently known as Barry Road) which divided their two estates. One final hindrance to uninhibited development of the estate was the payment of tithe, and the rent charge in lieu of this was redeemed in 1873.

The first building agreements were made with a number of builders in 1869. Minimum values of £200 and £300 were stipulated according to the location of plot, and the use to which the ground could be put was restricted to the building of dwelling-houses: offensive trades, cemeteries, burial-grounds, tan-pits, union houses, workhouses, nunneries, factories, steam-engine houses, and gasometers—the debasers of property values—were expressly forbidden. Although business conditions were generally favourable to rapid development of the estate, only about 150 houses, in various stages of completion, were standing on the estate at the end of the next six years, and well over half the estate remained under grass. In 1866 the key plan, on which the chief features were a church at Goose Green, two cemeteries, and two distant railway stations, had had an undeniably naked look to prospective builders. But the distance to the nearest railway at Herne Hill had been halved with the opening in October 1868 of North Dulwich Station. This was not, however, so easily reached, and the estate remained somewhat inaccessible.

The profits which were earned by this venture at this stage were, therefore, small. By June 1874 the total debit to the Land Account was £18,343, and the annual receipts consisted of £85 from unsecured ground rents, £470 from ground rents on 94 houses at £5 each, and £45 from the sale of grass: this made a total income of £600, or a rate of return of £3. 4s. per cent. The Building Account recorded a total debit of £28,321: expenditure included over £19,500 which had been advanced since December 1869 to fifteen builders in total amounts which varied from £300 to over £4,000, including an average rate of interest chargeable to them of about 3.3 per cent.; and a sum of over £13,000 which had been spent since 1870 in general repairs, building boundary walls, fencing, and finishing houses (presumably to individual tenants' requirements), and paying fire insurance; receipts included the proceeds from the sale of four houses for about £1,500, and from rentals of about £1,200 a year (including deductions for parish rates, taxes, water rates, and broker's expenses, amounting in all to £117 a year). A book-keeping entry to deduct ground rent at £5 per house (which had been reckoned to the Land Account) reduced the annual income to be set against the total outlay on building to £731, which was a return at the rate of £2. 12s. per cent. By 1874, therefore, the total investment of the company in this estate was £46,665, which was earning £1,331 a year, or £2. 17s. per cent. Whether the development of the remainder of the estate, which occurred between 1879 and about 1896, was any more profitable than this it is impossible to say, but it is clear that the business of estate development was not always a very profitable one, and that there were much better opportunities for remunerative investment elsewhere.

The Business of Speculative Building

That Victorian Camberwell was built on speculation is less surprising than it may sound, for speculative building means simply building houses in anticipation of the demand for them. This was not, however, an entirely guileless operation to contemporary eyes, and the term 'speculative builder' or 'speculating builder' came to acquire a peculiarly sardonic ring.[25] It was used to name not only a particular economic function but a meretricious scale of values and a dubious social status. "He found a solitude and leaves a slum"[26] was an observation which might well have belonged to any one of scores of scathing and frequently undiscriminating attacks on this breed of builder which appeared in Victorian periodicals and elsewhere.[27] Such popular generalizations were no doubt often misconceived, and the truth may be that the speculative builder's bad name properly belonged not merely to the scamping few of his kind but to certain landowners and money-lending solicitors and building societies who fixed some of the limits to his enterprise.[28] It might also have been applied more justly to governments which relied on indirect taxation on building materials at a time when the need for houses had never stood so high, and who failed moreover to develop an adequate code of building standards before the bulk of London's inner suburbs had been filled.[29]

The trade of speculative builder was moreover one in which even an informal apprenticeship could be disregarded. There were men who began in the building trades and who seized the chance of cheap money, when it was available, and a rapidly expanding market for houses, to lease a small plot of building land and to make of it a terraced frontage of small houses. One building trade often had a nodding acquaintance with another, and bricklayers, joiners, carpenters, plasterers, and masons often became successful speculating builders by combining several of these functions, or by variously sub-contracting some of the work.[30] Other men had such speculations thrust upon them by bad debts. Among these were the suppliers of building materials, whose terms were seldom net cash, and who sometimes found that the extension of credit to builders led them into the business themselves in order to recover what was due to them. Other involuntary speculators were the purveyors of capital, especially building societies, who sometimes found themselves engaged in speculatively building up half-completed houses on which they had had to foreclose. Still others launched into the trade to give employment to their savings, or as an alternative to gambling in the money market. There were speculative builders, therefore, who were not builders at all but were recruited from the most unlikely sources. Labourers and mechanics, servants and publicans, shopkeepers and merchants, lawyers and clergymen were all to be numbered among this invidious collection of speculative house-builders.[31]

What made entry to the business particularly easy was the ready flow of capital or the extension of credit to builders at the start of their operations, and the convention of sub-contracting the various trades, so that the speculative builder himself need have neither direct employees nor capital of his own. Moreover, what knowledge such builders needed in order to be on terms with those they employed, or in order to strengthen the slight competence they possessed could be got from a growing variety of technical literature which was some substitute for experience. Architectural pattern-books like S. H. Brooks' *Designs for*

Cottage and Villa Architecture (1839), or comprehensive treatises like J. C. Loudon's *Encyclopaedia of Cottage, Farm and Villa Architecture* (1833)[32]—many of which had been in effect so many elaborate circulars for their authors' wares—were by the 1850s being overtaken in publishers' lists by artisans' textbooks and builders' manuals.[33] Reliable primers for the building trades, such as *Weale's Rudimentary Series*—for which S. H. Brooks turned his hand to writing a treatise on *The Erection of Dwelling-houses; or, The Builder's Comprehensive Director* (1860)—became the best-sellers of their day.[34] These, together with the continuing stream of architectural works—like C. J. Richardson's *Picturesque Designs for Mansions, Villas, Lodges, &c.* (1870)[35] or C. Wilkes' *Handy Book of Villa Architecture* (1897)—and even books ostensibly aimed at householders—like J. D. Simon's *The House-Owner's Estimator* [*c.* 1870][36]—provided between them not merely a general outline of practically the whole conjugation of contemporary architectural style, but detailed, practical advice on the prime costs and suitability of building materials, constructional techniques, legal requirements, the drafting of specifications, and the provision of specimen bills of quantities, plans, elevations, and working drawings.[37]

The Builders of Camberwell

In these circumstances the number of speculative builders at work in the suburbs was bound to be large, even though the bankruptcy rate was high.[38] At the peak of building activity in Camberwell, in the years 1878–80, some 416 different firms or individual builders were actually engaged on the building of 5,670 houses. The following table sets out the main details.

Most of these builders had small businesses, for over half of them built no more than six houses in the whole three years; nearly three-quarters of them built no more than twelve.[39] Builders on this scale, however, provided little more than a quarter of the total houses built, and nearly one third of the total—about 1,800 houses—were built by only fifteen firms, each of which had an output of over 75 houses during the three years; the largest of them built 230 houses. The scale of such building

TABLE 4

HOUSE-BUILDERS IN CAMBERWELL, 1878–80

Size of Business (number of houses under construction)	*Number of Firms*		*Number of Houses*	
1 to 6	220	52.9%	699	12.3%
7 to 12	82	19.7%	769	13.5%
13 to 18	38	9.2%	594	10.5%
19 to 24	29	7.0%	620	10.9%
25 to 30	11	2.6%	304	5.4%
31 to 36	5	1.2%	162	2.9%
37 to 42	5	1.2%	199	3.5%
43 to 48	6	1.4%	268	4.7%
49 to 54	2	0.5%	105	1.9%
55 to 60	3	0.7%	169	3.0%
over 60	15	3.6%	1,781	31.4%
Totals	416	100.0%	5,670	100.0%

Source: District Surveyors' Monthly Returns.

operations had appreciably increased over the previous thirty years, for in another period of prosperity in the industry, 1850–1852, over 90 per cent. of builders were engaged in building twelve or fewer houses, and none built more than thirty houses all told. Very few of the firms in existence in the earlier period were still in operation in the later, and the great bulk of the builders at work during the boom of the 1870s appear to have set up their businesses only as the expansion took place. It is significant that so many of them—about a hundred—had so few resources as to have been capable of building no more than one or two houses, even on the very crest of the boom in 1878–80. The great majority of builders had local addresses, and very few whose headquarters were not in Camberwell came farther than Kennington, Brixton, Walworth, Bermondsey, or New Cross: those that did come from farther afield were generally building to contract and not on speculation. Probably nine out of ten of all the builders of houses in Camberwell in the 1870s were in fact building on speculation, and practically all the remainder were building under contract for some other builder or small capitalist whose venture was usually equally speculative.[40]

Contemporary accounts of his activities give the impression

that the speculative builder operated on a grand scale, but the evidence of the district surveyors' returns, as well as that to be seen on the ground, suggest that the building of Camberwell's streets was the unconcerted effort of many builders. There were, it is true, some streets which were wholly developed by one or two builders alone.[41] With a few exceptions, roads developed by a single builder were fairly short, and it was rare for one builder alone to develop a fairly lengthy street of, say, a quarter of a mile or more. But most development was, in fact, markedly heterogeneous, as is clear from some observation of the surviving houses on them.[42] There were also a good number of roads in which up to forty or fifty years elapsed between the filling of the first and the last building plots: on these the builders' names were practically legion.[43]

There were comparatively few streets and still fewer districts in which a single builder was either a solitary or a dominant figure. Although the largest builders were usually best known in a particular district, they tended nevertheless to spread their interests fairly widely within the parish rather than to concentrate them on a single estate of their own. This was true, for example, of the three largest builders in Camberwell in the 1870s —J. Dadd of Cemetery Road, Cooper & Kendall of Queen's Road, and W. Stubbs of Lambeth; these built 349, 296, and 243 houses respectively during the decade. For Dadd, his principal area of operations was Nunhead. He began building in Evelina Road in 1871, in Linden Grove in 1872, and in Kimberley Avenue in 1873; by 1880 he had built nearly 250 houses in the area, having completely monopolized the building in Howbury and Machell Roads in 1878–9. His other work was divided between two of the British Land Company's estates, Choumert Road at Peckham and Friern Manor Farm at East Dulwich, where he put up altogether about sixty more houses. Cooper & Kendall also built much at Nunhead: they began their operations there in Hollydale Road in 1876, and spread in the next three years to Lausanne, Crewys, Stanbury, and Lulworth Roads, in all of which they had built 177 houses by 1880; they also built some 55 houses in Brayard's Road, Peckham, in 1877–9, 25 houses in Wilson and Grace's Roads at Camberwell in 1878–9, and about 20 houses in Glengarry Road and East Dulwich Grove in 1880.

This was a firm, however, which also operated in other parts of London—for example, in Hammersmith in 1881. W. Stubbs of Lambeth divided his operations in Camberwell principally between two areas: in 1875–6 he started to build some 90 houses on Castlemain, Fendick, and Graylands Roads which had appeared on the remaining open space of the Rosemary Branch estate, and in 1878–9 he was ready to turn his attentions to the Vestry Road estate, where he erected 136 houses on Linnell, Lyndhurst, McNeil, Rignold, and Vestry Roads; in 1879, he switched his attention to East Dulwich and began to build on North Cross and Crystal Palace Roads.

The general pattern of development of these three builders was followed with some consistency by almost all the remaining builders whose scale of operations was large enough to allow them to spread their activities at all: Smith & Scarborough of Peckham, for example, though well rooted in the de Crespigny estates, also built much elsewhere; A. Bowles of Peckham Rye and W. T. Nicholls of Bromley built principally on the Selwyn estate, and F. Seiler on Bailey's estate, both at East Dulwich; R. Balaam of the Old Kent Road divided his work between Nunhead and East Dulwich; and this was the normal behaviour of many others, such as J. W. Hobbs, W. H. Cass, J. G. Dean, W. Cole, F. J. Johnson, W. Saunders, and G. & C. Acock.

There were, however, at least two instances of a pronounced concentration of effort by a speculative builder on a single estate. One was that of E. J. Bailey of Lordship Lane on his own freehold estate lying south-west of Goose Green. Between 1871 and 1878 Bailey built, or contracted to have built, nearly four hundred houses on this and the adjoining estates, and was undoubtedly the dominant influence in determining the general character of the district. The other instance of speculative building in the grand manner provides an excellent illustration of the way this was done and is therefore worth looking at in detail.

The Speculative Builder in Action

The builder in question was Edward Yates, who had his yard in Walworth Road just north of Camberwell Gate.[44] Yates was easily the largest builder at work in South London at the beginning of the 1880s and had in particular built hundreds of houses on some of the Ecclesiastical Commissioners' lands in Walworth. His business had all developed since 1867 when he had built a dozen houses in Nine Elms, Lambeth, with the help of a building society loan.

During the next thirty years Yates developed three estates in Camberwell. The first was on a small segment of ground on the south side of St George's Road, where he built Dragon Road in 1868–9.[45] The ground was leased from J. A. Rolls by a series of leases dated between April 1868 and December 1869, and the terms (which were for 69 or 70 years) were arranged to commence at dates between March 1867 and March 1869; the leases were drawn for groups of two, three, or four houses apiece. The ground rent was apportioned somewhat unevenly (presumably because of the variations in the size of the building plots) and ranged from £1. 9s. 6d. to £4 per annum. The completed estate consisted of 46 two-storeyed houses arranged in terraces down each side of the street. Yates reckoned their annual value at £26 a year and their prime cost at about £190 each. The total investment in the estate, probably including the provision of the normal essential services, was therefore about £8,750, and the property was insured against fire for £7,400.

Almost all the capital Yates needed to develop this estate he obtained by mortgage loans of 14 years' duration from building societies: from the London & Westminster he obtained three sums totalling £1,700, from the Planet six sums totalling £3,550, and from the Fourth City Mutual three sums probably amounting to about £1,250.[46] One other loan of £500 was obtained from a solicitor in Lincoln's Inn. The normal minimum rate of interest payable on such loans was 5 per cent.,[47] and if this were so for the loans in question it is clear that the whole venture can scarcely have been a very profitable one. Yates probably borrowed in all about £7,000, and on this his annual commitments in interest and amortisation cannot have been much below £850, to which should be added depreciation to cover the term of the leases, and sundry outgoings for rates, taxes, maintenance, and other overheads. The total ground rent payable to the ground landlord was £157 a year, so the total annual debit to his account was probably about £1,150. His annual income, if all the houses were occupied by punctilious tenants, was about £1,200. It follows that the margin of profit on his gross outlay may well have been no more than a half of one per cent. There seems little doubt, however, that speculative builders usually had less rigorous and more immediately practical methods of accounting than this. Most of their businesses lived from hand to mouth, and it had become a convention of the trade to raise a mortgage on one house, or even on one floor of it, in order to finance the next stage of development—be it the building of another storey, another house, another terrace, or another estate. This method of working normally involved none of the long-term financial considerations just mentioned because the average speculative builder aimed at selling rather than renting his houses.[48] By assigning the lease at a premium which covered the capital cost of building plus his own profit he disposed immediately of his indebtedness to the mortgagee and became involved in none of the cares of property management. But even when he preferred or was obliged to let his property he was unlikely to have accounted for his commitments in quite the same terms as above for he was unlikely to have created a sinking fund to cover depreciation, nor perhaps even at the start to reduce the mortgage loan. If his business prospered he might hope to make some large enough capital gains elsewhere, or to obtain enough land at a low enough rental to yield extra profits with which to meet his debts. Meanwhile, he found himself with some cash in hand, and he could begin the next speculation. In the case of Yates' speculation in Dragon Road, it was clearly by means of gains made elsewhere that he was able to redeem the majority of his mortgages before the end of their terms.

Yates' second speculation in Camberwell came in 1875 after six busy years of building in Walworth. The site of the estate was at the east end of Albany Road, where he built a neat *cul-de-sac* of twenty terraced houses to form Domville Grove.[49] Yates leased this estate for 75 years from J. A. Rolls at a total ground rent of £101 a year. The venture was probably financed, to be quite precise, by loans which had been raised on the security of some of Yates' Walworth houses, but Domville Grove in turn provided security for three further loans totalling £2,900 at 5 per cent. from a married woman at Tunbridge Wells who had already lent him over £5,000 on other property.

By this time Yates had abandoned his former practice of borrowing mainly from the building societies and was relying more and more on a series of connections he was making with various London solicitors, who frequently actually sought out Yates to discover what properties he had available as the security for specific sums of their clients' money. Actually, most building societies had already begun to turn away from the direct financing of speculative builders, who had been some of their biggest customers: there was no sudden switch on the part of the building society movement as a whole—as the revelations of the Liberator crash of 1890 made plain—but there was certainly developing a marked preference for lending instead to owner-occupiers. It may have been that the onset of the cyclical decline in house-building which coincided with Yates' first speculations made difficulties for him in raising as much capital as he needed from the building societies. That he had had to resort to five of them and one insurance company in 1868–9 certainly suggests this, and it is striking that although he was raising sums of £500 or £600 a time almost every month during this period, he had obtained no new capital on the Dragon Road estate between the end of 1869 and the middle of 1871. The last four houses to be mortgaged had been completed by September 1868, and when Yates had raised £500 more working capital on these in the summer of 1871 he had done so by tapping a solicitor. And it was to solicitors that he invariably looked for working capital in the years which followed.

The third Camberwell estate which Yates developed was easily his largest building project and one of the biggest enterprises by any builder throughout South London. This was what came to be known as the Waverley Park estate at Nunhead. It originally consisted of four fields of about nineteen acres in all lying on the east and south sides of the Nunhead Cemetery; a fraction of the estate actually lay in the parish of Lewisham. Yates bought the freehold of this land in 1877 from T. W. Evans, M.P. (who had come into possession of it as a mortgagee) for £6,300, £1,300 of which was paid as deposit on signing the contract, and the rest remained as a mortgage loan at 4½ per cent.

to be repaid at the rate of £500 after one year, a further £500 after two years, and the balance of £4,000 after three years. Yates realized that at a rate of about £330 an acre this property was a sound acquisition, but he appears at first to have been uncertain of his use of it. Cooper & Kendall, well established builders in the locality, made some proposals for taking part of the estate, and Yates would apparently have been willing to dispose of the whole of it at once had he been made a sufficiently tempting offer. He began, however, by turning part of it into a brickfield, and by the summer of 1878 was interesting local builders in his bricks.[50]

What may have decided Yates to develop the estate himself was the opportunity to lease from Christ's Hospital two pieces of land adjoining his own freehold land to the south. His original proposal, made late in 1879, was to take this land on a 99 year lease at £50 a year for the first five years, £100 for the next five, and £140 for the remainder of the term, and to build within ten years roads and sewers and to erect houses of a total value of not less than £10,000. After some very protracted bargaining, during which Yates also offered to buy the estate outright, and the Trustees of Christ's Hospital repeatedly tried to get Yates to raise his terms, a building agreement was finally made in December 1884 on the basis of an outlay by Yates of £45,000 on 120 houses of £350 to £450 each, and a ground rent of £225 a year. While these negotiations were pending Yates also bought, in 1881 or 1882, for £8,250 an estate of about 17½ acres adjoining the Christ's Hospital estate on its southern side; and early in 1884 he had both paid off the balance of the purchase price for the original land (which had been left on mortgage longer than had been originally arranged), and had bought another piece of ground of about six acres known as "The Vista" from a Mrs Nancy Scully. The acquisition of this land not only neatly extinguished a troublesome right of way along the cemetery wall but greatly facilitated the layout of the whole estate, so Yates was prepared to go to £5,000 to have it. The terms were for the payment of £1,000 down and for the balance to be left on mortgage at 4½ per cent., but this was actually paid off in two years.

By the end of 1884 Yates had in this way formed out of four

separate parts a reasonably compact and accessible estate of about fifty acres. He had begun in January of that year to erect the first houses in Ivydale Road, the back-bone of the estate, and this inaugurated a long and gradual process of making the superstructure to the estate, a process which was carried into a second generation twenty years later. Though its development did not supersede Yates' other interests in Walworth and elsewhere, the Waverley Park estate was the principal commitment of the business during the remainder of Yates' life, and its demands were sufficiently heavy to stay his hand on several other speculations, both distant and nearby which were put up to him in the next few years. Of the 2,345 houses which Yates owned in 1905, practically at the end of his business career, nearly one third were located at Nunhead.

There is an interesting feature of Yates' business activities which is worth noticing at this point. It is that during these formative years in the growth of the Waverley Park estate the output of his business did not conform at all to the normal cycles of prosperity and depression which were experienced by the industry as a whole. Characteristically enough, Yates had begun his business late in the up-swing of a building cycle, but this had ended abruptly in 1868. As we have seen, money had then been tight but not unobtainable and Yates' houses had not been left half-finished for lack of it. The slump lasted to 1872, but contrary to the general experience Yates' building operations never flagged: in 1871, his busiest year during this phase, he had built on lease 73 houses—mostly in Walworth—apart from a large contract he had had at the City Mortuary. To have kept growing in the exhilarating years of expansion down to 1881 was, of course, unremarkable for this was a time when even the humblest jobbing bricklayers and carpenters could be found measuring the leap into speculative building, and taking it. The surprising thing is that his output of houses should have continued unchecked and on such a scale into the prolonged period of *malaise* which followed this. The years between 1884 and 1895 were Yates' busiest, with a climax in 1888–90 when he was building around 150 houses a year. Apart from minor deviations the whole trend of his business was strongly upward for the whole twenty years down to the end of the 1880s, a period in which the

London housing industry as a whole experienced two slumps and a boom. The affairs of Edward Yates, whether measured in terms of his borrowings on mortgage or of numbers of completed houses was in the sharpest possible contrast to the mercurial behaviour of the London housing industry which was plotted in Fig. 4 above. His was a business with a rate of growth which neither the long-term rate of interest nor the vicissitudes of the capital market appear to have touched.

Yates, like all speculative builders, worked principally on borrowed capital, but, as with the Domville Grove speculation, the sums raised on the Waverley Park estate were probably used elsewhere, and the capital which was needed to launch that enterprise was raised by mortgage or by capital gain on different property again. By 1890 Yates' total mortgage indebtedness, an accurate index of the scale of his investment in his concern, was approaching a quarter of a million pounds, and in the absence of detailed accounts it is not possible to say just how successive loans were used.[51] By 1884 Yates had spent nearly £40,000 on the Waverley Park estate, yet he does not appear to have tried to raise money on any part of the estate before this date. Just how much he obtained of the £30,000 he was by that date seeking, however, is not clear, but some he must have received from a Northamptonshire clergyman, for insurance policies on the first houses to be completed on Ivydale Road were in their joint names. Yates evidently did not want to encumber the estate unduly with mortgage commitments while he was able to raise as much capital as he needed on his Walworth estates and by some very profitable land speculations in West London and elsewhere.[52] A loan of £6,000 which he raised on the original nineteen acres of building land in 1888 was thus a tiny fraction of the total value of that part of the estate, and was repaid in 1896. Even the £20,000 which he raised in 1895 on the Christ's Hospital section of it did not approach its real value, and it, too, was repaid in about seven years.

Journalists' likening of a speculative builder who was operating on this scale to a military commander were not entirely fanciful. In an enterprise of this sort, the builder had to ensure good access to the site for both building materials and potential tenants, to concentrate sufficient supplies of capital, of labour, and of raw materials at the right time, to superintend the interlocking processes of building construction, to attract and settle tenants in the completed houses, and to maintain the desired standards of sanitation and social status. Thus, Yates' first concern was to make a more direct road connection with the railway station at Nunhead, and this was accomplished by the end of 1882, after some nine months' importunate letter-writing and discussion with the railway company. But his next attempt two years later to get a still more direct connection with the railway came to nothing: he had tried to induce the company to provide him with a siding for ten trucks or so on his side of the line because, although he had arranged with several Kentish brickmakers and tilemakers to send large supplies by barge to the canal head at Peckham, he had hoped to lower his costs even below those for water carriage by avoiding the extra handling and road haulage entailed in bringing supplies by cart up the hill from Peckham. The outcome of the negotiation was a railway contract for the carriage of bricks, but to Yates' chagrin no siding resulted on the south side of the station. Yates was also unsuccessful in his attempt a few years later to get another station built between Nunhead and Honor Oak. But another question of accessibility shortly afterwards found him in a different mood, for when the Haberdashers' Company (who had a large estate on the slopes of Telegraph Hill beyond the railway line as well as the ground between it and the backs of the houses in Ivydale Road) approached him to get his agreement for a road between their two estates, Yates saw no point in "breaking up the privacy of my estate," and refused £3,000 as the price for doing so.

In the course of thirty years the technique of assembling large quantities of building materials on the site and of recruiting workmen became a routine. For part of the estate Yates was not free, of course, from the controlling hand of the Surveyor to Christ's Hospital, the ground landlord, but this superintendence does not seem to have affected very much either the programme or the nature of Yates' enterprise.[53] From the start, Yates prepared his own road plans and drainage plans for submission to the Metropolitan Board of Works and the local Vestries, and at the beginning he made his own roads, under the supervision of the local authority. By 1888 this work was sub-contracted, and in the 'nineties roadmaking on the Lewisham part of the estate was left in the hands of the local Board of Works, to whom Yates paid half of the total cost as a preliminary to adoption. The building of sewers was sub-contracted from the start. Gas and water supplies were procured by simply applying to the South Metropolitan Gas Company and to the Southwark & Vauxhall Water Company to connect their mains with the completed houses; street-lighting was provided by the Vestry. Practically all the remaining works were undertaken by Yates' own employees who appear to have worked—the skilled trades at least—on piece-rates which Yates fixed himself or agreed with the employee concerned: he paid no union rates.[54] His almost legendary personal inspections of the progress of the works, the establishment of an effective site office complete with private telephone line to head office, and vigorous complaints to all suppliers of building materials who gave short weight or supplied inferior goods were Yates' means of maintaining his relatively high building standards. And apart from fairly extensive advertising of the estate on railway stations in London and the suburbs, it was on the superior fittings and reasonable rents of his houses that Yates chiefly relied to attract his tenants.

His houses were modern, solid, and respectable, and Yates as landlord strove to maintain these suburban virtues: their exteriors proclaimed them to prospective tenants in terms of brass, bay windows, and stained glass, and the interiors in terms of back boilers, gas stoves, mahogany glass-fronted bookcases, numerous fitted cupboards, Venetian blinds, bathrooms, and separate washhouses. Most rentals were originally £28 a year exclusive of rates—which was about £4 a year cheaper than comparable houses in the neighbourhood—but by 1907 were available slightly more cheaply at £3. 5s. a month, inclusive of rates.

In time the estate acquired, too, most of the conventional amenities of suburban life. A few small shops—the nature of whose businesses Yates carefully determined[55]—came into existence almost at the start; by 1887 a pillar-box and a public-house, "The Waverley Arms", had appeared on Ivydale Road; by 1888 a temporary school of the London School Board and

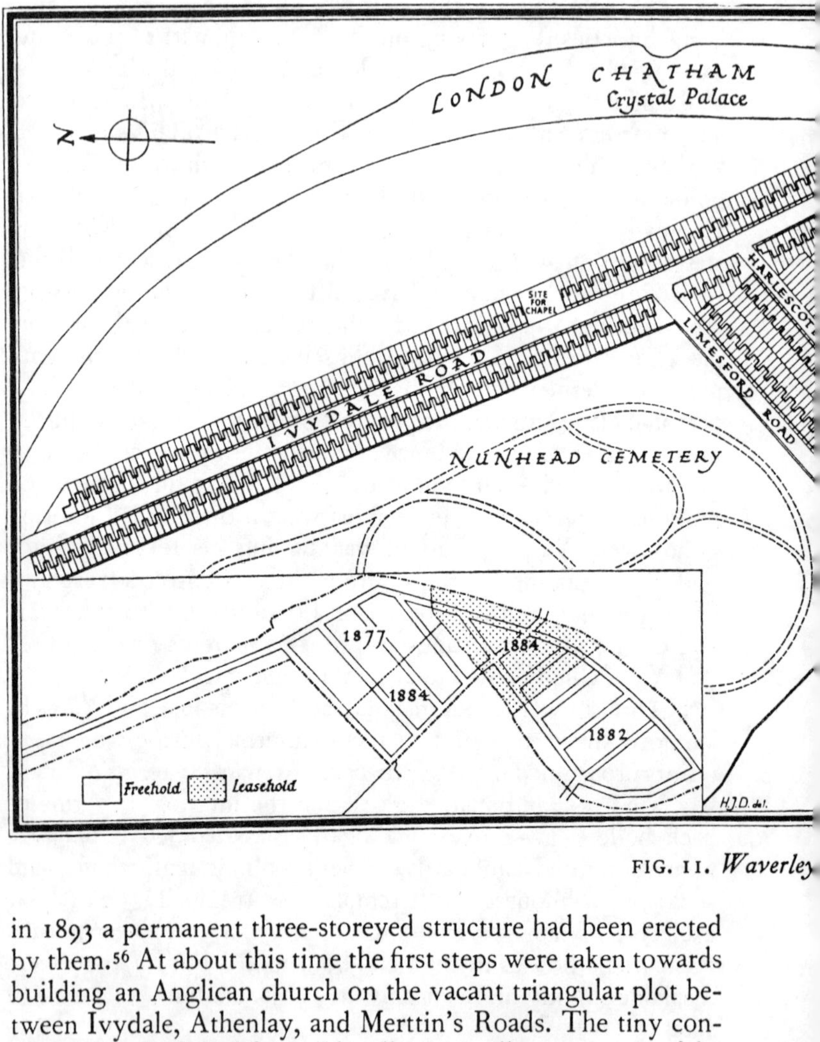

FIG. 11. *Waverley*

in 1893 a permanent three-storeyed structure had been erected by them.[56] At about this time the first steps were taken towards building an Anglican church on the vacant triangular plot between Ivydale, Athenlay, and Merttin's Roads. The tiny congregation which had formed locally originally met in one of the shops in Ivydale Road, moved to a temporary Mission Hall in Bellwood Road in 1896, and to its permanent home in St Silas' Church in 1903.[57] Meanwhile, a small Methodist chapel had been erected in 1895–6 at Nos. 149–159 Ivydale Road.[58] Apart from these, however, practically the only features to divert the eye

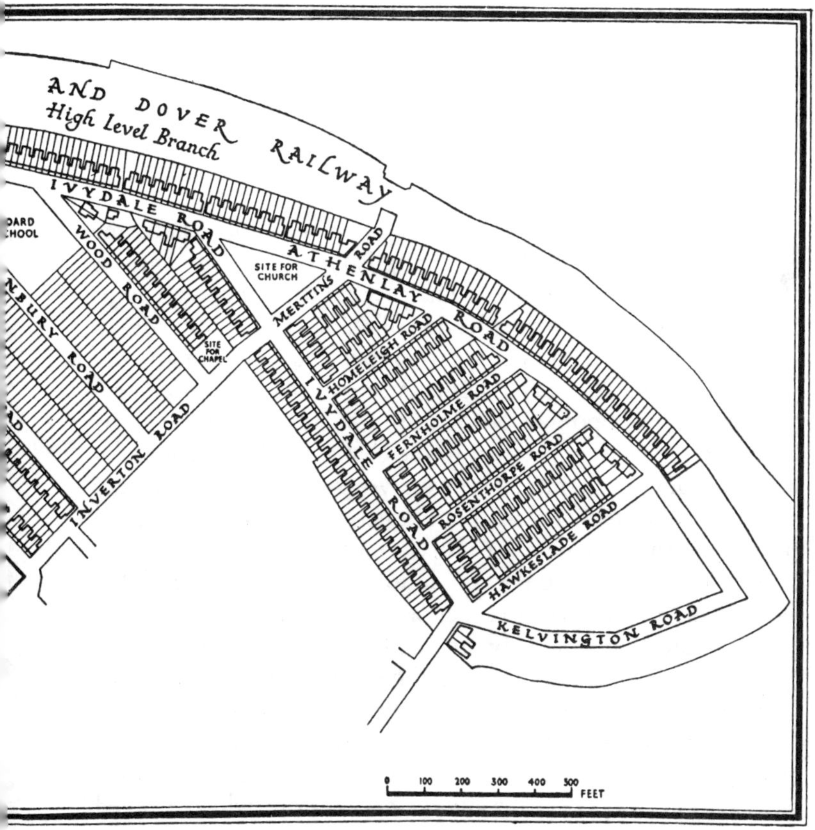

estate, about 1900

from the monotonous regularity of the streets were the railway, the waterworks, and the cemetery, and it was perhaps not surprising that clubs and associations were slow to form and to give to Yates' suburb a genuine life of its own.[59] In this it was not uncharacteristic of many of the new, battleship-trim neighbourhoods which were being formed for lower-middle-class suburbians on all sides of London in the last twenty years of the nineteenth century, and it is the provision of their amenities which must now be considered in the context of the general character of the suburb.

CHAPTER VI

THE PROVISION OF AMENITIES

The Framework of Local Government

CAMBERWELL grew to maturity as a suburb at a time when the whole fabric of English local government was being revolutionized. The process of change was complex for it involved the substitution of a single democratic organ of efficient local government for a complicated and inept array of largely undemocratic *ad hoc* bodies.[1] The formation of Camberwell into a metropolitan borough in 1900 came after a whole lifetime of belated adjustment to the changing circumstances of suburban development. These were years of fierce controversy in the world outside on the basic functions and forms of local government and on the content of the local franchise. At the very beginning of the period the conviction was still widespread that most of the requirements of a suburban community, as of any other, would be provided by unseen hands. The pursuit of self-interest was still thought to be the best mandate for the public welfare. There were perhaps some grounds for thinking this of the suburbs at the time, for the first suburbians were generally men of some position who knew how to protect their own interests and had the means and the connections which enabled them to do so. But this was naturally less and less true as the suburb filled up with people who could not afford the spaciousness and the detachment of the old days, and who demanded a voice in local affairs.

In one sense, the growing effectiveness and broadening justice of local authorities in the Victorian era were part of a far larger democratic process involving the reform of parliamentary institutions. In another, they were a response to the needs of a more complex physical and social environment which required new kinds of control. In neither sense were these changes in local government matters of the parish pump alone. Camberwell was part of London, the political controversies were part of a bigger argument about the functions of government itself, and the attack upon the antiquated machinery of local affairs was part of a general onslaught on the great structure of privilege built up by a ruling landed class. Looked at parochially, however, the transition from chaos to some kind of order in the local government of Camberwell turned on three dates—1834, 1855, and 1900.[2]

The year 1834 was a turning point in the local government of Camberwell as it was of every other parish in England because, among other things, it marked the beginning of a period in which the powers of the traditional organ of local government, the Vestry, were whittled down by the transfer of authority to other bodies. Hitherto the parish had in the main been governed by an open Vestry of the parishioners who, in the words of a minute of such a meeting, "ordered that a certaine number of the constant inhabitants and parishioners should be nominated . . . to meet once in every month in the parish church to consult with the minister and officers aboute the affairs of the parish and . . . to communicate from time to time (as occasion shall be) what they have inquired into and debated of, and at such time or times there shall be a generall meeting of the parishioners at the Church. . . ."[3] These were the Vestry's terms of reference at the Restoration, and they continued as the basis of the government of the secular affairs of the parish down to 1855.[4] The vicar was *ex officio* chairman of the Vestry, and the administration of the main business of the Vestry was entrusted to a small number of unpaid officials—the churchwardens and the overseers of the poor—and to a number of other officials who were rewarded in cash or in kind. In practice membership of the committee which decided the conduct of affairs as well as tenure of parochial office tended to be influenced by family connections; auditing of the parish accounts was done by the local gentry, and for at least one period by the vicar himself. The parish officials included the beadle, who was then the most highly paid of all, the Vestry clerk, collectors, ale-conners, and several others.

By 1834 the sovereignty of the Vestry had already been somewhat modified by the rise of other offices which either did not depend on Vestry sanction or tended to have an independent existence if they did. Thus, Commissioners of the Court of Requests had the responsibility from 1758 to 1846 of recovering small debts in the locality; the Surveyor of the Highways was, contrary to the original Act of 1555, appointed by the justices down to 1833; and since the Acts for lighting and watching Camberwell and Peckham and establishing a foot patrol had been passed in 1776 and 1787 two Lighting Trusts had come into being. When the Metropolitan Police came into being in 1829—the first step ever taken towards dealing with the whole metropolitan area as a single unit—the watching of the streets was handed over to them. One other aspect of local affairs which had never been the responsibility of the Vestry was drainage. The Commissioners of Sewers for Surrey and Kent were one of eight such bodies which had originally had the task of attending to land drainage and to the embankment of rivers, a task which they had discharged with quiet ineptitude until the invention of the water-closet, which was literally too much for them.

The Vestry in this period was still largely regulated by Common Law and local custom alone, though its powers had since the Vestries Act of 1818 been assailed by general legislation affecting the method of voting and, by implication, the franchise. The open Vestry was not an efficient organ of local government in a rapidly growing suburban parish, as Camberwell was in the 1820s and 1830s, and it was more than once severely criticized by commissions of inquiry. When the Royal Commission on the Poor Law reported in 1834 it alleged that the open Vestries were "the most irresponsible bodies that were ever entrusted with the performance of public duties or the distribution of public money." One of the provisions of the Poor Law Amendment Act was therefore to cut spending on the relief of the poor by, among other things, transferring responsibility for the poor from the open Vestries where everyone had a voice in the matter to newly constituted Guardians of the Poor who would be more discreet in applying the rates. In November of the following year such a body was set up in Camberwell, and the cost of the poor was reduced in the first year by 41 per cent. This was the first of the important functions of the Vestry to be handed over to statutory committees and it initiated a trend in the devolution of the executive authority of the Vestry by the establishment of special committees for different purposes, a trend which continued throughout the century.

The following year the General Highway Act gave to parish Vestries the power to appoint a representative board of management for the roads, and in this way a Highway Board came into being in Camberwell. In 1854 the adoptive powers of the Burial Acts, 1852–3, were used to establish a Burial Board which became responsible for the provision of parish burial grounds, and in particular a new cemetery at Forest Hill. In 1845 the Building Acts were applied to Camberwell as such and its own district surveyor appointed. He was responsible in the next ten years to a Registrar of Metropolitan Buildings who stood outside all the existing organs of local government in London. The local district surveyor was appointed by the Surrey justices, who in turn acted upon the advice of a small number of official referees appointed by the Commissioners of Works and Buildings.[5] The chief influence on the operations of the Vestry in these years was, however, the sanitary condition of the parish. The 1831 epidemic of cholera had already led to the creation of a local temporary board of health. When the cholera returned in 1849 it emphasized all the more urgently the need for sanitary reform. It is true that the previous year the several Metropolitan Courts of Sewers had been swept away and a Commission of Sewers for the whole metropolis put in their place. Yet this body, its membership constantly changing, was scarcely more effectual than its predecessors, and its activities or lack of them continued to be criticized on all sides. In Camberwell, the inadequacies of the Commissioners of Sewers were the subject of a public Vestry which met in June 1850 and again the following January. A resolution was then carried "for the entire removal of the present irresponsible, arbitrary, and most unconstitutional system, and its replacement by another which shall be alike simple, responsible, and constitutional." This was part of the general protest which resulted in 1855 in the summary dismissal of the Commissioners of Sewers and the establishment of the first body to have powers, few as they were, for the government of the whole of London. London meant the area used by the Registrar-General for census purposes, and was made up of a somewhat arbitrarily grouped number of Poor Law Unions and parishes.

The Metropolitan Board of Works was an indirectly elective

body which came into being under the Metropolis Management Act, 1855. The seventy-eight parishes of London outside the City were organized for local government purposes under twenty-three reformed parish Vestries, which included Camberwell, and the remainder under fifteen District Boards of Works which were elected by the Vestries concerned.[6] Vestrymen were elected by persons whose names had been on the rate-book for a year, and eligibility for office depended on the occupancy of premises rated at £40 or more a year. Camberwell was divided into six wards having twelve to eighteen vestrymen elected in each. The new Vestry was now invested with powers to deal with drainage and sanitation, which it used with vigour. These matters are dealt with in one of the following sections. Over the next few decades it also undertook new responsibilities, such as the upkeep of the disturnpiked roads (1865) and the implementation of the Artizans' and Labourers' Dwellings Acts (1866–75).

The trend towards the development of specialized committees in the locality to superintend new parochial undertakings, and the development of more comprehensive bodies to deal with certain affairs for the whole metropolitan area continued into this period. The district surveyor continued to be responsible for the implementation of the Building Acts, but his office now became yoked to that of the Superintending Architect of the Metropolitan Board of Works, to whom he submitted monthly and annual reports. The London School Board, which came into being in 1871, was another of the extra-parochial bodies whose influence reached deep into the local affairs of the parish. And the Vestry itself appointed other bodies of Commissioners, who derived their powers from general legislation—as did the Burial Board already noted—to attend to free public libraries and public baths. Meanwhile, other semi-public bodies had developed for the supply of gas and water.

The total effect of this multiplication of specialized bodies in London was to create, in the words of one informed critic at the end of the century, "a chaos which is not understood by any member of Her Majesty's government, and certainly not by the ordinary citizen."[7] The government of London as a whole as well as of its parts was also frustrated by numerous different divisions of the area for different administrative purposes. A start had, however, been made on tidying up this administrative confusion in 1889 when the Metropolitan Board of Works, which had got a bad name for jobbery and inefficiency, was supplanted by the London County Council. This change did not affect the Vestries, however, which continued to administer their allotted areas until 1900, when the London Government Act of the previous year created the twenty-eight metropolitan boroughs. Among these Camberwell was the fourth largest.

Water Supply and Sewage Disposal

There are a number of points at which this brief outline of the local government of the suburb needs to be supplemented in more detail. These are the supply of water and gas, and the provision of main drainage.

The supply of water to Victorian suburbs, though essential to their development, is not a matter which can be explored very effectively in parochial detail. Its history is principally administrative and financial, and the hefty volumes which contain what is known about the supply of water to Victorian London are reticent on the detailed chronology of development.[8] The beginnings of pumped supplies of water to Camberwell are traceable to 1804 when an association was formed to provide main supplies to the area which was then beyond the supply of the two existing water companies—the Southwark and the Lambeth companies—and the following year the South London Waterworks was formed. By the 1830s a reservoir had been brought into use at Kennington to receive the river water taken from the Thames at Vauxhall. This reservoir, however, became superfluous when the company amalgamated with the Southwark company in 1845 (and became known as the Southwark & Vauxhall Water Company), and the Vauxhall intake became obsolete in 1852 when the company was required, largely as a result of the inquiries which followed the disastrous cholera invasion of Camberwell in 1849, to collect its water above the tideway, at Hampton. Another six years passed before the first supplies were available from this source. At the same time, the company contemplated supplying the whole of its permitted area, which included

Camberwell and Peckham, and part of Dulwich, and for this purpose built its Nunhead reservoir, which also came into use in 1855.[9] Meanwhile, the Kent Water Company (formed in 1809) had begun to supply Hatcham and part of Peckham.[10] The Lambeth Water Company (formed in 1785) had by 1802 brought water supplies to Kennington, and later began to supply Walworth, Lambeth, Dulwich, and part of Lewisham.

Although by the end of the 1840s water undertakings were required by Act to supply pure water at constant pressure to any district within their area which demanded it, it was not until the 1870s that this provision was beginning to be made effective by the enforcement of legislative provisions, by constant and not intermittent supplies of water, and by the connection of a much larger proportion of houses with the main.[11] The cost of a barrel to store 36 gallons and a service pipe to the mains need not have cost more than 22s. 6d., according to one authority in 1849, but even this small sum was rarely incurred either by weekly tenants or their landlords in South London because neither was prepared to benefit the other financially.[12] According to Edwin Chadwick, distribution of water to "the wage classes" was, even in 1876, still "mostly by open butts in courts and streets, then in pots and pans in living rooms."[13] Water, the Vestry Surveyor had laconically remarked in 1859, was then "generally becoming a requisite of daily life,"[14] but it was not before 1897 that of the three companies operating south of the Thames the Southwark & Vauxhall Water Company alone could assert that every home in its district was constantly supplied with water.[15] How recent an innovation this has been is perhaps evident from the survival of the house-cistern system of water supply which had been the apparatus for receiving intermittent supplies.

What made intermittent water supply so obnoxious was the strong probability that in small houses cistern water would be polluted by gases escaping into the feeder pipes from sink traps, sewers, and water-closets when water supplies were turned off.[16] To annul the intimate connection between sewage disposal and water supply at its source was therefore matched by the necessity to maintain their distinction within the home and in the locality. Efficient house drainage and sewage disposal were accordingly amenities to be prized, the more especially when the incidence of cholera was shown to have been correlated with insanitary conditions of these kinds: in none of the outbreaks of cholera in London since 1832–3 had Camberwell escaped serious infection.[17] The extravagant claims put forward in auction particulars of new building estates which did have tolerable sanitary arrangements at this time serve to stress the unusualness of such provisions. The preamble to one in the early 1840s began: "Bath Road runs through the Estate and has a Famous Sewer already constructed from one end to the other, and there is a deep gravelly soil throughout this locality forming also a natural drainage which, together with the mild salubrious air for which the neighbourhood is proverbial, have gained for Peckham its present celebrity for promoting health and longevity."[18]

In general, however, sewerage arrangements in London suburbs before the 1850s were casually contrived, for, with no obligation placed upon the builder of a row of cottages or of an estate to provide adequate sewers or even adequate drainage, occupiers of suburban dwellings often had no other means of drainage than the common ditches, which usually came to perform the office of sewers as well as of land-drains and watering places for cattle.[19] An illustration of the conditions which frequently arose from such circumstances was given at a meeting of the newly formed Metropolitan Commission of Sewers in 1848, when the surveyor reported on the drainage of 87 houses at Peckham.[20] The basements, areas, yards, and gardens were overflowing with soil-drainage from adjoining cesspools: two or three of these, each of a capacity of about 10 cubic yards, were found in and about each house, and altogether 181 cesspools were discovered and emptied of their contents in 2,384 cartloads.[21] The process of substituting covered tubular drains for open ditches, and water-closets for privies and cesspools, had scarcely begun, and continued for at least another twenty years.

In 1856, when the reformed Camberwell Vestry came into being with the specific task of improving the sewerage and drainage, as well as the paving, cleansing, lighting, and general improvement of the parish, the parish was almost wholly undrained, and what sewers did connect with the open sewer which led away through Rotherhithe and Deptford were placed under its tidal influence.[22]

There was a lot to do, and the Vestry started its sordid task by the removal of cesspools and the provision of water-closets and dustbins, the latter mostly "for houses of superior class."[23] By 1871 the Vestry had succeeded—not without some goading by the ratepayers[24]—in abolishing some 4,352 cesspools and in providing instead an almost equivalent number of water-closets and fifty miles of covered sewers, at a cost to the ratepayers of over £100,000, most of which had been borrowed from insurance companies.[25] The opportunity to do much of this had come with the main drainage of London, on which work had begun in 1858, and which could be used for house drainage in Camberwell from 1864.[26] There remained, however, much still to do, for defective sewerage had to be renovated, and new estates incorporated into the system. The claim of the Vestry in a report to the Metropolitan Board of Works in 1871 that "at the present time (except here and there in the rural parts) there is scarcely a cesspool or privy anywhere in the parish," meant the achievement of a limited objective only.[27] The region between Goose Green and the Victoria tavern could, for instance, still be described in 1872 as an intolerable settling tank, and houses on the Newlands estate at Nunhead still had cesspools in 1883.[28] The sewerage of the parish was practically a standing item on the Vestry's agenda for the rest of its existence.

It may, incidentally, be interjected at this point that the maintenance of a sanitary code did not depend solely on the purity of water supplies and the efficiency of sewage disposal. Public health depended on more than public utilities. Thus, when the Nuisances Removal Acts, which had been discharged locally by two inspectors before the cholera of 1866 and four after it, were supplemented by the housing legislation of 1868–72, the Vestry's authority in controlling other threats to public health was greatly strengthened.[29] In 1872 a beginning was made under the authority of the Act of 1868 on the clearance of slums, which had already begun to appear in some parts of the parish, with the enforced demolition of six dwellings known as North Row Cottages in Crown Street.[30] Over the next few years numerous other single dwellings or rows of houses in Camberwell, Nunhead, and Peckham were similarly demolished by their owners by order of the Vestry.[31]

The Supply of Gas

The quality of suburban water supplies and the efficiency with which sewage was disposed of improved very rapidly in the last quarter of the nineteenth century. So it was, too, with the supply of new means of artificial lighting. But the supply of gas, like that of water, occurred almost without documentary trace.[32] A Camberwell Gas Company had spluttered into a brief, inactive existence in the early 1820s, but the first distributor of gas in the parish was the Phoenix Gas Light & Coke Company, which brought its mains to Camberwell Green, and thence along Coldharbour Lane and Peckham Road in 1824.[33] By 1831 it had 550 consumers in Camberwell, Peckham New Town, and South Lambeth. Meanwhile the South Metropolitan Gas Company—though it had not yet obtained the statutory powers it had twice sought—had begun to make and supply gas in the parish, and by the end of 1834 over twenty miles of mains radiated from its works on the Grand Surrey Canal along the Old Kent Road, New Kent Road, Walworth Road, and elsewhere in South London.[34] The history of the next twenty years is of desperate competition between these two companies, and with two others (the Surrey Consumers' and the London Gas Companies) for the supply of gas south of the river. Occasionally as many as ten sets of pipes would be laid in one street by the competing companies: in Walworth Road, each of the four companies had mains on both sides.[35]

Competition had the immediate effect of lowering prices and leading to the first installations in private houses in the area in 1842. From 1841 also began attempts at collusion of various kinds between the gas companies. After several attempts these reached final form in 1853 in a boundary agreement, which the Vestry regarded with some suspicion, but which was confirmed by the Metropolis Gas Act of 1860.[36] Before this sanction was obtained, however, the South Metropolitan Company, which was left in possession of virtually the whole of the parish of Camberwell, had to agree on a line of demarcation with the newly formed Crystal Palace Gas Company.[37] During the 1860s, when its charges (3s. 4d. per 1,000 feet) were the lowest in London, the South Metropolitan Company doubled its business, and would have done still more had not the costs of installation, just over £6 a house, been borne wholly by the consumer. In 1877 such limitations were partly removed by the company undertaking to pay the full costs of a normal installation of service pipe, and also by making gas-stoves available on hire; eleven years later they were to be had on hire purchase.[38] Gas was still practically unknown, however, in working-class homes, and it was not until 1892, when the company first fitted prepayment meters and undertook to install all pipes at a fixed rental, that gas began to be used practically everywhere for lighting and cooking.[39] Within six years over 80,000 penny-in-the-slot meters had been installed, and by 1905 this figure had more than doubled. At the same time the more economical incandescent mantle was being introduced. By now gaslight was almost as conventional a feature of the suburban home as running water and the water-closet had so recently become.

Retail Shops

The development of new techniques for selling gas in the vast suburban market was a symptom both of the changing character of the suburbs themselves and of retail trading generally. The retail shop was not a Victorian invention but this was the era of its most rapid development. In 1849 an architect was already writing of the tendency in the suburbs for shop fronts to be clapped onto the front gardens of houses: "one by one each house casts a proboscis forth in the shape of a long, low, narrow shop, covering the dull patch that once was dignified as the front garden."[40] On Southampton Street, for example, a third of the building done between 1845 and 1851 was of shops and shop-fronts.[41]

This was a trend which was enormously accelerated in the second half of the nineteenth century, when the distributive system was being influenced by the new wealth and tastes of an industrial society living in towns and their suburbs. As late as 1888 Thorold Rogers was able to speak of "the epoch of shops" as being a comparatively recent phenomenon. This was the period in which the retail shop was displacing the itinerant dealer, the market stall-holder, the wholesaler, and the craftsman. The shops themselves were becoming more specialized and shopkeepers less skilled, and their organization more complex.[42] With improved suburban communications, the long arms of the new departmental stores of Central London easily reached the metropolitan suburbs, and the multiple stores brought to them a brand new organization in the grocery, meat, footwear, chemists' goods, confectionery, tobacco, and a number of other trades. H. G. Wells' complaint about the decline of his father's shop at Bromley in the 1860s—that new residents came who "knew not Joseph and bought their stuff from the stores"[43]—was no doubt the cry of many such businesses throughout the suburbs.

The rise of the new generation of shopkeepers in Camberwell in the second half of the nineteenth century cannot very easily be detected in the parsimonious columns of the suburban directories. The first to appear, in 1860,[44] indicates very well the places where most suburban shopping was done, but what is not clear is the kind of establishment these places were. Entries for bakers, dressmakers, milliners, tailors, wardrobe dealers, hairdressers, and others, do not necessarily mean the existence of conventional shops. If mere numbers are any indication, however, they appear to have served the needs of their localities tolerably well and were only slightly less numerous, per head of the population, than they were fifty years later.

The largest group in 1860 was of 300 shops for the sale of food—about forty in each of the main trades. There were also about a score of dairies, and about a dozen confectioners, cheesemongers, fruiterers, and fishmongers. Clothing and household goods were each the business of about half the number of those engaged in the distribution of food. In clothing, easily the largest group was of over fifty boot and shoe makers, followed by less than forty tailors, about twenty milliners, and a few dressmakers, dyers, wardrobe dealers, staymakers, furriers, and hatters. Of those supplying household goods, chandlers of various kinds were the most numerous, though there were fewer than forty of them. Next came drapers, about twenty-five in all (including a few hosiers, lace warehouses, and Berlin wool repositories), about a dozen each of glass or china dealers, oil and colourmen, fancy goods dealers, and ironmongers, and a handful of upholsterers, furniture dealers, coalmerchants, and so on. Nearly as large a category as the last two was drink and tobacco, for apart from public-houses there were at least seventy beer retailers, and over twenty tobacconists. There was finally a large miscellaneous group which included about twenty chemists, a dozen stationers, hairdressers, undertakers, and watchmakers, and two or three newsvendors, florists, toy dealers, booksellers, photographists [*sic*], and pawnbrokers; there was also a solitary music-seller.

Most of these shops were to be found in groups on the main roads or on connecting side-streets, but there was a natural division here between those that could count on the continuous patronage of a relatively small but fairly heavily concentrated *clientèle*, and those that depended on the occasional custom of a larger number of people. The latter, such as berlin wool repositories, lace warehouses, watchmakers, furniture dealers, and so on, were to be found only on the main thoroughfares. There was seldom much scope in 1860 for more than two shopkeepers of a kind within a short walking distance of each other, and even in the busiest places there was therefore very little real competition between them. Around Camberwell Green, for example, the only establishments for which there were close substitutes were the public-houses, of which there were three, and the coffee rooms, cabinet-makers, bakers, and butchers, of which there were two apiece; the remainder, who had their trades to themselves, ranged from a baby-linen warehouse to a wines and spirits merchant.[45]

Such shopping centres as Camberwell Green in the 1860s were essentially different only in scale from the short parades of shops which were to be found on Camberwell New Road, Commercial Road, Southampton Street, and even at the foot of The Grove. The evolution of shopping areas having departmental and multiple stores was not perceptible for at least another twenty years. The full history of such changes has been recorded in fascinating detail both in the columns of contemporary street directories and in the advertisements which appeared in local blue books. In the 1860s it was only those with something unusual to offer who took advertising space, as was suggested by the jaunty patter of Wesson's "Original" Fancy Bazaar (est. 1850) in Camberwell Road, or by the unctuous disclosure of a "photographic artist" in Church Street that he was about to cut his prices.[46] By the middle of the 1870s, however, though some advertisers relied chiefly on the dates of their establishment as a recommendation, others had begun to stress special services, particularly of "families waited on daily," or lower prices: the 'sale' was imminent.[47] Meanwhile, the streets were still being scoured by a considerable number of street traders: smocked milkmen with pails of milk suspended from wooden yokes across their shoulders, or the cow herself to supply milk direct to customers' jugs; perambulating potmen from the local public-houses; sellers of water-cress, lavender, flowers, cat's meat, groundsel; itinerant costermongers; and gypsies, chairmenders, knife grinders, and many others.[48]

The changing structure of suburban retailing was naturally most evident of all in the late-Victorian development of a road like Rye Lane, which later became one of the leading shopping centres of South London.[49] Though it already had a number of well-established shops by the end of the 1860s, the new developments are probably to be traced to the founding of the drapery firm of Jones & Higgins there in 1867. The business opened at No. 3, and the following year expanded to include No. 5, and in 1871 No. 7, both of which were private houses in a terrace which had been put up on the west side of the road after 1850. The expansion of the next ten years added a further seven premises: 1873, Nos. 11, 13; 1876, No. 9; 1878, No. 15; 1880, No. 19; 1881, Nos. 17, 21. Another draper, Ely Thomas, had opened a shop in 1875 at No. 25, and E. H. Rabbits & Sons, the shoe firm, had also recently taken over a booksellers' which had hitherto existed at No. 1. About 1882 the beginnings of another important business occurred with the opening of Henry Holdron's "Market" at No. 53, and between 1885 and 1888 this had expanded to include existing shop premises on both sides, Nos. 51-57, and similar development continued steadily down to 1910. Ely Thomas also substantially increased his premises in 1893, and at the same time Jones & Higgins dislodged the shoe shop from No. 1.

It was from this date that Rye Lane began to be transformed by the appearance of a number of the multiple stores which were then being established in various parts of London and its suburbs. The Victoria Tea Company had had a brief existence at No. 55 before 1884, but it was the appearance of Lipton's Ltd., provision dealers, at No. 98 (formerly a private dwelling-house) in 1891 which marked the real beginning of this trend. Salmon & Gluckstein Ltd., tobacconists, opened next door to Lipton's in 1893. In 1894, Nos. 8-10, which had been occupied by two different shoemakers since the middle 1880s, were absorbed into E. H. Rabbits' expanding empire. The following year Dunn & Company, hatters, opened a shop at No. 106, where an oyster merchant had stood before; and the Singer Sewing Machine Company Ltd. opened one of their branches on the former premises of a dispensing chemist. In 1904, Rabbits' branch at No. 100 became part of the chain of shoe shops being created by Freeman, Hardy & Willis Ltd., and the same operation was repeated for Nos. 8-10 in 1909. Meanwhile, in 1907, three other components of larger concerns moved into Rye Lane: No. 102, which had had a long existence before 1905 as an artists' colourman and a year only after that as a mantle warehouse, was divided into two and occupied by J. Sears & Company, bootmakers, and the Maypole Dairy Company Ltd.; into No. 20 in the same year moved Boots Cash Chemists (Southern) Ltd. In 1910, a branch of the Home & Colonial Stores Ltd. was opened at No. 157, and J. Lyons & Company Ltd. opened a refreshment room at No. 26. Stead & Simpson Ltd., another multiple shoe firm, opened a shop at No. 89 in 1911. By this date, too, the three large drapers in Rye Lane had been joined by two others, Morgan & Collins at Nos. 61-67, and A. Trundle & Company Ltd. at Nos. 142-148.

By 1911 shops elsewhere in the parish had both increased greatly in number and altered somewhat in character. By that date there was one shop on the average for every 75 inhabitants —in all nearly 3,500 of them, of which about one-seventh were lock-up premises.[50] Social conventions were naturally changing and the new requirements of suburbians were evident from the new types of shops which were being established. Berlin wool repositories, for instance, had completely disappeared, bazaars were less prominent, fewer cheesemongers were to be found under that name, confectioners and pastrycooks had become as numerous as boot and shoe shops. And new functions were provided among others by numerous complete outfitters and clothiers, dyers and cleaners, and cycle shops.

Places of Amusement and Recreation

These new methods of retail distribution were evidence of a more general sophistication which was creeping into the economic and social relations of the Victorian suburb, and this was also to be seen in the development of various facilities for the use of leisure. This is not easy to document, even by reference to the changing physical superstructure of the suburb as recorded in contemporary directories. The spare-time pursuits of the countryside and the casually contrived social occasions of the local gentry were not snuffed out with the disappearance of the countryside itself. Gradually, however, there developed facilities for the use of the new suburbians' leisure which were on the whole more specialized, more regulated, and often more heavily capitalized.

An obvious symbol of this trend was the Camberwell Fair during its last shabby years. Boisterous enough an occasion in its rural setting, it became by the 1850s no more than a rowdy suburban spree, the pitch (it was said) for hundreds of cheats and thousands of dupes.[51] At one time it occupied The Green, at another it was wedged onto some vacant building ground, and about 1868 it disappeared altogether.[52] Survivals of suburban pleasure gardens[53]—like the extensive Flora Gardens in Wyndham Road before they were built over after 1863[54]—were also disappearing. Evidence of the appearance in the locality of new forms of recreation is inevitably random, but the general trend is clear enough. A large new public hall for musical and social occasions was opened in style in Rye Lane in 1884 by Princess Frederica; at the second concert the main attraction was the singing of Lady Edward Spencer Churchill.[55] At the same time the music-hall—like Mr Lovejoy's little "Peckham Varieties" in Southampton Street or the grandiose Oriental Palace which Dan Leno formed a company to build on Denmark Hill in 1896 —was in the process of becoming a suburban institution.[56] New play-houses had also come into the suburb by the end of the

1890s: the Théatre Metropole was opened at the corner of Denmark Hill and Coldharbour Lane in 1894 with the intention of bringing West End successes into the suburb, and the Crown Theatre was opened at Peckham three years later.[57] Nor, incidentally, was the cinema a very distant prospect: in 1911 four or five came into being in Peckham alone.[58]

These arrivals in the suburb were comparatively late in its development, and the institution that provided most opportunities for the use of leisure, at any rate for the working and lower middle classes, was the public-house. As a focal point for the social activities of these classes the 'pub' was unique and probably changed little as the suburb developed. The legal requirement of a justice's licence for the sale of beer and cider, which was introduced in 1869, may have put some beershops out of business, but the general provision of drinking premises was only a little less liberal at the end of the Victorian period, despite the great growth in population, than it had been at the beginning. In 1837 Camberwell had some 138 public-houses and 96 beershops;[59] in 1902 it had 307 public-houses, one in three of which sold beer and wine only, the remainder also selling spirits; and 134 off-licensed premises.[60] The principal information is contained in the following table.

TABLE 5

LICENSED PREMISES IN CAMBERWELL, 1903

(In selected wards)

Ward	*Public-Houses*		*Off-Licensed Premises*	
	Nos.	*Average Population per House*	*Nos.*	*Average Population per House*
All Camberwell	307	845	134	1,936
North Peckham	35	483	7	2,416
Addington	22	664	5	2,922
St Giles	14	740	5	2,066
Nunhead	13	1,074	12	1,163
Alleyn	1	14,631	11	1,330

Source: L.C.C., *Return of Licensed Premises in the Metropolitan Boroughs*, Feb. 1903.

Although the proportion of public-houses to the size of the population had fallen in the Victorian period, there was still on an average one public-house for every 845 inhabitants in 1903. Because of their uneven distribution, however, public-houses in most of the districts north of Peckham Road had still fewer potential customers apiece.

Of course, the public-house served more functions than the selling of alcoholic drinks. At least until the end of the 1860s it was the rendezvous for meetings of petty officials, or the head-quarters of a number of local builders, and remained for long after this date the customary venue for auctions of building land in the vicinity. Some of them were much more than sub-urban 'pubs'. "The Greyhound" at Dulwich, for example, had since 1772 been the meeting place for the Dulwich Club, to which had come Thackeray, Dickens, and Mark Lemon, and when it was sold for building development in 1897 its grounds included a couple of cricket fields and a pleasure garden.[61] The grounds of the "Rosemary Branch" also provided facilities for horse-racing, cricket, quoits, pigeon-shooting, and other pas-times.[62] It was here, too, that the traditional "free and easy"—a miniature music-hall, complete with stage and immaculate Chair-man to conduct the proceedings—was still being held regularly at the end of the period.[63]

The contributions which such 'pubs' had made to the social life of the suburb became especially clear when they came to an end. Thus, when the "Rosemary Branch" relinquished its cricket ground for building purposes about 1874 a forlorn attempt was made to retrieve it as a public recreation ground.[64] Generally speaking the growth of the suburb was bound to mean the loss of open space, both meadow and common, but it was not until the second half of the nineteenth century that any really strenuous efforts were made anywhere to preserve it.[65] The Metropolitan Commons Act, 1866, was some help in regulating the commons—five times more successful in terms of commons preserved south of the Thames than north of it[66]—and a number of voluntary bodies continuously lobbied municipal authorities in the attempt to preserve suburban open space.

In Camberwell the first successful rescue operation was in 1857, when the public subscribed £3,000 to preserve Camber-well Green, which had fallen into bad disrepair,[67] and in 1868 the entire interest of the lord of the manor in Peckham Rye, Goose

Green, and Nunhead Green was bought by the Vestry for £1,000 on condition that they remained open to the public in perpetuity.[68] These were laid out and opened under the authority of the Metropolitan Board of Works in 1882, and in the next few years the Metropolitan Public Gardens Association spent over £9,000 in laying out Myatt's Fields and St George's and St Philip's churchgrounds. Dulwich Park was formed by the London County Council in 1890, at a cost of nearly £36,000 out of 72 acres of land given by Dulwich College for the purpose; and the Peckham Rye extension, an area of about 48 acres of farmland, was laid out as a park at a cost of about £51,000 and opened in 1894.[69] Between 1897 and 1901 eight more small gardens and open spaces were added to these by the Vestry.[70] And since the summer of 1854, just overstepping Camberwell's southernmost border, had stood the Crystal Palace in its monumental yet fairy-tale landscape. Here was entertainment galore for almost everyone: concerts, exhibitions, displays of fireworks, spectacle, refreshment, and all the pleasures of the open air. It is clear from the map that Camberwell as a whole was not deficient in open space, though this was not very evenly distributed. For lack of open space there was, it was generally conceded, no blacker spot in London than the area stretching between Camberwell Green and the river,[71] but there was considerable justification elsewhere for the view expressed by an inhabitant of a Central London slum when he referred, with envy, to "Peckham and them airy parts."[72]

Churches and Religious Observance

Religious institutions were fewer in number and their distinctive contributions to the social life of the suburb probably less pervasive than most of the places which have just been considered. Camberwell was not, however, deficient in places of worship when measured by contemporary London standards. In 1851, there were 26 churches and chapels (among them 13 Anglican, 6 Independent, 2 Wesleyan, 1 Quaker, 1 Baptist), and these provided enough places for 30.2 per cent. of the total population, a proportion which was identical to that of London as a whole.[73] Anglican churches had just over twice the number of sittings which were available in the nonconformist churches.

TABLE 6

CHURCH ATTENDANCE IN CAMBERWELL, 1902–3

(Total Sunday congregations, with numbers of separate churches and chapels in brackets)

Denominations	*Camberwell*	*St George*	*Peckham*	*Dulwich*
*CHURCH OF ENGLAND	5,011(11) [23.7%]	5,064(11) [57.3%]	7,974(20) [28.1%]	3,587(5) [85.5%]
NONCONFORMIST	13,034(31) [61.5%]	2,919(10) [33.0%]	18,332(46) [64.5%]	607(3) [14.5%]
*§*Methodist*	2,010(4)	1,117(4)	1,928(6)	301(1)
**Baptist*	3,965(10)	621(3)	6,822(16)	269(1)
**Congregationalist*	4,014(5)	868(1)	2,724(7)	37(1)
Presbyterian	1,166(3)	—	—	—
Society of Friends	—	—	360(3)	—
**Brethren*	49(1)	238(1)	962(6)	—
Salvation Army	516(1)	75(1)	1,069(4)	—
†*Others*	1,314(7)	—	4,467(4)	—
ROMAN CATHOLIC	2,513(2) [11.9%]	—	2,020(1) [7.1%]	—
‡OTHERS	608(6) [2.9%]	855(3) [9.7%]	82(1) [0.3%]	—
Totals	21,166(50)	8,838(24)	28,408(68)	4,194(8)
Percentage of population attending church	[18.7%]	[10.8%]	[24.4%]	[32.8%]

Source: R. Mudie-Smith (ed.), *The Religious Life of London* (1904). There were recorded in addition 6 small chapels and mission-halls, the location of which cannot be traced: the congregations of these totalled 1,440.

* Including Missions.

§ Wesleyan, Primitive, United, New Connexion.

† Unitarian, New Jerusalem, Calvinistic Independent, Foreign Protestant, Christadelphian, Evangelistic.

‡ Including various Missions, Spiritualists, and others.

By 1902–3 there were in existence in Camberwell 156 churches, chapels, missions, and other institutions holding religious services, at which the congregations totalled some 64,000 persons (just under 25 per cent. of the total population) on a single

Sunday. To discover the number of actual worshippers these figures would have to be reduced by about a fifth to allow for those who attended twice in the day. The distribution of these churches and chapels and their relative strengths in terms of the size of their congregations are interesting. The table on page 157 summarizes the main data which were assembled in connection with the *Daily News* census of religious observance which was conducted throughout London between November 1902 and November 1903.

To try to measure the prevalence of religious conviction at all by statistical means is admittedly a speculative undertaking, and there are also special pitfalls in the way of dividing this up geographically. Churches were not always filled from the locality and nonconformist congregations in particular tended to be recruited from wide areas. Nevertheless, there are two broad conclusions which can be derived from these details.

The most noticeable contrast is evidently between church-going habits in St George and in Dulwich, with only one in ten of the population of the former going to church once in the week, and one in three in the latter. The difference was not one of denomination alone—though Dulwich had relatively speaking many more Anglicans and far fewer nonconformists than St George—but was primarily one of social class. The working classes in St George, as elsewhere, had stopped going to church for many reasons, among them the lack or loss of personal religious conviction. Partly, however, they tailed off because it was thought that religious services maintained class distinctions. Church-going had for the working classes none of the social prestige which doubtless impelled others. The dividing line between working-class and middle-class worshippers was not always fixed by the silken cord barring entry to rented pews, but wherever it was used this was a practice which inevitably put a premium on church-going. A reporter of the *South London Observer* was understandably jubilant when he described the opening of St Jude's, Peckham, having a seating capacity of 800, in 1876: "At last Peckham can boast of a Church of England," he wrote, "where the poor can go and say their prayers without living in terror of the pew rent collector."[74] As if to accentuate the innovation the seating was provided entirely by chairs. It was significant that when St George was wholly given up to the Trinity College Mission the first task of reconstruction was to remove the old high-backed pews.[75]

It was plain to contemporaries that congregations were composed in many cases as much by social propriety as by conscience, and that by the end of the century the working classes in the suburb had not only turned their backs on the churches but also to a large extent on the dilapidated mission-halls which had been built to serve them.[76] Nor were middle-class congregations being maintained, at least in the Anglican churches, at the strength of the middle 1880s, but appear almost everywhere to have declined.

The second inference which can be drawn from the *Daily News* census concerns the strength of nonconformity in the suburb. If, since the taking of the rather unsatisfactory census by the *British Weekly* in 1886, Anglican strength had been declining, that of the nonconformists had undoubtedly been increasing. Anglican congregations may not have shrunk by as much as the 39 per cent. suggested by a simple comparison of the 1886 and the 1902–3 figures, but what does seem certain is that Anglican numbers in Camberwell were falling much faster than in London as a whole, for which the total drop in congregations was of the order of 26 per cent. Meanwhile, the Baptists in particular could record some resounding successes. The South London Tabernacle more than doubled its congregation, from 661 to 1,615, over the same period, and the Peckham Rye Tabernacle, which was founded in 1895, had a congregation of over a thousand. Congregationalists, too, were thriving at East Dulwich Grove, in Barry Road, and above all at Camberwell Green. Such increases, among others, gave to nonconformists generally in Camberwell and Peckham a marked numerical superiority over the Anglicans there: the latter represented around one-quarter of the total church-goers in these areas in 1902–3, the former nearly two-thirds. The prosperity of a single church or chapel depended on so many circumstances, but the ability of the preacher to communicate with his congregation was the indispensable key to success.[77] The mere multiplication of churches and chapels in the suburb and the size of their congregations are not therefore easy to interpret. And perhaps the most that can be said with confidence is that their capacity was probably always adequate for the congregations which used them.

The question naturally arises: how were these churches and chapels founded, and by whom? There are as many answers to this question as there were separate institutions.[78] Financial resources inevitably varied a good deal, for some churches inherited their buildings and endowments, others received them almost as outright gifts from generous patrons, others again were built by the collective effort of many people. Though the majority of them were of Victorian origin there were a number, in addition to the parish church of St Giles, whose beginnings were more remote. Of several short-lived nonconformist congregations which had appeared in the parish from time to time, two were evidently viable by the end of the eighteenth century. When the Congregational Hanover Chapel was first designated as such in 1816 it had already had a continuous history as "The Meeting House" since 1657. Since 1775, too, another congregation had also been forming under the pastorate of a former Presbyterian minister in his own home at Bowyer House, and in 1797 this had been formed into the "Camberwell Meeting" which assembled in a meeting-house built onto the garden. In a similar fashion Rye Lane Chapel began in 1818 when a deacon of the Baptist Church at Blackfriars migrated to Hill Street, opened his house for prayer, subsequently provided a barn for the growing congregation, and finally took over the premises of a nearby Lancastrian School.[79] The formation of Camden Chapel in 1796 was the result of more collective initiative. The original eighteen trustees, known as the Countess of Huntingdon's Connexion, who had seceded from St Giles', provided £100 apiece to meet the cost of building their new chapel.[80] This was the original figure, too, for the shares of the proprietory chapel of St Chrysostom when it was opened in 1814 with 41 shareholders; later, the shares were raised to £150 each.[81] Grove Chapel was opened in 1819, at a cost of about £4,000, by part of the congregation of Camden Chapel, who had seceded from it when its trustees refused to install the popular preacher, Joseph Irons.[82]

With the exception of St Chrysostom's, the primary purpose of the chapels which had been built in the pre-Victorian period was not so much to provide additional facilities for new districts as to diversify provisions which had not yet become inadequate. But in the great programme of church building which followed the chief characteristic was not the establishment of new denominations—though these certainly appeared—but the proliferation of the churches and chapels of the old. Some of these undoubtedly owed their existence above all to the munificence of a few individuals. This was the case, for example, with Thomas Baily's gift of a chapel-of-ease at Goose Green in 1827,[83] or Sir George Lycett's large contribution to the building of Oakley Place Methodist Church (1874), or Mr Francis Peek's gift of St Clement's in Barry Road (1885),[84] or the Gooch family's building of All Saints', North Peckham (1894) as a memorial to Charles Cubitt Gooch.[85] And many churches had received their furnishing or a particular part of their fabric, or the land on which they stood, as a gift. But the building of most of the churches and chapels of this period was ultimately financed by the relatively small gifts, collections, and money-raising events from the congregations themselves, aided by loans and grants from the funds of the parent organization, from insurance companies, and probably from the banks. The sums they had to raise were often large. Among the largest were, for example: Camberwell Green Congregational Chapel (1853), 1,075 sittings, £8,000; St John's, East Dulwich (1865), 840 sittings, about £8,000; St Peter's, Dulwich (1874), 700 sittings, about £10,000; Herne Hill Congregational Church (1904), 450 sittings, about £9,500.

Financial methods were often quite literally matters of religious conviction. Herne Hill Methodist Church in Half Moon Lane, which cost £7,000 to build (1898–1900), was practically raised by bazaars and the zeal of the Ladies' Sewing Meeting alone.[86] Other bodies elsewhere relied on straightforward appeals for money. The beginnings of All Saints' in Blenheim Grove was typical of many such efforts, and is worth including here as an illustration of a general phenomenon. The first practical step was taken in 1866 by a missionary curate appointed by the Bishop of Winchester to form a new district church. First, a freehold site was bought for £750 with a loan from the South London Fund of the diocese and a letter dispatched to every house in the district explaining the whole project and inviting contributions towards the £8,000 which was thought necessary; a once-for-all contribution of £1,000 had been promised from diocesan funds. A semi-detached house, No. 60 Choumert Road, was meanwhile furnished for regular services, and the first congregation of 25 adults and numerous children assembled there in July 1866. Within eighteen months the congregation had grown to 300, and a school and a mission had been founded. Current expenses were met out of collections, and presently an influential committee was formed to enlarge the Building Fund; by the beginning of 1870 it contained £2,300; within another two years it had risen to nearly £7,000. Meanwhile, an architect was appointed and the contract for a building to seat 800 was let. The completed edifice in Kentish ragstone was consecrated in July 1872, paid for out of a sum of £10,000 which had been raised entirely by collections and contributions. The living was endowed with only £34 a year, but this was supplemented by pew rents:[87] at the time of its completion the church served a district of less than 5,000 people.[88]

The problems of finance were, in fact, seldom insuperable in the expanding districts in which the new churches were being built, and it was comparatively rare for congregations to continue indefinitely in the corrugated iron huts, converted dwelling-houses, theatres, public halls, public baths, and even tents or the open air in which so many of them seem to have begun. Often the new edifices were used before they were fully completed, and it was not uncommon for the extra features to be added when they could be afforded: the foundation stone of Barry Road Methodist Church, for example, was laid in May 1872, the church opened in March 1874, a lecture hall was added in May 1880, the spire completed in the 1880s, and galleries installed about 1890.

What, finally, did these various churches, chapels, and missions contribute to the life of their neighbourhoods? The bodies themselves were of every type from the struggling mission-halls housed under railway arches or in corrugated iron sheds, with their breezy evangelical proceedings and the doling of bread, clothing, boots, coal, soup, grocery tickets, and cash, to the Gothic edifices of the fashionable churches, with their eloquent preachers and the welcome problem of providing adequate facilities for their large congregations.[89] To take stock of the activities of them all is not possible in the present context. Most of them probably became focal points for the social activities of a larger proportion of the communities they served than the statistics of strict church attendance would suggest. These were usually in the form of debating societies, amateur dramatics, youth organizations and social clubs of various kinds, temperance and mutual improvement societies, and numerous benevolent activities.

To dip at random into the annals of a particular church is to transform these baldly conventional occurrences into human activities of a different dimension. St Chrysostom's church magazines for 1891–2, for example, produce evidence of a curious variety. Here, the Social Club was an all-embracing organization: there were mock-serious debates ("This house considers high heel shoes a danger to health!"); opportunities for self-help ranged from lessons in shorthand, mathematics, and fretwork, to a single authoritative lecture on chemistry; and there were picnics, outings, and productions of every sort—a picnic on Hayes Common, a visit to Mrs Jarley's Waxworks, the production of *The Blind Beggars*, a comic opera. The Young Women's Friendly Society braved a visit to Horniman's Museum to inspect its collection of moths and beetles. The "Dissolving View Entertainment," not yet known simply as the magic lantern, was put on for the Sunday Schools Fund, and the audience was regaled with an illustrated commentary on Tennyson's "Enoch Arden", and "The Curfew must not ring to-night." Mixed with these mild frivolities were some serious welfare activities; and, in anticipation of a Welfare State, readers of the magazine were informed that "Arrangements have been made by which really deserving cases can be fitted with artificial teeth,"—there was an accompanying illustration—"at Fees very considerably below the regular charges." Applicants were directed to the curate.

Schools

The education of the young of the Victorian suburb was fundamentally a matter of social class. There was throughout the period of its development much public debate on the scope and meaning of popular education, and on the rôle of the State in an educational system which would preserve political and religious liberties. The gradual advance of the State into the field of elementary and then of secondary education, its ultimate overshadowing of the voluntary schools, and the determined defence of the denominational schools, was evidence of this flux of opinion and of its slow hardening into specific legislation. The crucial stage in this development was reached in 1870 when School Boards were established to provide elementary education as a public service; and the complementary provisions for compulsory school attendance which were made in 1881, and for free education in 1891 completed this phase.[90] This was the principal trend in English education in the nineteenth century, and it naturally provides the theme for the history of education in a particular locality. Yet what influenced more directly the schooling of the individual suburban child at all times was the parents' capacity and willingness to pay for it. Except in unusual circumstances, the crucial factor which determined the kind of school to which he or she went, if at all, was the social status of the family. There were, in the main, schools for the middle and for the working classes. To go to the former cost £6 or £10 a year or more; to attend the latter cost 9d. a week or less.

The children of the middle classes were sent to a variety of independent schools, often run by a principal single-handed or with the help of a few assistants, and in several cases providing secondary as well as elementary schooling. 'Establishments' and 'seminaries' for young ladies, usually occupying large private houses—like Pelican House or Basing Manor House in Peckham Road or Dr Lettsom's mansion in Grove Park—multiplied rapidly from the 1830s, and to these was added the Mary Datchelor Middle Class Day School for Girls which was established in two private houses in Grove Lane in January 1877. The school was founded at the direction of the Charity Commissioners, who had been appointed in 1871 to consider the better use of the Datchelor Charity, an early eighteenth-century endowment in the City of London, which had been outdated by modern developments. The original idea of establishing "a day school for the education of girls of middle class" living in the original City parish had been abandoned as only one girl would have benefited by it, and instead the proposal centred on Camberwell where there were no such difficulties. Within four years of the school's opening the enrolment topped 300, and during the next few years the school was substantially enlarged and a training college for student teachers added.[91]

Another girls' school, which came into being in 1857, was that originally founded in 1741 by James Allen, Master of Dulwich College, for the poor children of Dulwich, but which was converted by Act into a girls' school on a fee-paying basis; by 1887, when it moved to new premises, it contained nearly 250 pupils at fees of six guineas a year.[92] Boys' schools at which all pupils were fee-payers were at first few, but became more numerous by the 1880s. St Mary's College at Hanover Park, which was organized under the National Society Middle Class School Committee in 1868, was one of the largest and most successful of these.[93] The establishment of public competition for entry to the Civil Service in the 1850s also brought into being a number of private schools. Two other schools of this general type were the Camberwell Collegiate School, formed in 1835 under Anglican patronage to accommodate 200 boys, but which quickly became a proprietary school and was closed about thirty years later, and the Denmark Hill Grammar School, which existed from 1837 to about 1870.

Throughout the Victorian period there were in addition to these only three public secondary schools for boys in Camberwell. One of these was the College of God's Gift—Dulwich College—which Edward Alleyn had founded in 1619 for the education of twelve poor scholars and, as he visualized, for up to 80 other boys who should pay fees. In its unreformed condition before 1857 the College was an almost complete failure as a grammar school, and the income from its endowment, which had by 1833 multiplied about ten times, was being misapplied. An attempt to allay criticism of its educational provisions led to the foundation of the fee-paying College Grammar School in the village in 1842, but the whole basis of the Dulwich College itself was plainly unsatisfactory and it was entirely reconstituted by the Dulwich College Act of 1857. In its new form of Upper and Lower Schools under a new head, the famous Dr A. J.

Carver, the College became within twenty years one of the leading schools of its type in the country. When it removed to its new premises in 1869 the roll increased to nearly 300; fees, apart from boarding, varied from £12 to £18 a year.[94]

Wilson's Grammar School, which had been founded alongside St Giles' Church at the beginning of the seventeenth century with the intention of providing a free grammar school for twelve of the children of the poor of the parish, had by the 1820s completely changed its original character: the Foundation scholars had been greatly outnumbered by and their needs neglected in deference to those of the private scholars whose fees were pocketed by the Master. The resignation of the Master for reasons of health, the disastrous fire which demolished the parish church and provided an opportunity for rebuilding it partly on the school grounds, and the unsatisfactory finances of the school (which had been greatly depleted by an expensive lawsuit) combined to close it down in 1845. It remained closed until 1880, by which time the development of the school land by building lease had provided sufficient capital to rebuild the school premises and a new Governing Body had been established by Order-in-Council. The new buildings were opened in 1882, and within four years had grown to about 300; fees were fixed at £10 a year. In 1894 the school began to receive annual grants from the L.C.C. in return for the allocation of twenty free places to Council scholars.[95]

Apart from the endowed grammar schools, working-class children depended before the 1870s for the most part on schools organized by the churches—Anglican, Nonconformist, and Roman Catholic—and by other benevolent bodies, such as the Ragged School Union. Most of the voluntary schools owed allegiance to one or other of the societies which were established at the beginning of the nineteenth century in the interests of the education of the poor, either to the British and Foreign School Society, which had an undenominational basis, or to the National Society, which was allied to the Established Church. The education of the poor was to the organizers of all these schools a kind of missionary activity which they could scarcely ignore at a time when the community as a whole was doing nothing directly about it. The growth in the numbers and activities of such schools is uncertain, but by 1871 there were altogether about 60 elementary schools of all kinds in Camberwell, giving instruction to nearly 7,000 children at fees of 9d. a week or less; the total number of children between 3 and 13 discovered by the London School Board visitors to require elementary education at this time was about 23,000.[96]

The barest details of the development of two of these schools must serve to illustrate the rest. One of these was the school begun by Thomas Cranfield, a leading figure in the Sunday School Movement, in Nelson Street about 1810. Although this school was closely connected with the Mansion House congregation, which had been established in the locality thirty years before, it came to be controlled by an independent committee under the patronage of the Duke of Sussex, and was known after 1813 as The Royal British Free School: it derived this name from its affiliation with the British and Foreign School Society, from which it received an annual grant from 1816. For a time fees of 2d. and 3d. a week were charged. The enrolment, which had once been as high as 300, soon fell by more than two-thirds, though something approaching the original numbers were recorded when the school was transferred, with a burst of enthusiasm, to a new school-house in Leipsic Road. The old premises in Nelson Street were then used as a ragged school.[97] In Leipsic Road the total enrolment soon exceeded the original figure, and evening classes were started on the premises about 1843 under the title of The Camberwell Institute for the Working Classes. In 1848 the committee of management decided by a majority vote to apply for a government grant, and it was on this basis that the school continued to 1871, when it closed. The Leipsic Road Board School, which superseded it, was opened in 1877.[98]

The other school to be mentioned owed allegiance to the rival organization, the National Society. This was the East Dulwich and Peckham Rye National School, which was opened in 1839 for 150 boys and girls. This school had begun nine years before as an infants' school attached to the East Dulwich Chapel at Goose Green, and its facilities had been expanded as the result of an appeal by the incumbent to the "opulent inhabitants of the neighbourhood," who immediately contributed £440 for "the moral and religious education of the poor" in the locality. The development of the neighbourhood required the building of larger premises in North Cross Road in 1871, and this was accomplished with the help of a government grant.[99] The school continued to have an independent existence, though its enrolment was temporarily affected by the opening of the Bellenden Road Board School in 1877.[100]

The coming of the Board Schools represented the last phase in the development of free primary education in the suburb. The first of them to be built especially for the purpose were opened in Canterbury Road and in James Street in 1874, and by 1880 another twelve had been built. These were large two- and three-storeyed structures which were usually intended to accommodate boys', girls', and infants' schools on the same premises. Many of them had places for nearly a thousand children, but they were quickly filled to capacity, usually with enormous classes of up to eighty or so children. It was here that the overwhelming majority of the children of the suburb went to school.[101]

CHAPTER VII

THE CHARACTER OF THE SUBURB

Topography and Social Structure: the pre-Victorian Legacy

TO recall the physical features and the social structure of the Victorian suburb is an uncertain task. This is not so much because the process of lifting from the surviving buildings the suburban trappings of later generations is difficult in itself. The reasons are that much of the physical apparatus of Victorian Camberwell has now disappeared and the nature of much of the evidence which is available of the social characteristics of the suburb is diffuse and impressionistic.

To seek the people of Victorian Camberwell literally at their home addresses is very seldom possible. There are, however, some things that can be said of the general nature of the houses they lived in, of the public buildings and the amenities which were available to them, and of the gradations of social status which marked different neighbourhoods at different times. This is the purpose of the present chapter. It is not intended to be a compendious parish guide, much less an introduction to its numerous celebrities. On the contrary, it is intended to be no more than a tentative appraisal of the general character of Victorian Camberwell.[1] As such it has three themes: first, the changing pattern and momentum of its geographical expansion and the increasing intricacy of its street plan; secondly, the detailed forms of its topographical features and their subtle modulation as their social functions changed; thirdly, the characteristics of the local communities themselves. These themes cannot be considered independently of each other, nor can they be adequately expressed by verbal description alone. There is no substitute in this respect for a careful scrutiny of maps and plans and of the streets and surviving buildings.[2]

There are two main periods into which these changes may be divided: from the 1840s to the end of the 1860s, and from the 1870s to the 1890s. These correspond very approximately to the periods before and after the coming of the railway and tramway to Camberwell—periods, it will be recalled, of moderate and rapid development respectively. The geographical divisions which it is convenient to use are: the area north of the Grand Surrey Canal; the whole belt lying between the canal and the Peckham Road and its extensions; the rest of Camberwell, Peckham, Nunhead, and East Dulwich; and Dulwich itself.

Apart from the general direction of development imparted to it by its position on the south side of London and by the pre-existence of the principal main roads and some earlier human settlement, the growth of the built-up area of Victorian Camberwell had no close links with any purely geographical features. The first extensions of London's built-up area into Camberwell had naturally occurred along the main roads which approached the parish from the north, that is the Old Kent Road and Camberwell Road, and this kind of settlement had linked up by the 1840s with the existing village nuclei of Camberwell and Peckham and with the development which was occurring along their interconnecting road. Along both the Old Kent Road and Camberwell Road, as well as along Albany Road which ran between them, had by this date appeared practically continuous ranks of small and medium-sized houses, which were rather raggedly dressed to their own building lines and grouped for architectural effect or financial expediency in terraces or 'places' of varying length but almost uniform address. Those on parts of the eastern end of Albany Road, for example, were exceptionally elegant, especially those that had the extra distinction of being fronted by a continuous colonnade or being arranged in a crescent. But except for the occasional stuccoed double-fronted house or a mansion or church withdrawn from the road, the ground plan of these northern approaches to the parish consisted in the 1840s of long terraces which were broken only by the intersecting roads, or by breaks in the alignment which marked the limit of one man's enterprise from that of the next.

It is worth noting, incidentally, that since the right suburban address was to the resident primarily a social requirement, it was nearly as much a matter of nomenclature to him as it was of site or of architecture, and sophisticated builders knew this. The monotonous but purposeful recital of Debrett—Burlington, Montague, Addington, Melbourne, Devonshire, Bedford, and so on—was, therefore, a special characteristic of the pre-Victorian and early Victorian suburban address.[3] Such styles, however, were more often pretentious than accurate pointers to the social status of the residents, and there was often little to choose between the quality of such houses and those which the builder had named after his relations or to advertise the amenities of the district, or simply to denote their essential characteristics—as, for example, did Alfred Place, Canal Place, Prospect Place, and Cottage Place. There was often no telling what the terminology might conceal. Thus, Clarence Place on the eastern side of the Walworth turnpike was an elegant terrace of twenty-two late-Georgian three-storeyed houses, with basements and attics, built to pleasing proportions in brick and tile with characteristic wooden door-cases and a short flight of stone steps to the front door—a stylish address. On the other hand, Chatham Place, on the north side of the Old Kent Road, though belonging to the same period and embodying some of the same architectural conventions, was built to rather pinched dimensions on two floors only, with a more prosaic entrance—a much less fashionable address. By the 1840s, the earlier ribbon development which was taking place along the main roads was rapidly being modified by intakes of meadow or market-garden behind them, either for the building of streets which yawned onto the countryside beyond, or for squares and interconnecting streets which shut it out.

North of the canal the only concentration of new streets of this kind lay in the triangle formed by Albany Road, Cobourg Road, and the canal. Some building had occurred here in the 1820s, particularly in Cobourg Road, where a row of about twenty rather spare and severe semi-detached brick-built houses had appeared on its eastern side. Each pair was bracketed together by a common gable, and was arranged on two or three floors plus basements, with the principal entrances placed at the side. These were reached by short garden paths and flights of steep stone steps. Most of the building which had recently occurred off Albany Road was, however, on a much smaller scale, mostly on the pattern of the slightly-built terraced cottages which were being put up around 1840 for the lower orders flush with the pavement in Neate Street.

Between the canal and Peckham Road were two systems of

new streets in the course of being laid out away from the main roads. The first and most extensive was arranged on both sides of Southampton Street and in the area north of Elmington Road. Here was a medley of houses and cottages of all sizes, schools (notably the St George's National School near the church, founded in 1824, but given new premises in 1840),[4] one or two factories, public-houses, chapels, and the District Church of St George's. Dwelling-houses varied in style from the discreet respectability of the solid, brick town houses on the east and west sides of Addington Square to the stuccoed ornamental cottages and small villas in the rural atmosphere of Parkhouse Street, from the modest semi-detached villas in Havil Street to the gregarious collection of tiny dwellings which were already being packed into the suburban alleys behind the Green Coat School on the north side of Camberwell Green. The best addresses in this area were undeniably to be found to the east of Southampton Street, where the massive presence and classical form of St George's (Francis Bedford, 1822–4) not only brought to the neighbourhood a refreshing change in architectural scale but conferred on it the essential element in its social prestige.

An area of recent development in another part of northern Camberwell was New Peckham, where Peckham Park Road and Asylum Road were salients for encompassing the market-gardens which were enclosed between the Old Kent Road and Deptford Lane, later known as Queens Road. At right-angles to Park Road itself new terraces like Brunswick Terrace and Belgrave Terrace had begun to push out westwards into the market-gardens at the rear, and Leyton Square had also been laid out; on its eastern side Friary Road and Carlton Road had already begun the process of parcelling out the intervening land towards the Old Kent Road. Much the same was also occurring to the east of Asylum Road.

South of Peckham Road were also two principal areas of development. One of these was Peckham itself, where Highshore Road, Elm Grove, Holly Grove, Blenheim Grove, and Choumert Road had recently begun the long trek across the fields to the only other major extension of the built-up area in the region of The Grove and Champion Park. The first two of these were by 1840 practically filled up by a variety of terraces and small

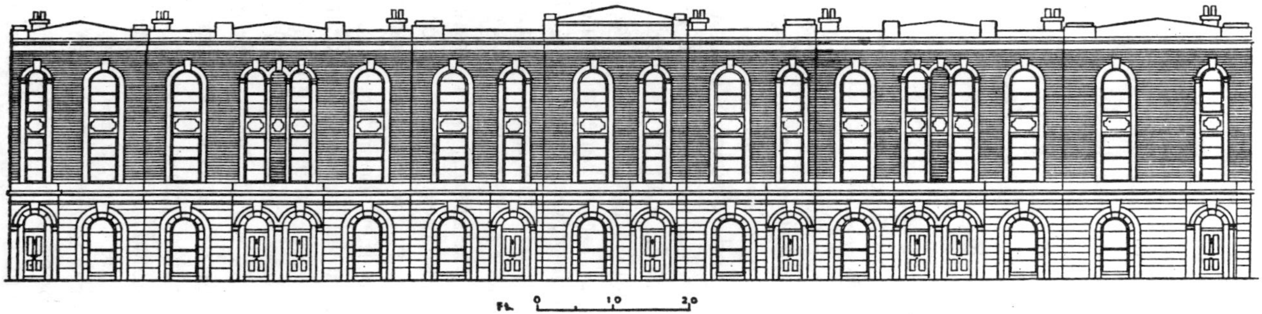

FIG. 12. *Nos. 2–18 Clifton Way, built in 1846–47*

semi-detached and detached houses set in ample gardens. Highshore Road had a special elegance which it would not otherwise have possessed by the presence in it since 1826 of a Friends' Meeting House of simple but distinctive design. The other three streets, though experiencing a similar development, were still at a much more primitive stage and, except for South Grove (on one side of which had been built a pretty row of modest villas), were practically bare of houses. Their prospect beyond the intervening fields and farm buildings to the west was, however, quite different.

By the 1840s The Grove had had at least half a century of continuous development. It contained by then a series of late-Georgian terraces and semi-detached houses whose careful alignment and splendid proportions made the very most of the straight, wide avenue which rose gently to the top of the hill. Its development was virtually complete by 1840, except for The Crescent which was not finished, and it also included on the west side the simple edifice of Grove Chapel (D. R. Roper, 1819), and on the opposite side of the road the white brick, Tudoresque building of the Collegiate School (Henry Roberts, 1834) and the ornamental Fountain Cottage. Grove Lane, which ran nearly parallel to The Grove a stone's throw to the west, lacked its regularity of building line, its width, and its straightness, but it, too, contained a few presentable late-Georgian terraced houses towards the crest of the hill. Here also in the grandiloquent mansions on Grove Hill, Champion Hill and thereabouts was to be found the very apex of Camberwell society. Here in particular, where Lettsom Street now marks the southern boundary of its grounds, stood the house of Dr Lettsom, an imposing brick villa, ornamented by some symbolical bas-relief and, along the line of the roof, a balustrade capped by Grecian urns: this, the overseers rated as highly as any house in the parish. Near the foot of The Grove stood the old parish church of St Giles, a rather shapeless structure with a square tower surmounted by a turret. There were still traces in 1840 of the original building mentioned in Domesday, but more obvious than these were the additions made from the end of the seventeenth century to enlarge its capacity—galleries in 1688 and 1708, the brick-built extension to the south aisle in 1786, and the enlargement of 1825. The whole of it was destroyed by fire in 1841 and a new, much larger Gothic edifice of Kentish ragstone, designed by George Gilbert Scott and W. B. Moffatt, was built and consecrated by the end of 1844. Not surprisingly, it immediately took its place as one of the largest parish churches in the country: it had cost £24,000.

Neither of these localities south of Peckham Road, however, was comparable in extent or in the rate of its development with the neighbourhoods which were coming into being to the north of it. Yet even there the unequal struggle between town and country was by no means concluded when the Victorian builder appeared on the scene, for enclosed meadow land and market-gardens in abundance were still to be found contesting the claims of suburban houses and factories, gasworks, and breweries. The rusticity of this area was so far intact indeed as to allow the common snipe and even the spotted crake to nest and to breed there.[5]

The Beginnings of a Suburban Continent

The developments of the next twenty to thirty years principally concerned the more intensive use of all these areas and the forging of new road links between them.

North of the canal in this period numerous new streets were being cut and fewer vacant building plots were surviving on the old. Here, Cobourg Road alone among the principal streets was virtually complete by about 1870, but there was space for no more than a short terrace of cottages on Neate Street and on Albany Road; and the narrow side-streets had mostly been filled by a miscellaneous collection of cottages and factories, and a sprinkling of chapels, schools, and public-houses. One exceptionally large piece of ground (which had formed the bulk of one of Rolls' estates) between the backs of the houses on Albany and Cobourg Roads was, however, still untouched by the speculative builder, and remained so for almost another twenty years. This whole area was sealed off on the east by the purely residential development which had now begun on the Trafalgar Avenue estate, and which had been preceded by the making of Glengall Terrace and Glengall Road some thirty years before. These made a graceful estate of about fifty small semi-detached and

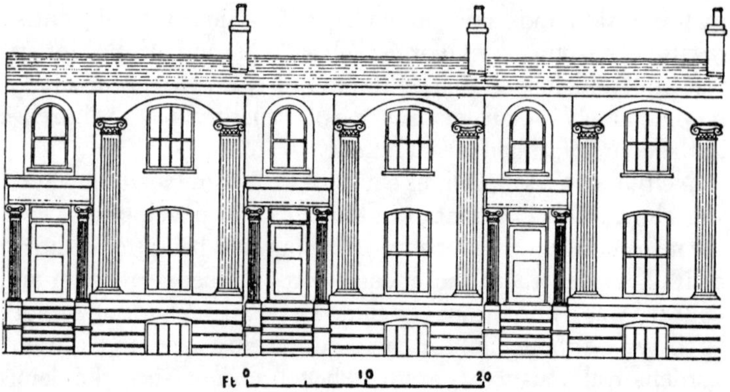

FIG. 13. *Nos. 1–3 Glengall Terrace, built between 1843 and 1845*

terraced houses of Grecian design. Between this point and the intersection of the canal and the Old Kent Road the character of the area again became miscellaneous: by the end of the 1860s it consisted of Cottage Farm (the lane to which was presently straightened to form Ossory Road), several acres of open ground, a whiting works, a brewery, a patent safe factory, and a number of small cottages.

These general characteristics of mixed development belonged also to the district on the north side of the Old Kent Road: Rowcross Street, Cooper's Road, and Mawbey Road had been completely developed by the building of small terraced houses in the 1840s and 1850s, Marlborough Place had been begun about 1850, though not completed for at least another thirty years, and there were in addition two large tracts of land still being used as market-gardens—one on the site of the present Avondale Square, and the other between the canal, the South London Railway, and the Rotherhithe New Road. There was also a distinctively industrial area in the alleys and turnings which had congregated around Lovegrove Street since about 1845: the industries included the manufacture of linoleum, japanned goods, collars, leather, beer, woollen goods, whiting, size, and chemicals. Farther down the north side of the Old Kent Road this industrial zone was extended by the massive installation of the South Metropolitan Gas Company. This not

FIG. 14. *Nos. 16–20 Trafalgar Avenue, built in 1852*

only gave to the neighbourhood a pronounced whiff of carburetted hydrogen and a mutable skyline of gasometers and coke-ovens, but brought to it a new physical and social influence. This was powerful enough in 1868 to transplant Christ Church from the site it had first occupied thirty years before in the heart of the works area to its present position on the other side of the Old Kent Road; it brought the surrounding streets to a number of dead-ends; and it contributed to a general depression of their social status.

The area in which occurred the most dramatic changes in the period before 1870 was, however, the broad belt of building land lying between the canal and Peckham Road. The streets around Southampton Street and Elmington Road spread laterally during this period. On one side they embraced the region lying between Camberwell Road and Camberwell New Road, and on the other they made a connection, by means of Commercial Road and its congeries of side-streets, with the thriving neighbourhoods of New Peckham beyond Hill Street, and of Hatcham Park. The western extremity of this area, that is the segment lying between Camberwell Road and Camberwell New Road, still remained relatively uncongested. Comber Grove, Councillor Street, Redcar Street, and one or two other terraces had started their development in the 1840s, and the main roads which bounded the area had already been lined by a variety of public buildings, especially on Camberwell New Road. Here were the Lambeth County Court building, a Masonic Hall, a post office, a National school, and a Roman Catholic chapel. There was still a considerable expanse of open space on either side of the railway in the rear of these. Nor was the initial coverage of open land much more advanced north of Wyndham Road, where the Sultan Street-Hollington Street slum was still being made.

Nearer the hard core of development in this part of the parish, on the eastern side of the Camberwell Road between Elmington Road and the canal, few building plots were still untaken and many were being developed still more intensively for small dwellings, shops, public-houses, and industrial premises. Practically all these roads around Wellington Street* and Picton Street had had their genesis in the 1840s, or much earlier, and those south of Waterloo Street had also begun their development by the end of the 1860s. Practically the whole area lying east of this, between the canal, its Peckham branch, Peckham Road, and the line of Havill and Wells Streets, was by the end of the 1860s covered by small terraced and semi-detached houses (which generally had few embellishments beyond the lower storey bay-window which was by this time fast becoming *de rigueur* in all grades of suburban houses), and the shops and other facilities which had come into being to meet the needs of their occupants. The reduction of this area of market-gardens and meadows had begun gradually about forty years earlier, with the building of a grid of streets on both sides of Commercial Road and by the encroachment of Peckham Grove. The most rapid extensions of these streets onto the open ground between them occurred in the 1860s, when Cator Street, East Surrey Grove, and Camden Grove were pushed to their northern limits and St George's Road was driven parallel with the canal to square them off. Gloucester Grove was also built at this time, as were numerous *culs-de-sac* which were formed to take full advantage of the available building land, but which could not interconnect with other estates which had already been completed. By the end of the 1860s virtually the only open ground,

* Formerly ran parallel with Picton Street, now disappeared.

FIG. 15. *Nos. 49–52 Vicarage Grove, built between 1866 and 1868*

apart from isolated building plots, was the "Rosemary Branch" quoit and cricket ground.

The differences between the physical and social characteristics of this district and the remainder of the area north of Peckham Road, *i.e.* between Hill Street and Old Kent Road, were not marked. Though neither area was homogeneous in these respects, the Peckham part probably contained on the whole more substantial houses than were to be found on the other side of the canal branch. But even here more recent building set lower standards than had prevailed ten or twenty years before. The houses on the west side of Montpelier Road or on King's Grove, for example, noticeably lacked the ample proportions of the houses which had been built in the 1840s and 1850s, for example on Asylum Road, Culmore Road, Clifton Way, and York Grove. Despite more extensive building hereabouts between the 1830s and 1850s a larger proportion of ground remained unused by builders in 1870 than was the case farther to the west. Most of the land between the canal and Peckham Park Road was still open, as was practically the whole area between Meeting House Lane and Commercial Road; the southern end of Peckham Park Road still ran across broad acres of market-garden. The legacy of early Victorian building in this whole area, coupled with some rather extemporaneous estate development, and the intrusion of the brick viaduct of the South London Railway, served to accentuate both the diversity in the style and the social status of the houses and the clumsy articulation of the streets. Despite its priority in development, this locality had too few public buildings off the main roads to leaven its residential lump. There were, it is true, the generous and restful proportions of the Licensed Victuallers' Asylum, completed in 1831, at the top of Asylum Road,[6] a few small nonconformist chapels, an assortment of schools (Ragged, Birkbeck, National, and independent), the stuccoed and battlemented Gothic façade of the Anglican proprietory chapel of St Chrysostom[7] (1814) on Hill Street, and the early French Gothic pile of St Andrew's (1865) on Glengall Road. These were not enough, however, to modify the severely residential aspect of this large area.

South of Peckham Road the same processes of converting the available land to more intensive uses and of interconnecting these developments by means of new roads were afoot. They were less conspicuous in this area before the end of the 1860s, however, than they were to the north of this dividing line. In Peckham, the roads which had in the 1840s protruded like ribs from the backbone of Rye Lane had within the next two decades become linked together, and across the fields which had divided them from Camberwell the new Grove Park Road now stretched to Camberwell Grove. Eastwards from Rye Lane the beginnings of entirely new districts had been laid by the making of Clayton Road, Gordon Road, Brunswick Road, and their associated crescents and groves. By the end of the 1860s the suburban islands which had been located twenty-five years before in the northern and north-western tips of the parish, at Peckham New Town, at Peckham, and at Champion Hill, were beginning to lose some of their geographical, if not their social, distinctness and to congeal into a new suburban continent.

The Crowded Years

Measured simply in terms of the physical fabric and the aggregate population of the suburb, the most crowded years of all in Camberwell's development occurred in the period from the

FIG. 16. *Nos. 28–34 Sandover Road, built in 1882*

1870s to the close of the century, and particularly during its first fifteen years. The process had then quickened too much for most map-makers, and the builders of petty villadom were usually too astute to leave over the doorways of the houses they built an indelible record of their age. However, the Vestry clerk and the district surveyor, each with a pecuniary purpose, noted in detail the accumulating houses, and the meticulous entries of the latter in his monthly returns to the Superintending Architect of the Metropolitan Board of Works, still preserve at least the main outlines of the chronology of events.

The process of building up the whole of North Camberwell was virtually completed during the 1870s and 1880s. The remaining vacant building land was taken for more houses, and some of the existing houses now entered a decline which eventually brought them either into the hands of a demolition contractor, or some small manufacturer, or a retailer whose business did not require fastidiousness. The diminutive and crudely-built brick boxes of the Barkworth Road estate off Rotherhithe New Road swallowed up the last tract of market-garden in the area between 1878 and 1885, and practically immediately were occupied by a poverty-stricken community which depended on the precarious employment to be had along the canal or in the nearby gasworks.[8] During this period also scores of lofty and repellent late-Victorian, plebeian versions of the narrow-fronted town houses of a century before—the very epitome of the thickening of taste in domestic architecture over the previous fifty years or so—had been wedged onto the Sandover Road estate off the south side of Albany Road. In these lived together the poor and the comfortable working class. During this period, too, the last vestiges of a suburban frontier in North Camberwell, a couple of cricket fields, were capped by terraces of dwelling-houses. One of these grounds disappeared under the respectable cover of Avondale Square, and the other beneath the bodged brickwork of the Grenard Road estate, which was reminiscent of Sir Walter Scott, alas, only in name.

There were only three other large estates still remaining to be developed in this period. The first of these was the area on the southern edge of the canal at Glengall Bridge, and this was built over by means of Unwin, Reddins, and Haymerle Roads, all unmistakably working class, between 1875 and 1883. The second estate covered the market-gardens lying between Meeting House Lane and the back of the Licensed Victuallers' Asylum, part of which was built up by Nutcroft, Naylor, Studholme, and Springall Roads in 1876–8, and the remainder, consisting of Pennethorne, Kincaid, and Geldart Roads, in the middle 1880s. All these roads were occupied by fairly comfortable working-class families who tended, if anything, to raise the tone of the district. The third estate was the area of rather similar development between Fenham Road, Marmont Road, and Furley Road, which were built between 1876 and 1882.

These streets were the last additions to an area in which physical and social decay was already at work in some of its parts. There were still some oases of moderate wealth and respectability, such as Brunswick Park and Vicarage Grove, Peckham Grove, Camden Grove, Asylum Road, Glengall Road, and Avondale Square. There were also roads which the moderate earnings of clerks, foremen, schoolmasters, printers, travellers, mechanics, and so on, kept unstained by poverty. But the overwhelming majority of these streets were, by Booth's reckoning, either mixed or poor, consisting of households in which the

FIG. 17. *Nos. 90–93 Avondale Square, built in 1875*

lowest average earnings were about a pound a week. A simple measurement of the social metamorphosis which had occurred within the previous fifty years is provided by the fall in the pew-rents of St George's from £600 a year to vanishing point. By 1885 the vicar was ready to deliver up the welfare of a block of about six thousand of his poorest parishioners into the hands of the Trinity College Mission which was established there.[9] There was also a number of streets in which the inhabitants were in chronic want, and a tiny residue which had bad police records. Among the former were Lovegrove Street, the west end of Verney Road, Tilson Road, and Ethnard Road. Among the latter were Bridson Street, an Irish colony notorious for its drunkenness and improvidence, and the Sultan Street area, a veritable citadel of outcasts.

The most conspicuous changes in the physical superstructure of this whole area were not to be observed in the comparatively few new houses which appeared between 1870 and 1890, but in the buildings which were now raised above their rooftops. The most obvious of these were the nine or ten three-decker Board Schools which shot up from about 1875 onwards, and four grim blocks of model dwellings—the first of a number to appear in the vicinity of Camberwell Road in the next few years—which were raised at the western end of Albany Road. Some new churches were also added during these years: notably the stock brick Normanesque structure of St Jude's in Meeting House Lane in 1876, the stock and red brick church of St Luke's[10] on Rosemary Road in 1877, the Dutch-inspired brick edifice of St Mark's on Cobourg Road in 1880, and the solid brick church of All Saints' in Davey Street in 1894.[11] A large new Secular Hall was being built in New Church Road in 1885.[12]

None of these additions to the built-up area of North Camberwell in the 1870s and 1880s did much, however, to modify the general characteristics which these districts had already developed, and the arena for the most dramatic scenic changes of these decades lay south of Peckham Road. In this virgin suburb the intricacies of the street plan of North Camberwell, which had been much more contorted by narrow expediency than it had been controlled by even the most rudimentary considerations of accessibility, were largely left behind. It is true that even here whole estates were sometimes no more than elaborate dead-ends until the surrounding land was laid out, and short terraces were sometimes isolated for years from any similar development nearby. Nor did streets always run in the most rational directions. But at least their average width was greater for their having been laid out almost wholly under metropolitan by-laws, and they were eventually better articulated in many cases for their having been conceived by land companies and others, who laid them out in much larger blocks.

The suburban process of growth by accretion was inevitably faster and more comprehensive in this area than circumstances would allow north of Peckham Road. A typical growing point was the little intersection of closely-built streets, occupied mostly by clerks and skilled workers, between Wilson Road and Vestry Road, which were first laid out in the early 1870s on the grounds of Wilson's Grammar School. The chain of building activity begun here was extended street by street into the neighbouring area between Linnell Road and Lyndhurst Grove in the years 1878 to 1882, and then connected up with the distinctly more prosperous servant-keeping area which had been spreading westwards north of the railway from Lyndhurst Road since the 1850s. Here were some of the houses which George Gissing described as belonging to the ambitious middle class of Camberwell—houses like those in De Crespigny Park, where "each house seems to remind its neighbour, with all the complacence expressible in buff brick, that in this locality lodgings are *not* to let."

South of the railway the Denmark Park estate, which was laid out for middle- and lower middle-class occupation between 1872 and the early 1880s on the land formerly occupied by the Denmark Hill Grammar School, dramatically accelerated the extension of Choumert Road, which had been in the making for about twenty years beforehand, and completed the link with The Grove by means of Bromar and Ivanhoe Roads by 1882. South of this again was the vast area of hundreds of acres stretching between Grove Vale and the beginnings of Forest Hill, in which many of the roads had not had their full complement of houses even after twenty years of sporadic over-building, which had had the effect of lowering rents and attracting poor tenants. Bailey's estate alone, which was built in the years 1873 to 1885, was developed with dispatch, and many of the remaining streets between Oglander Road on the Selwyn estate in the north and Underhill Road on the British Land Company's estate in the south were still uncompleted in the 1890s.

The social composition of this area was very mixed. Between Oakhurst Grove and Peckham Rye and on parts of the British Land Company's estate farther south was a number of well-to-do streets occupied most by professional people, but the majority of the houses in East Dulwich, some of them designed for two families and others used as though they had been, were occupied by the working classes. A seven-roomed house, with bath and garden, could be had here at the end of the period for £30 a year plus taxes, but in the poorer streets a seven-roomed house cost 13s. a week. The difference between renting rooms in such localities was similarly slight—four rooms for 9s. a week in the better, three rooms for the same rent in the poorer streets.

East of this area, on both sides of Peckham Rye Common, the extension of the built-up area left fewer enclaves of meadow, market-garden, and builder's waste, and the land between the future Peckham Rye Park and the Nunhead reservoir remained

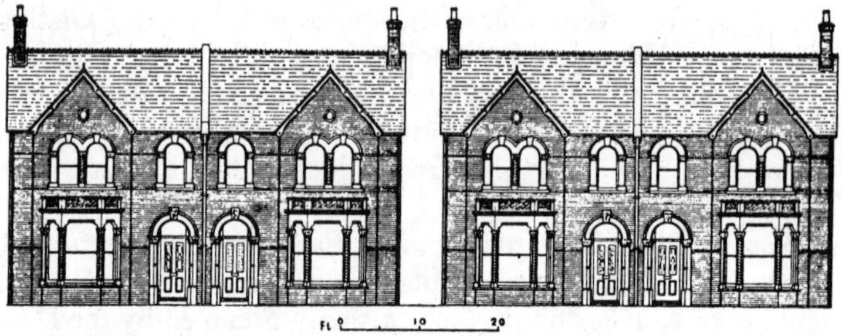

FIG. 18. *Nos. 65-71, Oglander Road, built in 1879*

therefore almost untouched until the last decade of the century. Apart from this uncommitted land, and the half-finished Newlands estate between Stewart and Cheltenham Roads and Yates' giant enterprise on the Waverley Park estate, practically the whole of Nunhead as far north as Lugard Road was completed during the 1870s and 1880s. This, too, was an area in which social class varied a good deal between the extremes represented by the impoverished community of gravediggers and labourers occupying the little nest of streets on the north-west of Nunhead Cemetery, and the ranks of the professional classes living at the top end of St Mary's Road. One other area which should be noted as being developed at this time was the extensive Minet estate lying south of Camberwell New Road. The bulk of this had remained market-garden until the middle 1860s, when the first service roads were put across it as a preliminary to some good class residential building. Some building had begun by 1871, but not more than half the building plots had been taken by 1890. In 1889 over fourteen acres in the centre of this area were given by William Minet to the L.C.C. as recreational ground, and this became Myatt's Fields.

Comparatively few of the houses which were built on the whole of this area south of Peckham Road during this period were basically different from each other in architectural style. The fairly limited range of building materials available and the conventional requirements of lower middle-class and working-class families who needed accommodation at between, say, 30s. and £3 a month, inevitably meant some general conformity in

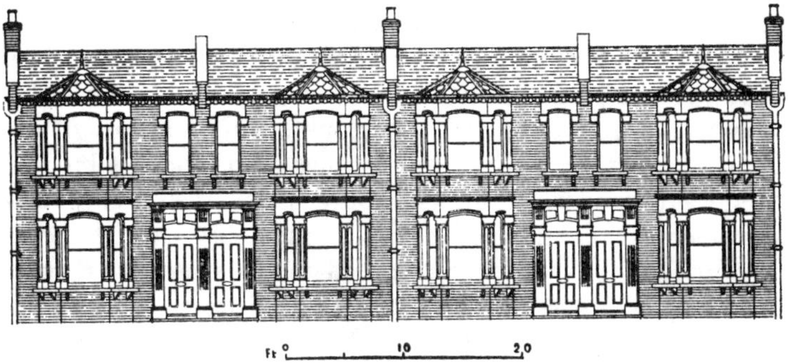

FIG. 19. *Nos. 51–57 Ivydale Road, built in 1900*

their appearance and internal arrangement. Even so there was some scope for individual embellishment.

The two-storeyed brick terrace was the almost standard component, even for fairly substantial houses, which might signify their superiority by an extra storey (if only an attic with a dormer window) or by a wider frontage. Brickwork varied in colour from grey to yellow and red, and these colours were frequently used together in the decoration of porches, lintels, and eaves, or in providing some contrast in variegated courses of brickwork. Sometimes the brickwork was also incised or laid at an angle to accentuate the effect. The principal roofing material was blue Welsh slate, sometimes cut to a petal shape or surmounted by a fretwork of ornamental red ridge tiles, and terminated at the gable ends by narrow wooden or even leaden barge boards; on the larger houses the barge board almost became a piece of architectural millinery, an elaborate frippery which was intended 'to do something' for the whole appearance. The bay-window on at least one floor had by now become a vogue, even in the cheapest houses, and it was here and in the construction of the porch that most of the distinctive embellishments of the better order of houses were concentrated. These usually took the form of plaster mouldings to make sham balustrades to unusable balconies above the bay-windows, or to form tooled columns which were often of absurdly bulky or slender dimensions. It was no rare thing for each of the capitals to these—usually composed of fossilized fruit and unidentifiable foliage—to be quite different from each of its fellows on the same house, but to be repeated (in a different permutation) a few doors away. Such individuality was also occasionally cultivated in the variety of coloured leaded panes in the front door and its surround, and in the design and fixing of brass door furniture. Further scope for this kind of thing was offered by the multi-coloured tiles—their multiplicity was practically an index of the rate of the house—which paved the porch and the short path which led up to it. Gates and railings to enclose front gardens, the proportions of which again varied subtly to suit the standing of the house, were invariably of cast iron in a single pattern for a whole terrace.

There were, it should be said in passing, few of the obvious social distinctions in the nomenclature of the streets that there had been at an earlier date. Public men were less honoured in this way, and before the Boer War there were fewer feats of arms worthy of note. New street names in the last quarter of the nineteenth century tended to have a hybrid and faintly romantic air to them—as Allendale, Daneville, Bramcote, Beauval, Fernholme, Landcroft, and Willowbrook. There were, too, estates whose street names had a common theme: there were, for example, the geographical place-names of Bailey's 'Derbyshire Colony', the literary allusions of the Grenard Road estate, the genealogical references of the de Crespigny estates at Camberwell and Peckham, the acknowledgment of the legal profession in the Talfourd Road estate.

In the lower grade streets the houses conformed to their prototype when they were first built with the mechanical fidelity of a production line, but human habitation usually meant some variation between them in time, however slight. The builder naturally played a fundamental rôle in such matters when he decided upon the front elevation of his houses or spaced out trees along the street. The geometry of the ground plan tended to settle some of the social issues from the outset, for the longer and straighter and flatter the street the fewer pretensions it normally had. The choice of trees, too, had its social overtones: planes and horse chestnuts for the wide avenues and lofty mansions of the well-to-do; limes, laburnums, and acacias for the middle incomes; unadorned macadam for the wage-earners. Within such limits, however, the occupiers themselves also had plenty of scope for little acts of symbolism, as, for example, in the furnishing of the front windows or in the arrangement of the front garden. The idiom in which these acts were performed varied from class to class. The aspidistra half-concealed by carefully draped lace curtains, the privet hedge of carefully determined height, the geometrical perfection of minute flower-beds edged with London Pride, the window-box trailing fern and periwinkle—these were some of the elements in one situation. Ivy-scaled walls, great round clumps of laurels, rhododendrons, lilac, and laburnum, lawns infested with sparrows and set with pedestalled urns, and gravelled drives—these were the elements in another. It would be a mistake to think of these features solely in terms of personal taste. They gave scope, it is true, for the outward expression of romantic idiosyncrasies, but they were equally emblems of different shades of respectability, some of suburbia's badges of rank, and their collective expression was a subtle acknowledgment of a locality's status in suburban society.[13]

The non-residential additions to the superstructure of this area in the last thirty years of the century were mostly limited to new churches and chapels, and to the ubiquitous Board Schools. Two of the most prominent church buildings actually came into being in the 1860s. These were the rather ungainly Wesleyan chapel at the junction of Harder's Road with Queens Road in 1864, and the district church of St John the Evangelist at Goose Green in 1865.[14] Two Kentish ragstone edifices were completed for All Saints', Blenheim Grove in 1872, and St Peter's, Dulwich, in 1876; St Antholin's, Nunhead, a red-brick Victorian Gothic structure, containing a reredos attributed to Grinling Gibbons (a relic from the Wren church of the same name which had been demolished in the City in 1875) was completed in 1878.[15] St Clement's, perpendicular Gothic in red brick with stone facings, was opened in Friern Road in 1885.[16] These were also years of steady building by nonconformist congregations. A brick chapel was opened by the Lordship Lane Baptist Church in 1873,[17] and the Barry Road Methodist Church came into use in 1874. A small brick and stone Gothic chapel was built by a congregation of Primitive Methodists in Sumner Road in 1875,[18] the large red brick South London Tabernacle Baptist Church was opened in

1884 to replace the corrugated iron building which had been in use on Peckham Road since 1880, and in 1890 another Gothic structure, the Dulwich Grove Congregational Church, was opened in East Dulwich Grove.[19] Another public building of importance, which was opened in 1884, was a public hall in Rye Lane capable of seating 1,200 persons.[20]

The last area to be considered is Dulwich. To cross Lordship Lane into Dulwich in this period was less of a geographical excursion than it was an historical one, for Dulwich remained in 1900 in the condition in which East Dulwich had been well over thirty years before. It was the same unblemished rural spot, blessed by some splendid elms and poplars and a broad belt of green fields, which Mr Pickwick had selected for retirement nearly a century earlier.[21] Hardly any marked concentration of buildings of any kind had yet occurred beyond the village, except for the large villas in the vicinity of the Crystal Palace and around Alleyn Road to the south. Graced as it was by some elegant Georgian brick houses discreetly withdrawn from the road, one side of the main street of the village itself, the east, was more fashionable than the other, but the whole effect was unusually pleasing—as it still is despite much rebuilding. The prettiness of Dulwich Village was in 1900 quite unmarked by the kind of unthinking development which had lately occurred so close to its northern edge in East Dulwich.

What obviously dominated the landscape in every sense, however, was Dulwich College—Alleyn's College of God's Gift, founded in 1619 by Edward Alleyn, the actor. It had three components. First was the Old College, a picturesque group of buildings in which modifications and additions—not to mention the depredations—had been made from time to time since the seventeenth century. Second was Sir John Soane's inimitable Art Gallery, which he had designed for the collector Noel Desenfans in 1811 and which had since come into the possession of the College, and which had made Dulwich a little mecca for the artistic world of Victorian London.[22] Third was the elaborate silhouette made by the group of red-brick and terra-cotta buildings which the younger Charles Barry had designed for the new College in the Italian manner; this was built in College Road, half-a-mile away from the other buildings, between 1866 and

1870. These comprised the architectural centrepiece of the College's autocratic domain. The only other building of note was the church of St Stephen's, another Gothic edifice in ragstone, which had been raised in the same road, but on the other side of the tollgate, in 1868. Perhaps it happened that the proceeds of the sale of land to the Chatham railway, which largely financed the building of the new College (which had cost £100,000), had avoided for the time being any need to increase the landed income by building development.[23] The College's gift in 1884 of seventy-six acres of land between Court Lane and Dulwich Common Road for a public park was another happily inspired tactic to preserve the unblemished character of the College lands by the creation of a peaceful buffer state in the path of the suburban invaders from the north.[24] Invaders of a different kind and whose presence in the locality was a more conspicuous landmark than building operations in one year at least were the gypsies whose rambling encampment adjoined Lordship Lane.[25]

It is clear from the variety of human condition and physical environment to be found in Camberwell at the end of the nineteenth century that it would be rash to generalize very much about them as a whole. The general tendency was, it seems, for practically every district, except those strongly fortified against social change by sheer remoteness or by the configuration of the surrounding streets, to deteriorate in status as the relatively prosperous moved farther out and poorer families moved in. Once neighbourhoods had begun to deteriorate new and badly-built houses sprang up, which deceived the ignorant by their fresh, facile appearances. The satisfying of the large new demand for houses in the suburb from the 1870s inevitably meant the abandonment of former social standards and a more intensive use of the land, which completely changed both the superficial appearance and the human content of the suburb. "The people with whom you travel and the mode of their travelling are alike in tone with the life which is most common in a multitude of the 'mean' streets of the locality," observed two critics of Camberwell life in the 1890s,[26] who noticed this "even where the houses have been erected within the last few years and make some pretence—with coloured glass in the panels of the doors, brass knockers, and electric bells—to comeliness." The inflexion in such reporting is as unmistakable as it was general. In the curious, unobtrusive way in which such collective reputations are acquired Camberwell had in the second half of the nineteenth century almost become a symbol of social uniformity, its social structure a kind of lowest common multiple of suburbs everywhere as the lower middle class poured into them. When, in 1866, Matthew Arnold wanted to pour scorn on the illiberal dismal lives of the middle classes it was to Camberwell he turned.[27] It was here, in the Peachey household in De Crespigny Park, that Gissing set one of the searing scenes of suburban desolation he recalled in his novel *In the Year of Jubilee* (1894).[28] And it was Camberwell which C. F. G. Masterman pilloried as prominently as any when he wrote his angry essays on the drab stuff out of which the suburbs of Greater London seemed to him to have been made.[29]

It is hard to tell how true these judgments were. It is, of course, extremely doubtful whether Camberwell, with all its social complexity, was the very seat of such mediocrity, but there can be little meaning in discussing the proposition on such uncertain grounds. What alone is possible is to point to numerical data of a kind. The rateable value per head in Camberwell was, for example, the lowest in South London by the early 1890s.[30] Some 27 per cent. of all property in the parish at that time was rated at £20 per annum or less, which was an unusually large proportion of small properties for a London suburb.[31] Camberwell contained in 1901 easily the largest concentration of clerks—over 7,000 of them[32]—to be found anywhere south of the river. These are, however, no more than very crude hints about some aspects of the general character of the suburb at practically the limit of its expansion. They are admittedly suggestive, but they cannot be definitive for the whole subject of the structure of Victorian suburban society and its institutions needs a full-length study of its own.

EPILOGUE

BY the end of the nineteenth century the great days of Camberwell as a suburb were almost over. There were already whole districts in the north of the parish for which the designation suburban was a piece of flattery, and many others which had not stood on the suburban frontier for nearly half a century. It is true that there were also many acres of potential suburb in the south which still remained a green oasis encircled by the grey streets. But it was becoming increasingly difficult to think of most of the parish in any but purely urban terms, and those parts of it which did retain suburban characteristics were becoming merged in the almost anonymous domain of suburbia.

To walk its streets to-day is to witness the culmination of this process in an inescapable way. The process which began with the carving up of the old estates and the driving of straight new streets across the serpentine walks of the big houses was an initial phase which has been superseded. The houses and the public buildings of Victorian Camberwell are now being put to new uses—re-faced with shop-fronts, split into flats, converted into garages, laundries, workshops, offices of all kinds. The original fabric of the Victorian suburb has not, however, merely been overlaid by the paraphernalia of the two or three generations which have used it since, but is nowadays being reduced to rubble and being carted away to make room for an entirely different collection of buildings. Though there are fewer people to house within the area now than at the end of the nineteenth century, buildings are having to grow taller to accommodate them. More of the land has been taken for business premises, and the shortage of building space coupled with the development of much more liberal standards of housing for all have compelled expansion to be upwards rather than outwards, as it was in the Victorian period, and the whole landscape is changing swiftly and radically as a result.

The whole of the area north of the Peckham Road is being rapidly renewed, and remnants of the fabric of an older Camberwell will soon be hard to find. Streets of terraced houses, already thinned by war, are being demolished on a Haussman-like scale, and all that are left behind are the public-houses, the Board Schools, and the churches, each of which still has some functions to perform. The condition of these is not, however, what it was. The new dignity of 'secondary' status which has been thrust on some of the old schools, the emptiness of the church pews vacated by congregations which have melted away to more distant parts, and the incongruity of the appearance of the old 'pubs' in their new settings, seem to make the Victorian scene a more distant prospect still. It might be added, however, that the social and physical upheavals which have accompanied the passing of suburbanity have involved a re-appraisal of domestic belongings of all kinds, and sometimes more tangible evidence of the old state of affairs is to be found in the local second-hand furniture shops and junk stalls at jumble sales, which have become the temporary repositories for many of its moveable relics. Even in the south, where the land has not yet been put to such intensive urban use as it has been in the north, there are obvious signs of change. Many of the meadows of Dulwich have been set out as playing-fields for the employees of various firms, or bulldozed into new shapes around small blocks of L.C.C. flats, or scarified by allotments. Encroachments upon its woodland for well-concealed luxury flats have so far been discreet. The skyline, however, has been irrevocably changed. The Crystal Palace, once visible by night and day from the windows of so many Camberwell houses, has been replaced by a symbol of another generation—the towering mast of the B.B.C.'s television transmitter.

To be well-informed about this whole changeable landscape the topographer has to have an eye both for what now is and for what will shortly cease to be, and to be alert for the first signs of the demolition squad. Pencilled jottings about the buildings of the disappearing suburb sometimes suddenly become invaluable as the only tangible evidence one has to recall the look and the feel of an architecture now gone. In some ways indeed it is almost reasonable to speak of it in archaeological terms.

Thus it is that much of this history must remain inscrutable. Much was too trivial to record when it happened, and many of the records of the growth of the suburb have either been discarded for their sheer bulk, or have been destroyed in war, or have been pulped for re-use. What remains is nevertheless enough to assess not only the force of the diverse influences which governed the pace and the character of the physical development of Victorian Camberwell and to throw some light on the means by which this occurred, but to hint at its changing social structure. And more than this it throws some light at the same time on the origins and the characteristics of the genus itself—the Victorian suburb.

NOTES

Street Names

Place-names present a special difficulty in an urban study because they tend to change fairly quickly. For the sake of simplicity the street names given throughout this book are accordingly those now in use. Most of the earlier names can be found in the Metropolitan Borough of Camberwell's *Street List* (Jan. 1954).

Abbreviations

AP Auction particulars. The great majority of these are contained in a grangerized version of W. H. Blanch, *Ye History of Camerwell* (1875), which was enlarged by the author's assistant, W. F. Noble, by insertions of all kinds down to 1912. The whole work is now contained in 16 large foolscap volumes, and forms part of the Surrey Collection of printed books and other materials which is housed at the Minet Public Library, Knatchbull Road, S.E.5.

AR *Annual Reports of the Camberwell Vestry*

B *The Builder*

BHJ *Journals of the Bridge House Estates*

BHM *Minute Books of the Bridge House Estates*

FC *Freeholder's Circular*

GSCM *Minute Books of the Grand Surrey Canal*

JRSS *Journal of the Royal Statistical Society*

JTH *Journal of Transport History*

LS *London Statistics*

LTB *Annual Reports of the London Traffic Branch to the Board of Trade*

PP *British Parliamentary Papers*

SLP *South London Press*

T *The Times*

VM *Minutes of the Camberwell Vestry*

CHAPTER I

PAGE

19 1 The statistical data have been taken from the *Censuses of England and Wales, 1801–1911*, and from W. Ashworth, *The Genesis of Modern British Town Planning* (1954), Chap. I.

20 2 Leyton 133.3 per cent., Willesden 121.9 per cent., Tottenham 95.1 per cent., and West Ham 58.9 per cent.

3 Percentage increases were: Ilford 277.6, East Ham 193.6, Southend-on-Sea 117.9, Walthamstow 105.3, Willesden 87.4,

PAGE

Edmonton 84.8, Wimbledon 61.6, Leyton 56.7, Acton 55.9, Gillingham 52.4, Tottenham 43.3, and West Ham 30.5. For more information on this general trend see T. W. Freeman, *The Conurbations of Great Britain* (1959); there are also some interesting comparisons with other European cities in I. Svennilson, *Growth and Stagnation in the European Economy* (1954), 77 *et seq.*

21 4 For a valuable and comprehensive appraisal of the work of the geographers W. Christaller, A. E. Smailes, R. E. Dickinson, and F. H. W. Green in this field, see H. C. Brookfield, *Urban Development of Coastal Sussex* (unpublished Ph.D. thesis, University of London, 1950), 249 *et seq.*; also, V. D. Lipman, *Local Government Areas, 1834–1945* (1949), Chap. XII.

5 James Kenward, *The Suburban Child* (1955), 74.

23 6 William Cowper, *Retirement* (1782), especially lines 481 *et seq.*

24 7 H. J. Dyos, "Urban Transformation: the objects of street improvement in Regency and Early Victorian London," *Intern. Rev. Soc. Hist.*, ii (1957), Pt. 2, 259-265.

25 8 A valuable effort has been made by the National Central Library since 1946 to preserve Victorian and pre-Victorian fiction, including children's and foreign books. The Metropolitan Joint Fiction Reserve now contains about 20,000 items which are farmed out among the metropolitan libraries.

26 9 The Smiths first appeared two years before this in *World and His Wife*, a magazine founded by Mr Leicester Harmsworth on the lines of the American *Ladies' Home Journal*; they were originally suggested by Harmsworth, who first wanted them settled in a £26-a-year house, and then elevated them to £600 a year (Keble Howard, *My Motley Life* (1927), 218-21).

10 Other parts of the southern suburbs were used for *The Unclassed* (1884), *Thyrza* (1887), and *Odd Women* (1893).

11 Sir Walter Besant, *South London* (1899), 320. See, too, Charles Booth, *Life and Labour in London* (1900–03), 1st Ser., i, 289.

12 D. Pasquet, *Londres et les ouvriers de Londres* (1913), 413.

27 13 Daniel Defoe, *A Tour Thro' Great Britain*, ed. G. D. H. Cole (1937), i, 161.

14 Charles Knight, *Excursions from London* (1851), 5; Augustus Mayhew, *Paved with Gold, or The Romance and Reality of the London Streets* (1858), 41.

15 D. Pasquet, "Le Developpement de Londres," *Annales de Géographie*, viii (1899), 43 ; G. A. Sala, *Brighton as I have known it* (1895), 13; S. J. Low, "The Rise of the Suburbs," *Contemp. Rev.*, lx (1891), 547; T. A. Welton, "On the Smaller Urban Districts of England and Wales," JRSS, lxviii (1904),

PAGE
26-9, and "Note on Urban and Rural Variations according to the English Census of 1911," *ibid.*, lxxvii (1913), 304.
27 16 [W. S. Clarke], *The Suburban Homes of London* (1881), vii (this work originally appeared in serial form in *The Citizen* in 1878).
28 17 See F. Pick, "The Organisation of Transport," *J. Roy. Soc. Arts*, lxxxiv (1936), 213, and G. S. Wehrwein, "The Rural-Urban Fringe," *Econ. Geog.*, xviii (1942), 217.
30 18 See W. Pett Ridge, "Faults of the Londoner," *Nineteenth Century*, lxvi (1909), 303. The concept of a Londoner is interestingly discussed in H. A. Mess, "The Growth and Decay of Towns," *Pol. Qutly.*, ix (1938). The danger to villages and small towns of losing their individualities when becoming suburbs of expanding cities is noticed by Professor W. H. B. Court in writing of the Black Country in his historical sketch to *Conurbation* (1948), 63. For a notable exception that proves the rule, see the work of William Margrie ("The Sage of Camberwell"), especially *My Heart's Right There* (1947), and *The Poets of Peckham* (ed. 3, 1956).
19 John Ruskin, *Praeterita* (1886), i, 41-3.
31 20 D. Lysons, *The Environs of London* (1796–1811), i, 68, 80-1; vi, 423-4.
21 B, viii (1850), 68; P. M. Johnston, *Old Camberwell: its History and Antiquities* (1919), 122; and H. Williams, *South London* (1949), 241.
22 For an impression of the range of domestic architecture in London's outskirts generally at the beginning of the nineteenth century, compare the aquatints of elegant mansions in John Hassell's *Picturesque Rides and Walks* (1817) with the etchings of tumble-down cottages in J. T. Smith's *Remarks on Rural Scenery* (1797). An interesting view of Herne Hill is in T. M. Baynes, *Twenty Views in the Environs of London* (1823), Plate 14.
32 23 W. E. Tate, "Enclosure Acts and Awards relating to lands in the County of Surrey," *Surr. Arch. Coll.*, xlviii (1943).
24 16 Geo. III, Cap. 26.
25 P. 558.
26 *V.C.H. Surrey* (1912), iv, 34.
33 27 *Ibid.*, 25, and *SLP*, 20 Aug. 1870; *Household Narrative*, Aug. 1854, 183.
28 Priscilla Wakefield, *Perambulations in London and its Environs* (ed. 2, 1814), 439.
29 *The Table Book*, May 1827.
30 The Census figures are: 1801, 7,059; 1811, 11,309; 1821, 17,876; 1831, 28,231. No separate figures are available for

PAGE

Camberwell, St Georges, Peckham, and Dulwich Registration Sub-Districts.

33 31 For example, B. P. Capper, *A Topographical Dictionary of the United Kingdom* (1808), unpag.; H. Hunter, *History of London and its Environs* (1811), ii, 122; G. A. Cooke, *A Topographical and Statistical Description of the County of Surrey* (1817), 110-11; T. K. Cromwell, *Excursions in the County of Surrey* (1821), 140, 143; and S. Lewis, *Topographical Dictionary of England* (1835–40), iv, 246.

CHAPTER II

34 1 G. Unwin, *Industrial Organisation in the XVI and XVII Centuries* (1908), 219, and *Gilds and Companies of London* (1908), 308; S. E. Rasmussen, *London: The Unique City* (1937), 63. See, too, J. L. Archer, *The Industrial History of London, with special reference to the Suburbs, 1630–40*, (unpublished M.A. thesis, University of London, 1934).

2 J. Strype, *Stowe's Survey of London* (1720), 32; S. Kramer, *The English Craft Gilds* (1927), 65 n.

3 T. F. Reddaway, *The Rebuilding of London* (1940), 42-3.

4 G. B. Harrison, *The Elizabethan Journals 1591–1603* (1938), i and ii, *passim*; and *Remembrancia*, i, ii, iv, vi, and viii, *passim*.

35 5 Strype, 33.

6 G. Brett-James, *The Growth of Stuart London* (1935), 69.

7 Harrison, i, 178, and *Remembrancia*, ii, 263.

8 31 Eliz., Cap. 7, 35 Eliz., Cap. 6; Harrison, ii, 47, 78; Brett-James, 76.

9 Reddaway, 43, note 5 gives the chief sources; see, too, J. L. Lindsay, *Bibliotheca Lindesiana, Handlist of Proclamations* (1886), Nos. 30 and 55.

10 *Acts of the Privy Council*, 1613–14, Col. 589; 1616–17, Col. 206.

11 *Acts and Ordinances*, ii, 1223–34.

12 A Citizen, *Survey of London* (1708), 516; O. H. K. Spate, "The Growth of London, A.D. 1660–1800" in *An Historical Geography of England before A.D. 1800*, ed. H. C. Darby (1935), 538.

13 Anon., *A New View of London* (1708), ii, 452, 545; J. Summerson, *Georgian London* (1945), 256.

14 PP, 1911 [Cd. 5972], xxxiv, 179.

36 15 Orazio Businο, quoted by H. & P. Massingham, *The London Anthology* (1950), 455.

16 Strype, ii, 27-31.

17 J. Noorthouck, *A New History of London* (1773), 681.

PAGE

36 18 Compare *The Little London Directory of 1677* with *Kent's Directory*, 1754.

19 J. C. Lettsom, *Village Society* (1800), 5.

20 Geological data have been taken from W. Whitaker, *Guide to the Geology of London and the Neighbourhood* (ed. 6, 1901), and H. B. Woodward, *Soils and Subsoils from a Sanitary Point of View, with especial reference to London and its Neighbourhood* (ed. 2, 1906). For an interesting study of the influence of physical factors on the development of the built-up area in an adjacent parish, see G. M. Hickman, *The Origins and Changing Function of Settlement in South East London with special reference to the Flood-Plain Section of the Borough of Deptford* (unpublished Ph.D. thesis, University of London, 1951).

37 21 C. E. N. Bromehead, "The Influence of its Geography on the Growth of London," *Geog. Journ.*, iv (1922), 132; Sir J. Prestwich, *The Waterbearing Strata around London* (1851), 250, and address to Geological Society, 1872, reprinted in *Qu. J. Geol. Soc.*, xxviii (1872), liii.

38 22 See Howard Roberts (ed.), *Survey of London, Vol. XXV: St George's Fields* (1955), Chaps. V, VI; P. M. Carson, *The Provision and Administration of Bridges over the Lower Thames, 1701–1801* (unpublished M.A. thesis, University of London, 1954), and H. J. Dyos, "The Growth of a Pre-Victorian Suburb: South London, 1580–1836," *Town Plann. Rev.*, xxv (1954), 67 *et seq.*

23 These were formed in 1786 into the Surrey New Roads Trust, under the management of the Trustees of the Surrey and Sussex Roads. The best, though incomplete, account of the development of metropolitan roads will be found in LTB, PP, 1911 [Cd. 5972], xxxiv, Appendix H.

24 One proposal had fallen through in 1806, but a modified scheme and a petition which had been enlarged by the signatures of landowners in Camberwell and Peckham had been successful three years later: *J. H. of C.*, lxi, 1806, 101; lxiv, 1809, 55; lxviii, 1812–13, 85, 129; lxix, 1813–14, 70.

25 See Rev. J. Richardson, *Recollections, Political, Literary, Dramatic, and Miscellaneous of the Last Half-Century* (1856), 3-4.

26 *Hackney Coach Rates within the Bills of Mortality* (1771); *The Shopkeeper's & Tradesman's Assistant* (1773, 1805); *Cary's New Itinerary* (1821).

39 27 C. Hadfield, *The Canals of Southern England* (1955), 91-4. Ralph Dodd's *Plan of part of the Grand Surrey Canal*, 1801, shows cuts between Rotherhithe and Kingston, with branches

PAGE

to Deptford, Borough, Peckham, Vauxhall, Croydon, and Epsom.

39 28 Sir J. G. Broodbank, *History of the Port of London* (1921), i, 131.

29 Hadfield, 94; *Extracts from the Proceedings of the Trustees of the Surrey and Sussex Roads* (1829), 14; GSCM, 7, 28 Sept. 1810; 11, 18 Jan. 1811; 28 Sept. 1837, 14 June; 1838 BHJ, 12 Sept. 1856.

40 30 48 Geo. III, C. cxvi.

31 53 Geo. III, C. cxci, 130 acres of open field had been enclosed under an Act obtained in 1805: *Glebe Estate Terrier*, held by Messrs H. M. Grellier & Son, Palace Chambers, Bridge Street, S.W.1.

42 32 *Gent. Mag.*, lxv (1795), 618, 738.

33 The descent is complicated by intermarriage between the Bowyer and Windham families: see W. H. Blanch, *Ye Parish of Camerwell* (1875), 34, recital of indentures in Private Act, 59 Geo. III, c. 39, and *Abstract of Assignments of Estate of Sir Edward Smijth*, Jan. 1849: L.C.C. Deeds. Information about the contemporary topography and terms of tenure of lands on the Smijth estate has been taken from the *Smijth Estate Terrier* (1830), in the Minet Library.

46 34 H. A. Shannon, "Bricks—a Trade Index, 1785–1849," *Economica*, N.S., i (1934), 309; A. D. Gayer, W. W. Rostow & A. J. Schwartz, *The Growth and Fluctuation of the British Economy, 1790–1850* (1953), ii, 705; A. K. Cairncross & B. Weber, "Fluctuations in Building in Great Britain, 1785–1849," *Econ. Hist. Rev.*, 2nd Ser., ix (1956), 291-3. Additional statistical information based on the District Surveyors' quarterly returns during the years 1828–31 is contained in PP, 1831–2 (505), xliv, 409-46; 1833 (22), xxxiv, 35-43.

47 35 These estates were about equally divided between Camberwell and Peckham; the former covered most of the area enclosed between Champion Hill, Love Walk, Grove Lane, and the open ground near the foot of Dog Kennel Hill; and the latter various plots of land in the area between Peckham High Street, Consort Road, Rye Lane, and Nunhead Lane; there were also plots of land on Meeting House Lane and in the angle between Denmark Hill and Coldharbour Lane. The *de Crespigny Estate Terrier* (1840), has recently come to light and been deposited in the Minet Library.

48 36 This estate [358-386 Old Kent Road, and the area enclosed between Trafalgar Way, Pepler Road, and Waite Street] was one of the metropolitan estates whose revenues helped to provide the income for the maintenance of London Bridge.

PAGE

48 37 BHJ, xiv, 24 July 1777, 72-4.

49 38 Quoted Brett-James, 219.

39 *Ibid.*, 340.

40 Josiah Tucker, *Four Letters on Important National Subjects* (ed. 2, 1773), 45.

50 41 W. Cobbett, *Rural Rides*, 4 Dec. 1821, 8 Jan. 1822 (ed. G. D. H. & M. Cole, 1930), i, 39, 60.

42 See *Cobbett's Weekly Register*, 11 Dec. 1824, lii, 641-70.

43 J. Fenimore Cooper, *England, with Sketches of Society in the Metropolis* (1837), iii, 70; see, too, Lord Byron, *Don Juan* (1824), Canto XI, xx. A particularly interesting commentary on this trend is contained in L. Simond, *Voyage en Angleterre pendant les années 1801 et 1811* (1817).

CHAPTER III

51 1 The Author of "A Mechanic's Saturday Night," *Saint Monday, a poem* (1833), xliv.

2 F. Harrison, *The Meaning of History* (1894), 433-4.

3 *Westminster Review*, April 1866.

52 4 Wilkie Collins, *Hide and Seek* (1861), 16.

5 For example: [Mrs Tonna], *The Perils of the Nation* (1843), 4; F. Chambers, jun., "The Architectural Advantages and Deficiencies of London," B, vii (1849), 220-1; [G. A. Sala], "The Great Invasion," *Household Words*, v (1852), 69 *et seq.*, reprinted in *Looking at Life* (1860), 366-76; C. M. Smith, *Curiosities of London Life* (1853), 362-7.

6 "Growth of the Map of London," *Edin. Rev.*, civ (1856), 52.

7 B, xxxiv (1876), 716-7 (italics mine). This development had been going on since about 1850, when Marlborough House and a 1,000 yard extension of Marlborough Road were auctioned: *ibid.*, xiii (1850); advts., 6 July, 12 Oct.

53 8 *Ibid.*, xxxv (1877), 784.

9 16 Oct. 1875.

10 For a comparative analysis of more fundamental causes of urban development in the nineteenth century, see P. Meuriot, *Des Agglomérations Urbaines dans l'Europe Contemporaine* (1898).

54 11 T, 25 June 1904.

12 A. F. Weber, *The Growth of Cities in the Nineteenth Century* (1899), Table CLXV, 463. A useful cartographical representation of this is given in K. G. Grytzell, "Befolkningsforskjutningar inom Londonomradet, 1801–1911," *Svensk Geografisk Arsbok* (1948). See, too, R. Price-Williams, "The Population of London, 1801–81," JRSS, xlviii (1885), 376.

PAGE

54 13 A. K. Cairncross, "Internal Migration in Victorian England," *Manch. School*, xvii (1949), 72.

14 The figure for the area of the parish varied in almost every decade as more accurate surveys improved on the reckoning of 1831. That used here was arrived at for the 1891 census. The "Registration District" was abandoned as the principal unit of census enumeration in 1911 and was then superseded by the Metropolitan Borough. The acreage was affected by the London Government Act of 1899 which made numerous boundary adjustments, but although large areas were involved the exchanges between Camberwell and her neighbours almost exactly compensated each other; none of these occurred before 1901.

55 15 That is to say, in the Registration Division (later, County) of London. Fulham and Paddington alone exceeded this rate of growth, but neither of these formed separate Registration Districts before 1881 and 1891, respectively.

16 Subsequent Census data are: 1921, 267, 198; 1931, 251, 294; 1951, 179, 777.

56 17 The calculation has been based on (1) total population increase per decade, and (2) the decennial figures of recorded births and deaths since 1871: *Supplements to 45th, 55th, 65th, and 75th Annual Reports of the Registrar-General*, PP, 1884–5 [C. 4564], xvii; 1895 [C. 7769], xxiii, Pt. I; 1905 [Cd. 2618], xviii; 1914–16 [Cd. 8002], viii.

57 18 It would have been possible to correct the acreages used by deducting the areas given to open spaces and inland water, but such a result would still have given a somewhat illusory impression of actual densities since it would not have been possible to correct it for agricultural land, unoccupied building land, or untenanted houses.

58 19 It would have been possible to trace such migrations in more detail had the enumerators' tallies for the Censuses after 1851 been available for sampling, but these, unlike the earlier Census material which is available in the Public Record Office, are still in the hands of the Registrar-General and are not therefore open to inspection.

20 The figures of decennial migration on which this and subsequent statements are based have been calculated from census birthplace particulars which have been progressively reduced by the application of the appropriate death-rates. This method of calculating actual migrational flows was first outlined by Brinley Thomas, "The Migration of Labour into the Glamorganshire Coalfield, 1861–1911," *Economica*, x (1930), 275-94, and subsequently enlarged by H. A. Shannon, "Migration

and the Growth of London, 1841–91," *Econ. Hist. Rev.*, v (1935), 79-86. Data for South London have been taken from H. J. Dyos, *The Suburban Development of Greater London, South of the Thames, 1836–1914* (unpublished Ph.D. thesis, University of London, 1952), 84-122 and Appendices I-III.

58 21 Except for the 1840s: Shannon's figures for net immigration into London per decade, expressed as percentages of total mean population (with South London figures, excluding intra-metropolitan migration, in brackets), are: 1841–51, 19.9 (12.1); 1851–61, 12.1 (12.0); 1861–71, 11.8 (12.4); 1871–81, 15.3 (16.0).

59 22 The Censuses give details on the basis of Registration Districts in London for 1851 and 1861 only, but the distribution of birthplaces of the inhabitants of Camberwell is very similar in these years to that of South London inhabitants generally.

23 See E. G. Ravenstein, "The Laws of Migration," JRSS, xlviii (1875).

24 For example: Booth, 1st Ser., i, 277, 296; *Labour & Life of the People* (1891), ii, 450; The Economic Club, *Family Budgets, 1891–4*, (1896), 21. It has been calculated that in the long intercensal gap from 1931 to 1951 the net movement of population was on the average only about 5 per cent. of the gross: E. C. Willatts & Marion G. C. Newson, "The Geographical Pattern of Population Changes in England and Wales, 1921–1951," *Geog. Journ.*, cxix (1953), 446.

25 Booth, 3rd Ser., vi, 88.

26 See Improvements & Town Planning Committee, *The City of London: A Record of Destruction and Survival* (1951), 165.

27 *S.C. on Artizans' and Labourers' Dwellings Improvement*, PP, 1882 (235), vii, QQ. 2,116-9.

28 Booth, 1st Ser., i, 87.

60 29 SLP, 16 Jan. 1877.

62 30 Booth, 2nd Ser., ii, 372; iii, 480, 489. At this date, Camberwell contained more clerks than any other part of London (21,576, 11.9 per cent. of the total), and was among the three most important areas for employees in hat-making (1,317, 13.4 per cent. of the total) and the printing trades (8,681, 10.5 per cent. of the total).

31 *Kelly's P.O. London Suburban Directory*, 1860 and 1884, *passim.*

32 L.C.C., *Rept. Stat. Off. on inadequacy of workmen's train services on Sth. London Rlys.* (1897). The completed questionnaires themselves have unfortunately not survived.

63 33 Cf. K. K. Liepmann, *The Journey to Work* (1944), 156-62, in which a sample inquiry based on the *New Survey of Life and*

PAGE

Labour in London (1929–30), showed that in the four boroughs of Stepney, East Ham, Tottenham, and Willesden at that date, the proportions of the working classes in local employment or making no demand on the transport services were approximately 57 per cent., 30 per cent., 48 per cent., and 38 per cent., respectively. There were in addition large variations in these proportions according to sex and age. It should also be noted that more recent surveys of daily journeys to work confirm that the proportion of London workers not using public transport for this purpose has remained high: over 40 per cent. used other means for reaching work in London in 1949 and 1954, and of these between a third and a half made no use of public transport because of the nearness of their work (L.T.E., *London Travel Survey* (1950), 24-5, (1956), 18, 20). A recent analysis based on the 1951 Census volume on workplaces shows that in 1951 two in every three Londoners were employed locally; in Camberwell the percentage of the night population working within the borough or in an adjacent one was 67 (J. Westergaard, "Journeys to Work in the London Region," *Town Plann. Rev.*, xxviii (1957–8), 50-1. See, too, R. Lawton, "The Daily Journey to Work in England and Wales," *ibid.*, xxix (1959), 241-57).

64 34 *E.g.*, an arterial road from Southwark Bridge through Walworth, Camberwell, Peckham, Penge, and Beckenham: S. Low, "The Tangle of London Locomotion," *Nineteenth Century*, lii (1902), 936-8. Apart from purely local additions and improvements, the road system of London as a whole had not changed throughout the nineteenth century: 3 LTB, 1910, PP, 1911 [Cd. 5472], xxxiv, 2.

35 2 AR, 1857–8, 17.

65 36 *S.C. on Turnpike Trusts*, PP, 1864 (383), ix, Q. 2,864.

37 J. E. Bradfield, *Notes on Toll Reform and the Turnpike and Ticket System* (1856), 10. See *County Report of the Secretary of State* [*on Turnpike Roads*]*: No. 2, Surrey*, PP, 1852 (1458), xliv.

38 *S.C. on Turnpike Trusts*, *loc. cit.*, Q. 792 [J. E. Bradfield]; QQ. 2,886-91 [Sir J. Paxton].

39 *S.C. on Metropolis Turnpike Roads*, 1856 (333), xiv, QQ. 914-48, 1,455.

40 T, 31 Oct. 1865.

66 41 14 AR, 1869–70, 7. 44 AR, 1899–1900, 273.

42 By the end of the period three government departments had become concerned with street traffic, yet none was responsible for the whole of it. The most urgent need was for simplification and concentration of responsibility, both municipal and

PAGE

national: *S.C. on Motor Traffic*, PP, 1913 (278), viii; 6 LTB, 1913 [Cd. 7190], xli, 10.

66 43 Probably in both directions, though the evidence is not clear: PP, 1834 (45), li, 37.

67 44 H. C. Moore, *Omnibuses and Cabs: their origin and history* (1902), 10 *et seq.*

45 SLP, 16 Oct. 1886.

46 *Robson's London Directory* (ed. 17, 1837), 781 *et seq.*; (ed. 23, 1842), 904 *et seq.*

47 *Watkins's Commercial and General London Directory* (1852), *Kelly's P.O. London Directory* (1857).

48 The details are in: Edmund Yates, *The Business of Pleasure* (1879), Chap. IV; Moore, 80 *et seq.*

69 49 SLP, 16 Oct. 1886. On the eve of the motorized age, in 1905, he had 7,000 horses: for more details of the development of his business, see John Tilling, *Kings of the Highway* (1957). On the economics of omnibus operation generally in mid-Victorian London, see J. E. Ritchie, *Here and There in London* (1859), 188-199, and E. Chadwick, "Results of different principles of legislation and administration in Europe," JSS, xxii (1859), 392, note.

50 *S.C. on Metropolitan Communications*, PP, 1854–5 (415), x, Q. 1,340. See G. A. Sekon, *Locomotion in Victorian London* (1938), 8-13.

51 L.C.C., *Rep. Stat. Off. on Workmen's Trains on L.B. & S.C. Rly. and City & Sth. London Rly.*, 1896, 2.

52 *The London Omnibus Guide and Local Conveyance Directory* (1865), 4-15.

53 See *Kelly's P.O. Guide to London in 1862*, 379-84.

71 54 "Railways Strangled and Railways Developed," B, xxvi (1868), 613-4.

55 R. W. Kidner, *The London, Chatham & Dover Railway* (1952), 10. P. S. Bagwell, "The Rivalry and Working Union of the South Eastern and London, Chatham & Dover Railways," JTH, ii (1955), 69.

72 56 AP, 1867 (estates at Hanover Park and Bushey Hill).

57 Between Barrington Road Junction (East Brixton) and Cow Lane Junction (Peckham Rye) the Brighton Company built an extra pair of lines for the exclusive use of the Chatham Company, and between Barrington Road Junction and Wandsworth Road Junction (Wandsworth Road) the Chatham Company did the same for the Brighton Company. Each company owned the sections of line which it had built. (Kidner, 10-11; Sekon, 171-4.)

74 58 C. M. Smith, *The Little World of London* (1857), 94.

PAGE

74 59 See C. E. Lee, "The English Street Tramways of George Francis Train—II," JTH, i (1953), 100-4.

60 VM, iii (31 Oct. 1860), 84-5.

61 See B, xix (1861), 672.

62 This company was amalgamated with the Metropolitan Street Tramways Company into the London Tramways Company Ltd. in 1873, and this was finally taken over and operated by the L.C.C. in Jan. 1889. Chronological details and the microscopic topography of the routes can be had from the series of 1:2,500 maps drawn by F. Merton Atkins, *London's Tramways* [1951–].

75 63 It had been launched as the Peckham and East Dulwich Tramways Co. Ltd. The whole proceedings between 1882 and 1898 were reprinted in VM, 14 Dec. 1898. See, too, *Tramway Annual Returns*, PP, 1884–1901; LS, xvii (1906–7), 330; and 1 LTB, Appendix C—II, 107.

64 It should be added that the London Southern Tramways had linked Camberwell Green with Brixton and Vauxhall via Coldharbour Lane by an infrequent service of single-deckers since 1884. An afternoon service also ran from this date between Camberwell Green and Norwood.

77 65 For a discussion of the relationship between railway demolitions, workmen's fares, and suburban migration in Victorian London generally, see H. J. Dyos, "Railways and Housing in Victorian London," JTH, ii (1955), 11-21, 90-100, and "Some Social Costs of Railway Building in London," *ibid.*, iii (1957–8), 23-30; see, too, "Workmen's Fares in South London, 1860–1914," *ibid.*, i (1953–4), 3-19. A brief examination of some aspects of this is also contained in "Counting the Cost of Railways," *Amat. Hist.*, iv (1957), 191-7.

66 The volume of traffic has been estimated on the basis of the third-class (or equivalent) seating capacity on both local and metropolitan public transport services available between the approximate times of 7.30 a.m. and 8.30 a.m. The details of street traffic have been taken from L.C.C., *Locomotive Service: Return of Services and Routes by Tramways, Omnibuses, Steamboats, Railways and Canals in the County of London and in Extra-London, Pt. I* (1895). The second instalment of this Report, which was to have covered railways and canals, was never presented. The details of train services have been taken from *Bradshaw's General Railway & Steam Navigation Guide*, Jan. 1895. The third-class seating capacity of trains on the different lines has been estimated on the assumptions: (1) That their average corresponds closely to the amount of similar accommodation on workmen's trains which were then

PAGE

available: it is certain that the L. C. & D. Railway always used ordinary trains for its workmen's services at that date, and made up none specially for this purpose; and there is some direct evidence, apart from other grounds for believing that this was probably a standard practice, that the L. B. & S. C. Railway did likewise. (2) That little change in these facilities had occurred in the previous twelve months. *Bradshaw's Guide* has therefore been supplemented by *Copy of Statements furnished to the Board of Trade by the railway companies having termini in the Metropolis*, PP, 1894 [C. 7541], lxxv, 12-14, 33-39.

78 67 1 LTB, 26.

79 68 L.C.C., *Locomotive Service*, 1895.

69 This Company had been acquired by the L.C.C. in 1889 (LS, xvii (1906–7), 330), but services were not running until ten years later.

70 E. L. Ahrons, *Locomotive and Train Working in the Latter Part of the Nineteenth Century* [1951–4], v, 43.

71 The total number of workmen's trains available from Camberwell stations increased about three times between 1892 and 1903: L.C.C., *Rept. Public Health & Housing Cttee. on Workmen's Trains South of the Thames* (No. 21), Feb. 1892, and L.C.C., *Qutly. Ret. Workmen's Trains*, Aug. 1903. The rôle of the L.C.C. in liberalizing and expanding these facilities is recorded in L.C.C., *Workmen's Trains: An Account by Stat. Off. of the action of the L.C.C. respecting Workmen's Trains*, Feb. 1904.

72 L.C.C., *Rept. of Stat. Off. on Inadequacy of Workmen's Train Services of Sth. London Rlys.* (No. 365), March 1897, *passim.*

73 SLP, 29 Oct. 1881, 22 June 1889, 15 Feb. 1890. One such meeting, which was held 1 Feb. 1883, was organized by a body which called itself the South of London Railway Passengers' Protection Association. The chair was taken by the Chairman of the Camberwell Vestry (Handbill).

80 74 For a comprehensive analysis of the factors determining the general level of building, see C. E. V. Leser, "Building Activity and Housing Demand," *Yorks. Bull. Econ. Soc. Research*, iii (1951), 131-149.

75 W. W. Rostow, *British Economy of the Nineteenth Century* (1948), 49, 59. This relationship is explored by E. W. Cooney, "Capital Exports and Investment in Building in Britain and the U.S.A., 1856–1914," *Economica*, N.S., xvi (1949), 347-54. Cf. F. M. L. Thompson, "The Land Market in the Nineteenth Century," *Oxford Econ. Papers*, N.S., ix (1957), 302.

81 76 The data are obtained from the annual totals of fees received by the District Surveyor (under the Metropolitan Building

PAGE

Act, 1855), which were printed in LS, annually. The relative magnitudes of total fees for new building received by the District Surveyor for Camberwell in boom years were: 1868, £825; 1869, £837; 1878, £2,853; 1879, £2,352; 1880, £2,757; 1898, £990. The comparable figures for slack years were: 1871, £463; 1872, £463; 1891, £181.

81 77 For an estimate of variations in the supply of new houses and empty property in London from 1871 to 1916, see J. C. Spensley, "Urban Housing Problems," JRSS, lxxxi (1918), 170. In Camberwell, the proportions of unoccupied houses as percentages of the total at the censuses were as follow: 1841, 4.1; 1851, 9.9; 1861, 5.6; 1871, 10.9; 1881, 11.0; 1891, 5.8; 1901, 3.6; 1911, 5.5. It is worth noting that the proportion of empty houses to the net increase in their number in Camberwell remained around 28% between 1851 and 1881, and rose to over 35% by 1891, and to nearly 60% by 1901 (calculated from the Censuses).

82 78 National Freehold Land Society A.G.M.: FC, 10 Mar. 1885; cf. *ibid.*, 26 Mar. 1872, 9 Mar. 1886, 28 Feb. 1887.

79 *Lordship Lane*—159 occupied, 72 unoccupied, 19 building; *Barry Road*—107 occupied, 44 unoccupied, 12 unfinished; *Crystal Palace Road*—215 occupied, 105 unoccupied, 9 unfinished (B, xli (1881), 831).

80 Letter from Trustees of Edward Yates to Town Clerk, Camberwell, 16 Sept. 1907.

81 *Rept. on Dwellings, Paris Universal Exhibition, 1867*, PP, 1867–8 [3968—II], XXX, Pt. II, 260.

83 82 Collins, 19.

83 S. E. Rasmussen, *London: The Unique City* (rev. ed., 1937), 405-13. By 1871, site values in London and its suburbs stood in the ratio of about twenty to one; thus, when the average value of land in the City of London was £1 a foot, the cheapest suburban land was available at a shilling a foot: see report of a paper by Edward l'Anson, "London: its Commercial Centres, and their Influence on the Value of Land," B, xxix (1871), 420-1, 462-3. For an economic analysis of the determinants of urban property values—principally of general accessibility and of special local amenities—see Ralph Turvey, *The Economics of Real Property: an analysis of property values and patterns of use* (1957), especially pp. 52-4. It is interesting to notice in this connection that it would appear that the rate at which population density almost invariably falls off between the centre and the circumference of large cities is an exponential function, whatever the actual rates of decline of density in different cities. This was true of London throughout the

PAGE

nineteenth century, despite the tendency, as the whole metropolis expanded, for the population density to fall off less sharply between the heart of the city and its extreme suburbs: Colin Clark, "Urban Population Densities," JRSS, cxiv (1951), Ser. A, 490-6; and "Transport—Maker and Breaker of Cities," *Town Plann. Rev.*, xxviii (1957–8), Fig. 1, 247.

83 84 R. M. Hurd, *Principles of City Land Values* (1903), though dealing mainly with the valuation of building plots in American cities, provides a valuable suggestive outline of the local circumstances governing the character and pace of development. See, too, R. M. Haig, "Towards an understanding of the Metropolis," *Qutly. Journ. Econ.*, xl (1926), 179 *et seq.*, 402 *et seq.*

CHAPTER IV

87 1 The powers of trustees of settled estates to grant building leases were not defined at all before the Settled Estates Act, 1856, and this and the Act of 1877 provided the necessary authority on certain conditions; by the Settled Land Act, 1883, tenants for life could sell on certain conditions without recourse to the courts. Charity and ecclesiastical lands could be developed by building lease from the dates of the Charitable Trusts Act, 1854 and the Ecclesiastical Leasing Act, 1842, respectively.

2 For an outline of legal developments and tables of precedents, see A. Emden, *The Law Relating to Building Contracts, the Improvement of Land by, and the construction of, Buildings* (1882). *The Builder* and some other trade journals regularly carried reports of legal cases. For political controversy on this matter see, for example, G. C. Brodrick, *English Land and English Landlords* (1881), F. Banfield, *The Landlords of London* (1890), J. Kay, *Free Trade in Land* (ed. 2, 1879), and J. B. Kinnear, *Principles of Property in Land* (1880).

3 Some others were: E. B. Sugden, *A Series of Letters to a Man of Property, on the Sale, Purchase, Lease, Settlement, and Devise of Estates* (1809); Lord St. Leonards, *A Handy Book of Property Law* (1863); and Fowler Maitland, *Building Estates: a Rudimentary Treatise on the Development, Sale, Purchase, and General Management of Building Land* (1883). Cf. David Spring, "The English Landed Estate in the Age of Coal and Iron: 1830–1880," *J. Econ. Hist.*, xi (1951), 3-24.

88 4 The whole process is well described in C. H. Sargant, *Urban Rating, being an Inquiry into the Incidence of Local Taxation in Towns* (1890).

PAGE

88 5 *S.C. on Town Holdings*, PP, 1886 (213, Sess. 1), xii, Q. 7,924 [PP Surv. Inst.].

6 AP, 15-16 Oct. 1889.

7 AP, 14 July 1879.

89 8 Bedford Street, Covent Garden was originally developed by building lease dated 1630; *S.C. on Town Holdings*, PP, 1887 (260), xiii, Q. 11,313 *et seq.* [London steward to Duke of Bedford]; Q. 7,083-8 [Edward Yates]. The convention of fixing the date of the lease in the building agreement and of granting leases for single or groups of houses when completed had the effect of causing a great variety in leasehold terms. By the end of the century sixty-year leases had become uncommon. 'Long leases' were for 999 years.

9 14 Mar. 1889.

10 *E.g.*, "Leasehold Tenures and Frail Structures," B, vi (1848), 616-7; "Leasehold Houses and their Results," *ibid.*, xxxvii (1879), 1083-4.

90 11 Of 3,903 houses within 12 miles of the City which were sold at the Auction Mart in 1884, 1,332 were freehold, 2,443 were leasehold, and 128 were copyhold; *Trans. Surv. Inst.*, 31 Mar. 1885.

12 This is a more meaningful statement of the distribution of ownership than one based on ground rents because many of these were quite nominal: 63 houses in Adys Road, for example, were held by one individual under two leases for a combined ground rent of £5, while comparable houses in Maxted Road were leased individually at £5 each. Of the total ground rents, 53 per cent. were paid by absentee leaseholders, 23 per cent. by occupying leaseholders, 12 per cent. by builders, 6 per cent. by investment associations, and 3 per cent. each by insurance companies and by land and building societies. (Derived from AP, 15-16 Oct. 1889; *Kelly's London Suburban Directory*, 1888; and District Surveyor's Monthly Returns, 1871–88.)

13 *S.C. on Town Holdings*, PP, 1889 (251), xv, 15.

93 14 BHJ, 23 Apr. 1840, 11 Sept. 1840.

15 BHM, 13 May 1842.

16 BHJ, 18 Dec. 1840.

17 He built nine of the fourteen: BHJ, 11 Oct. 1844. The builder of the remainder may have been Joseph Johnson, the landlord of the "Lord Nelson": BHM, 3 June, 10 June, 4 July 1842. The District Surveyor recorded three as having been put up by T. Burtenshawe.

18 *Bridge House Contracts*, xi, 76, and Plan (1903). The building agreement gives some indication of the structure of the well-built house. It stipulated, *inter alia*, that grey stock bricks were

PAGE

to be used in lining and best second malm stocks of uniform colour were to be used for facing (*i.e.* made from the malm soil of the south-eastern counties, which is rich in lime and potash); roof slates were to be copper-nailed; timbers to be of sound oak or yellow fir of approved dimensions; gutters were to be made of 7 lb., hips and ridges of 6 lb., and flashings of 5 lb. lead. Numerous trades were specifically excluded from the completed premises: tallow chandler, soapmaker, distiller, slaughterman, beer dealer, butcher, and so on. The lease was for 61 years at £12:12s. per annum.

93 19 BHM, 26 Apr., 10 May 1844. The school was formed following a public meeting six months before for the purpose of establishing a school for the education of the children of the poor (P.R.O., Close Roll 13,388 No. 7).

20 *Ibid.*, 24 Nov. 1843.

21 BHJ, 12 Mar. 1841 (the tenant was a William Couldry, who had occupied a cottage on the land for forty years); BHM, 10 Mar. 1848.

22 BHM, 21 Nov. 1851. Robert Wallbutton (of Wallbutton & Moggudy, Great Trinity Lane, City); and J. B. Cooper and S. H. Bottomley, of East Street, Old Kent Road: this partnership was dissolved in November 1856: BHJ, 14 Nov. 1856.

94 23 *Bridge House Contracts*, xii, 35-6.

24 *Ibid.*, 50. A proposal of Wallbutton's to take the same plot as a builder's yard had already been rejected.

25 BHM, 12 Mar., 2 Apr., 12 Nov. 1852.

26 *Ibid.*, 23 Apr. 1852; 8 July, 16 Sept. 1853.

27 *Ibid.*, 15 Sept. 1852. The cost of making what was later Pepler Road was estimated by the Corporation's architect to be about £250, or 2s. 6d. a foot.

28 BHM, 14 May, 15 Sept. 1852.

95 29 BHJ, 13 June 1856. The sub-committee considered the levy too high, but the subject is not mentioned again, and the presumption must be that the works were completed under that arrangement.

30 *Ibid.*, 8 Apr., 13 May 1859.

31 *Ibid.*, 12 Sept. 1862.

32 The total cost was estimated to be about £500. Other contributors included the local landowners and licensees: *ibid.*, 12 Sept. 1856.

33 BHM, 10 Feb., 13 Oct. 1865.

34 VM, 9 May 1866.

35 BHM, 12 Apr. 1867, 14 Feb. 1868.

36 He had been in partnership with a Mr H. T. Tubbs in developing surplus land when the Metropolitan Railway built its line

PAGE

between Aldersgate and Moorgate. They were also chiefly responsible for the development of the Farringdon Market area, after which they extended their field of operations to Old Street. The present firm of Messrs Tubbs, Lewis & Co. Ltd. of Finsbury Pavement is in an entirely different line of business (information from Cecil B. Tubbs, Esq.).

95 37 VM, 29 Apr., 13 May, 1 July 1868. BHM, 10 July 1868. Victory Place and Brontie Street which had been planned as *culs-de-sac* were required by the M.B.W. to be given two entrances.

38 BHM, 16 Oct. 1868: 86-110 (odd) Trafalgar Avenue (now derelict). New shop-fronts were built over the forecourts in 1879–80 (*D.S. Returns*). The opposite side of the street was being built up at about the same time, and by 1869 re-numbering was possible.

96 39 BHM, *passim*. Lewis's ground rent of £300 was apportioned as follows: public-house, Trafalgar Avenue, £10; 12 shops, Trafalgar Avenue, £4:10s. each; 72 houses, Pepler Road, £2 each; 26 houses, Nile Terrace and Waite Street, £1:10s. each; 53 houses, Aboukir Street, Brontie Street, Victory Place, £1 each (*ibid.*, 16 Oct. 1868).

40 The London School Board had in 1883 contemplated the compulsory acquisition of land in Pepler Road, but had been successfully opposed by the City Corporation: BHM, 9 Feb. 1883, 25 Feb. 1884.

97 41 Now absorbed into the grounds of the William Booth Memorial Training College (designed by Sir Giles Gilbert Scott), which was opened in 1932.

42 The Champion Hill Residents' Association was formed some time before 1845 and lasted to at least 1903. This is the period covered by the Association's Road Book, a small octavo account book, in the possession of Messrs Strutt & Parker, Lofts & Warner of Berkeley Square, London. The Association concerned itself with the upkeep—including gas-lighting, gravelling, cleaning, and drainage—of Champion Hill, and employed their own full-time roadman, as well as others when necessary, to carry this out. Before 1883 there were few years in which a credit balance could be carried forward: expenditure rose about the middle 1860s from around £60 per annum to well over a £100, and rose to between £200 and £300 per annum from the end of the 1870s. Income was allowed to fluctuate by the adjustment of the rate levied on the residents, usually between 3d. and 8d. in the £ on the parish assessment. The membership increased from 13 in 1845 to around 30 in 1900. Only once, in 1863, did the bills for repairs get to the point at which the desirability of transferring the road to the

PAGE

parish was seriously considered: the idea was rejected, unanimously.

98 43 Rye Lane Baptist Chapel had been founded in 1818, and migrated to a site which became Peckham Rye station after 1863 (Members' Handbook).

44 Scylla Road was not, however, wholly adopted by the Borough Council until 1926.

45 J. Jenkins of Walworth, who built 25 houses in Scylla Road in 1877–8.

100 46 AP, 6 Aug. 1868.

47 Dulwich College Governors, *Minutes*, 8 Mar. 1859.

48 B, xliii (1882), 649.

49 Prospectus, Tulse Hill and Dulwich Estates Co. Ltd., 1885; Estates Governors, *Minutes*, 12 Mar. 1896; and information from W. J. C. Kane, Esq.

101 50 Authorized by Act, 53 Geo. III, Cap. 191, and developed principally under an agreement dated 1 Jan. 1821 between the vicar and a George Spence, who agreed to develop the 600 foot frontage between the Vicarage and the Workhouse at 7s. 0d. a foot, or £210 per annum gross, and to erect houses of at least £600 in value: *Glebe Estate Terrier* (1840) held by Messrs H. M. Grellier. Spence appears to have made some arrangement with Joseph Hains, carpenter and builder, to carry out the work on at least one of the houses: L.C.C. Deeds.

51 59 Geo. III, Cap. 40 (1819).

103 52 Borsley appears from the District Surveyor's returns to have delegated the building to another firm, Humphries and Company.

53 AP, 13 Aug. 1863, 28 Mar. 1866, 26 June 1867.

54 The carcass of a house was usually taken to comprise the bare walls roofed over, but containing only partitions and joists, with no plastering, flooring, nor furnishings of any kind.

55 It gave ecclesiastical corporations power to grant building leases not exceeding 99 years, with the consent of the Ecclesiastical Commissioners.

104 56 Into a wall on the west side of Benhill Road opposite the present Elim Church is let a stone inscribed: "The land five feet eastward from the face of this stone belongs to the Vicarage Road Estate comprised in a lease now the property of John Roycroft April 12 1865." An earlier lease of the corner plot on Church Street, dated December 1851, had been granted to Stirling, but this interest was also demised to Helling with the remainder from Midsummer 1862 for 88 years at £122 per annum; the value of the houses was to be at least £400 apiece (the premium which was charged to sub-lessees was £410).

PAGE

104 57 For some years a partner to Edward Yates of Walworth, the subject of the last section of this chapter.

58 Blanch, 59.

105 59 AP, 18 Aug. 1864.

60 B, xxxii (1874), 993-4; SLP, 6 Oct. 1877.

106 61 Blanch, 265-6, 349.

62 The estate, which had been the property of Miles Stringer in 1839, was first advertised for letting on building leases in 1850 (B, 25 May 1850), and was bought by the British Land Company in 1857.

63 AP, 28 June 1866, 2 July 1867.

64 B, xxv (1877), 784.

107 65 AP, 30 Nov. 1880.

66 A hall was erected at the back of the house between 1882 and 1884, and a church at the side of it in 1892–3: information from Rev. D. W. Norwood, St James's Church.

67 It had probably been built around 1711 by the first baronet, and stood on what became the corner of Denmark Hill and Love Walk.

109 68 A particularly spectacular development took place between 1890 and 1910 on the Dulwich House estate between Herne Hill and North Dulwich stations. Ten substantial mansions and their grounds on Herne Hill, Half Moon Lane, and Red Post Hill were auctioned in eight lots, but were acquired, presumably, in one. This allowed the streets to be arranged in a coherent plan, which conformed to the general limitations imposed by its own boundaries. The streets concerned are those between Ruskin Walk, Danecroft Road, and Ardberg Road.

69 AP, 20-28 July, 3-11 Aug. 1882. The rents of these houses varied from 4s. 3d. to 6s. od. a week. This formed part of the Edmonds estate, which was sold following a suit in Chancery (1881, E. No. 127, Palmer v. Buchanan and others).

111 70 "Our Ragged School" [Nelson Street], *Ragged Sch. Union Mag.*, x (1858), 185.

112 71 G. H. Duckworth [collaborator with Charles Booth], "The Making, Prevention, and Unmaking of a Slum," *Journ. R.I.B.A.*, 3rd Series, xxxiii (1926), 327-337.

72 L.C.C. Deeds (unsorted).

113 73 Booth, 1st Ser., ii, 88-9.

CHAPTER V

114 1 S. J. Price, *Building Societies, their origin and history* (1958), 59-62.

PAGE

115 2 F. E. Gillespie, *Labor and Politics in England, 1850–67* (1927), 83, 94-5.

3 *Household Narrative*, Sept. 1850. See, too, J. H. James, *A Guide to Benefit Building Societies* (1849), 27; FC, 1 Jan. 1853; *Freehold Land Times*, 1 July 1854.

4 FC, 1 June 1852, 26 Aug. 1855; A. Scratchley, *Industrial Investment and Emigration, being a Treatise on Benefit Building Societies* (ed. 2, 1851), 158.

5 FC, 1 May 1854.

6 Price, 128.

7 *Lambeth Building Society, 1852–1952*, 17.

8 *S.C. on Friendly and Benefit Building Societies*, PP, 1871 (C. 452), QQ. 6,172-3 [Sec. to Temperance Soc.].

116 9 The St Pancras & Marylebone Building Society at one time owned the Hall Rd-Stuart Rd estate: AP, —1867.

10 Temperance Bldg. Soc., *Bd. Mins.*, vi, 1-55, *passim.*

11 See Sir Harold Bellman, *Bricks and Mortals* (1949).

117 12 FC, 1 July, 2 Aug., 1 Nov., 1852 and 1 June 1853.

13 This was without interest for the first year, and thereafter at 5 per cent., though this did fluctuate a little according to the state of the long term capital market, rising in 1858 to 8 per cent. Alternatively, part of the advance could be commuted for a rent charge of $5\frac{1}{2}$ per cent., or 5 per cent. on a lease for 99 years (*ibid.*, 23 Dec. 1858, 26 Aug. 1856). Some other freehold land societies and land companies were related in the same way, *e.g.*, the Conservative Land Society and the United Land Company.

14 FC, 27 June 1868.

15 There is a very slight historical account in [W. C. Marsh], *The Centenary of The British Land Co. Ltd., 1856–1956* (1956). For more information, see FC, 28 June 1856, 15 Mar. 1867.

16 Brief references to these appeared from time to time in FC, 1862–75.

119 17 AP, June 1864. All unattributed information on the subsequent development of this estate comes from some of the Company's original papers and accounts which are now in the hands of the Phoenix Assurance Company. The British Empire Company (which had amalgamated with the Pelican Assurance Company in 1904) was absorbed by the Phoenix in 1908.

18 The Land Account of the company was debited altogether with £18,343, but this included surveying, drainage, and road works. Undeveloped building land in such suburbs was probably then worth on the average up to about £500 an acre, though higher prices were being paid if other land was already

PAGE

being developed in the vicinity (*Freehold Land Times*, 15 May, 1 June, 15 Aug. 1854; cf. R. W. C. Richardson, *Thirty-two Years of Local Self-Government* (1888), 16, 18, and Howarth and Wilson, *West Ham* (1907), 25-6). Some indication of the effect of development on adjacent land may be gauged by the rate of £1,362 an acre which was paid in 1885 for three acres on Barry Road, part of this self-same estate (SLP, 30 Aug. 1885).

119 19 The company had also developed a small estate of 32 houses at Plaistow by 1873.

20 18 AR, 1873–4, 108.

120 21 Post-war historical research among records which were kept on business premises in London has many disappointments of this kind: enemy action during the last war, I am told, destroyed all the Perpetual's records, and few of the Phoenix's papers either rose from the fires.

22 The Perpetual Building Society submitted accounts to the British Empire Life Office to cover surveying, drainage, and road works for the years 1867–9, in which the actual charge was one half the total cost. By 1871 the Perpetual Bldg. Soc. (est. 1851) had invested nearly £22,000 in its East Dulwich estate, and almost as much altogether in four other estates in the suburbs of London (*Building Societies' Guide, and Land, Loan, & Investment Directory*, 1871).

23 VM, 31 Oct. 1866, 9 Jan., 6 Feb., 27 Mar., 3 July, 1867; 15 July, 25 Nov. 1868.

24 The surveyor's fee was based principally on a unit charge of 8s. od. per plot.

122 25 This is the theme, for instance, of much of the evidence on the subject as given to the *S.C. on Manufactures, Commerce, and Shipping*, PP, 1833 (690), vi, and to the *S.C. on Town Holdings*, PP, 1887 (260), xiii.

26 B, xlviii (1885—I), 896.

27 *E.g.*, F. Cross, "The Present Position of Land Societies v. Land Transfer," B, xix (1861), 229; J. W. Penfold, "On Speculation and Competition," B, xvi (1858), 176-8; C. M. Smith, *Curiosities of London Life* (1853), 362-8; Wilkie Collins, *Hide and Seek* (1861), 17.

28 Booth, 2nd Ser., i, 51; "The Urban Tenant and his Landlord" (ed.), B, lvi (1889—I), 403-4; *S.C. on Town Holdings*, PP, 1886 (213—I), xii, Q. 8,183 [Ryde, P.P. Surv. Inst.].

123 29 Viz., the window tax and the brick and timber duties, which were abolished in 1851. For a contemporary analysis of the effects of these, see B, viii (1850), 121.

30 See J. W. Papworth, "On houses as they were, as they are,

PAGE

and as they ought to be," B, xv (1857), 220; and "Contractors and Sub-contractors," x (1852), 693-4, xi (1853), 29.

123 31 Letter from District Surveyor for Nth. Battersea: B, xxxv (1877), 42.

124 32 Loudon's references to earlier works of this kind are valuable. Less often noticed is his compendious *Suburban Architect and Landscape-Gardener* (1838).

33 John Betjeman's Rede Lecture, *The English Town in the last Hundred Years* (1956), provides an interesting commentary on this trend.

34 The first volume in the building series was E. Dobson, *Rudiments of the Art of Building* (1849): it had gone through thirteen editions by 1890 and had by then been joined by similar works on every practical aspect of house-building. These were small octavo volumes of about a hundred pages each, and sold for two shillings or so. When John Weale died in 1862 his series had become too successful and valuable for Batsfords to bid for it and it went instead to Crosby, Lockwood & Son: H. Bolitho (ed.) *A Batsford Century* (1943), 12.

35 It reappeared in 1896 in a new format under the title *The Englishman's House*.

36 A first edition cannot be traced: the second appeared in 1875, a fifth in 1900.

37 Ralph Dutton, *The Victorian Home* (1954), contains some more references to books of this kind; R. Harling, *Home: A Victorian Vignette* (1938), examines among other things the literature devoted to interiors.

38 *The Law Times*, lxxv (1883), 130.

39 A reckoning based on a single year would naturally show a larger proportion of firms engaged in building on this scale: in 1880, 79.4 per cent. of firms were building twelve houses or less, and their aggregate output was 40.4 per cent. of the total houses under construction in Camberwell; for South London as a whole, the proportions were 83.1 per cent. and 47.5 per cent., respectively, which, incidentally, come very close to the comparable figures for London as a whole (83.3 per cent. and 47.7 per cent.). The writer is at present engaged in an analysis of the all-London figures.

125 40 Part I of the District Surveyors' Monthly Returns gave details of 'builder' and 'owner': as these appear to have been scrupulously entered, it has been thought reasonable to assume that all houses entered as being built and owned by the same person were in fact being built on speculation. The proportion of houses built on speculation in London suburbs

PAGE

in the 1880s was thought by a leading real estate dealer to be 99 per cent.: *S.C. on Town Holdings, 1887*, Q. 2,963 [E. Tewson].

126 41 The best examples are: Barset Rd. (J. Dadd, 1877–81), Bonamy St. (G. Whitaker, 1876–81), Braybourne Gro. (G. Avis, 1878–9), Coll's Rd. (J. W. Hobbs, 1874–6), Grimwade Cresc. (C. Grimwade, 1877–8), Howbury Rd. (J. Dadd, 1878–86), Kimberley Rd. (C. Grimwade & J. Dadd, 1873–8), Parkstone Rd. (Standing & Marten, 1872–4), Sansom St. (S. Sansom, 1879–84). The names are of builders, the dates mark the start of building operations and the final adoption of the street by the Vestry.

42 For example, Ausdell Rd. (6 builders, 1873–6), Avondale Rd. (15 builders, 1874–81), Crofton Rd. (13 builders, 1877–80), Barry Rd. (49 plus builders, 1871–88).

43 For example, Asylum Rd., Bellenden Rd., Choumert Rd., Cobourg Rd., Lausanne Rd., Rosemary Rd.

127 44 I am extremely grateful to the Trustees of the Estate of the late Edward Yates for their courtesy in making all surviving business records available to me. These included copies of several thousand letters, property ledgers, and other account books. They are to be made the basis of a separate study of Yates' business activities as a whole. All unattributed references in the account which follows are from Yates' letters.

128 45 E.Y., Property Ledger, i, 7-27. The financial details which follow for the Dragon Road estate are unique in their relative completeness, and it has been thought worthwhile therefore to give them more or less in full.

46 The actual details are not recorded in the property ledger, but it is reasonable to assume that Yates raised about the same sum on the twelve houses concerned as he did on others in the same road; if anything, the figure used here is likely to be an under-estimate.

47 4 per cent. on freehold property: *S.C. on Building Societies*, 1871, QQ. 5,649-50 [F. Cooper, Sth. London builder].

129 48 *S.C. on Town Holdings*, 1887, Q. 2,781 [Tewson].

49 E.Y., Property Ledger, i, 374-94.

131 50 His prices ex Nunhead were 33/- and 34/- per 1,000.

133 51 *Property Ledgers, passim.* By no means all business transactions were concluded by letter, and in spite of the large number which survives much information is lacking on specific points.

52 Principally at Blythe Road, Kensington.

134 53 The heavy correspondence which Yates had with the landlord seems to show that although he had to approve the

PAGE

layout of the streets, the construction of the houses, the naming of the streets, and so on, he was powerless to insist on matters which were not part of the building agreement.

135 54 The arrangement appears to have been that the individual workman undertook the preparation and/or fixing of specific items at an agreed rate and was paid a weekly sum which approximated to the work actually done; accurate settlements seem to have occurred rather irregularly at intervals of between one and six months, or even more. A carpenter named White, for example, contracted between April 1884 and May 1885 to prepare and fix some 1,192 pairs of window sashes and frames (which, with Venetian frame fitting, was an almost unvarying employment for him for at least five years) to Nos. 2-200 (e) Ivydale Road at a rate of 5s. od., reduced to 4s. 5d., per pair: his total earnings for this period, less £2. 15s. for the "use of a machine," were £292. 18s. 4d., of which he received in weekly instalments £281. 18s. 4d., and a final settlement in September 1885 of £11. When in work, which was practically continuous, White was receiving on an average about £5 a week. Tradesmen like him frequently employed their own labourers. (E.Y., *Workmen's Book* [1877–89], 171-2, and information from Mr Thompson, Manager, Waverley Park estate.)

55 Having let one shop to a cheesemonger and provision dealer, Yates called on two existing shopkeepers in the same road to stop selling such goods.

136 56 The price paid by the Board for the land was between £4,000 and £5,000.

57 *Church Mag.* (Jubilee ed., 1953), 8. Yates contributed £500 to the building fund, and appears to have planned a church for this site almost from the beginning.

58 Yates contributed £50 to the building fund. The building is now a small organ factory.

137 59 See F. Willis, *101 Jubilee Road* (1948), and *Peace and Dripping Toast* (1950), both of which are based on first-hand experience of suburban life in this part of late-Victorian and Edwardian London.

CHAPTER VI

138 1 See B. Keith-Lucas's excellent short history, *The English Local Government Franchise* (1952). The standard authorities for the period before 1835 are the Webbs. The relevant volumes of their work on *English Local Government* are: *The Parish and the County* (1907), *The Manor and the*

PAGE

Borough (1908), *The Story of the King's Highway* (1913), and *Statutory Authorities for Special Purposes* (1922).

139 2 Some details, including data from parish registers and churchwardens' accounts, especially for the period before 1834, are contained in Blanch, Chap. 10, which has been used here.

3 *Ibid.*, 99.

4 For an account of the legal prescriptions and practice of local government in this period, see *Report of the Poor Law Commissioners on Local Taxation*, PP, 1843 [486], xxi.

141 5 See Ida Darlington, "The Registrar of Metropolitan Buildings and his Records," *Journ. Soc. Archiv.*, i (1955). The professional evolution of the District Surveyor is described in Bernard Dicksee, "An Enquiry into the Origin of the Office and Title of 'District Surveyor'," *Journ. R.I.B.A.*, 3rd Ser., xii (1905), 256-8, and in C. C. Knowles, *A History of the London Building Acts, the District Surveyors, and their Association* (author's MS., 1947, deposited in Members' Library, County Hall, London). Before 1845 part of the parish of Camberwell was administered by the District Surveyor for Lambeth under the London Building Act of 1774.

142 6 On this see L.C.C. Reports on *London Local Areas* (1894) and *Vestry and District Board Representation* (1894), both reprinted in LS, iv (1893–4), 589-616. A useful general treatment of the legal position of the Vestry is W. H. Macnamara (ed.), *Steer's Parish Law* (ed. 4, 1881).

7 G. L. Gomme, *London in the Reign of Victoria* (1898), 189. On the tangle of local government in London generally, see S. Webb, *The London Programme* (1891), especially Chap. III, and W. A. Robson, *The Government and Misgovernment of London* (1939); the standard history of the L.C.C., which is deficient for the early period, is Sir G. Gibbon & R. W. Bell, *History of the London County Council, 1889–1939* (1939). Though they contain very little specifically about Camberwell, the Blue Books still constitute the principal source of information on local government in London generally during the era of the M.B.W.: *S.C. on Local Taxation and Government of the Metropolis*, PP, 1861 (211, 372, 476), viii, and *S.C. on Metropolitan Local Government*, PP, 1866 (186, 452), xiii; 1867 (268, 301), xii.

143 8 H. W. Dickenson, *Water Supply of Greater London* (1954) is the standard work, which can usefully be supplemented by: H. C. Richards & W. H. C. Payne, *London Water Supply* (ed. 2, 1899); H. Jephson, *Sanitary Evolution of London* (1907); W. R. Baldwin-Wiseman, "The Increase in the

National Consumption of Water," JRSS, lxxii (1909), 248-292, and T. F. Reddaway, "London in the Nineteenth Century III: the Fight for a Water Supply," *Nineteenth Century*, cxlviii (1950), 118-30. Met. Water Bd., *London's Water Supply, 1903–1953* (1953) also contains a short survey of earlier developments. The most valuable introductions to original material are two reports: L.C.C., *Rept. on London Water Supply* (1905), which gives a detailed narrative, an analysis of the financial implications since 1879, and a most comprehensive descriptive bibliography of municipal and parliamentary sources; and L.C.C., *Synopsis of Reports before Royal Commissions and Parliamentary Committees relating to the Water Supply of London* (1890) which covers the general history of London's water supply down to 1852. See, too, R. W. Morris's well-mapped and documented study, *Geographical and Historical Aspects of the Public Water Supply of London, 1852–1902* (unpublished Ph.D. thesis, University of London, 1941).

144 9 Dickenson, 84. Four covered service reservoirs were built at Peckham in 1871.

10 *Ibid.*, 95.

11 Under the Waterworks Clauses Act, 1847 (10 & 11 Vict., Cap. 17), local boards of health were empowered to take action to enforce the supply of water to designated areas. As to its purity, according to the Medical Officer of Health for the City, the Southwark & Vauxhall Water Company not only remained grossly inefficient throughout the 1860s in the management of its apparatus for subsidence and filtration, but had continued "to distribute as part of their supply the interdicted tidal water of Battersea Reach": Jephson, 192.

12 W. Clay, *Remarks on the Water Supply of London* (1849), 22-3.

13 E. Chadwick, "The System of Water-Supply of the Metropolis," *Sanitary Record*, iv (1876), 243.

14 3 AR, 1859, 15.

15 LS, vii (1897), 545.

16 See W. M. Stern, "Water Supply in Britain: the Development of a Public Service," *Roy. San. Inst. Journ.*, lxxiv (1954), 1001.

145 17 Deaths attributed to this cause had been: 1832–3, 107; 1849, 504; 1854, 553; 1866, 46 (11 AR, 1867, 88).

18 AP, 18 Nov. 1845, and another (N.D.). This was the Peckham Road estate, consisting of Clifton Grove, Peckham Road, Clifton Road, Bath Grove, Bath Road, and Asylum Road.

PAGE

145 19 *S.C. on Buildings Regulation and Improvement of Boroughs*, PP, 1842 [372], x, QQ. 1,007-8 [Wm. Lawrence, builder]. Gen. Bd. of Health, *Mins. of Information on Drainage of Land forming sites of Towns, road drainage, and the facilitation of the drainage of suburban lands*, PP, 1852 [1471], xix, 9.

20 Reported in B, vi (1848), 596-7.

21 The cost of the whole operation, including mains, branch pipes, drains, sinks, traps, and water-closets, was about £500, or £5. 15s. per house. Over-flowing cesspools were the worst feature of drainage in Regent Street, Melon Ground, and parts of New Peckham, as well as in "wealthier localities," according to the Medical Officer to the Vestry: 2 AR, 1857–8, 35.

22 *S.C. on Local Taxation and Government of the Metropolis*, 1861, loc. cit. QQ. 2,225-30. For subsequent legislation affecting the rôle of the Vestry in this field, see J. Scholefield & G. R. Hill, *The Law Relating to the Paving and Sewering of New and Private Streets* (ed. 2, 1911).

146 23 2 AR, 1857–8, 33. The Vestry began the collection of household refuse in 1876, instead of sub-contracting it (*Sanitary Record*, iv (1876), 250).

24 *I.e.*, by letters to the local press, public meetings, and some caustic pamphleteering. One particularly severe critic of the Vestry was G. Clifford, *The Camberwell and Peckham Ratepayers' Association defended against the Camberwell Vestry* (1864).

25 15 AR, 1870–1, 18-22. The loans were: 1864, Pelican, £8,000 @ 4½ per cent. for 20 years; 1865, Hand-in-Hand, £13,000 @ 5 per cent. for 20 years; 1866, Atlas, £26,000 @ 5 per cent. for 30 years, and London, £10,000 @ 5 per cent. for 30 years; 1867, London, £23,000 @ 5 per cent. for 30 years (18 AR, 1873–4, 108).

26 8 AR, 1863–4, 10. Its course and general relation to the main drainage system of London are mapped in *R.C. on Metropolitan Sewage Discharge*, PP, 1884 (C. 3842-1), xli, Appendix D.

27 15 AR, 1870–1, 22.

28 SLP, 13 Jan. 1872, B, xlv (1883—II), 199-200.

29 For a list of the duties of inspectors of nuisances, see 11 AR, 1866–7, 26.

30 17 AR, 1872–3, 29.

31 20 AR, 1875–6, 25-39.

147 32 Gas company minutes do survive, but maps of gas mains were amended and discarded from time to time, so that none now remains to illustrate the development of the service area

in South London. One historical account, based mainly on minute books, is a long series of articles by W. F. D. Garton, "History of the South Metropolitan Gas Company, 1814–1949," *Gas World*, cxxv-cxxvi (1952). This is the source of any unattributed information on gas supply contained in this section. See, too, H. Chubb, "The Supply of Gas to the Metropolis," JRSS, xxxix (1876), 350-80.

147 33 There were four companies in London by this time, supplying over 60,000 private and 7,000 street lamps: D. Chandler & A. D. Lacey, *The Rise of the Gas Industry in Britain* (1949), 72.

34 It removed to its new works in 1865.

35 *S.C. on Metropolis Gas Bill*, PP, 1867 (520), xii, Q. 1,433 [Engineer to Phoenix Co.]; Chandler & Lacey, 74.

36 *S.C. on the Gas (Metropolis) Bill*, PP, 1860 (417), xxi, QQ. 4,048, 4,090 [Manager of Camberwell public lights]. The South Metropolitan subsequently absorbed the Surrey Consumers' Gas Company (1879), the Phoenix Gas Company (1880), and two Woolwich companies (1885).

37 Formed in 1854–5 and incorporated in 1858.

148 38 Between 1885 and 1898 the numbers of such stoves grew from 3,499 to 40,601 (*S.C. on Metropolis Gas Companies*, PP, 1899 (294), lxxx, Appendix No. 4).

39 Chubb, 365. The common dip candle, which normally provided the only artificial light, was relatively expensive: at 6d. a pound such candles gave 5¾ hours light for a penny; but comparable illumination by gas at 3s. 9d. per 1,000 cubic feet cost a penny for 52 hours.

40 B, vii (1849), 221.

41 4 shop-fronts, 7 shops, 31 houses: *D.S. Returns*.

149 42 For an excellent introductory analysis of this phenomenon, see J. B. Jeffreys, *Retail Trading in Britain, 1850–1950* (1954), Chap. I, and F. G. Pennance and B. S. Yamey, "Competition in the Retail Grocery Trade, 1850–1939," *Economica*, N.S., xxii (1955), 303. Of considerable value are Booth's notes on retail trades, *op. cit.*, Final Volume, Appendix.

43 H. G. Wells, *Experiment in Autobiography* (1937), ii, 65.

44 Kelly's *P.O. London Suburban Directory* (1860).

150 45 The full list also included: tailor, dressmaker, beer retailer, greengrocer, poulterer, glass dealer, hosier, bookseller, corn dealer, shoemaker, stationer, fishmonger, ironmonger, confectioner, marine store dealer, hairdresser, grocer, and cheesemonger.

151 46 The terms are interesting. Wesson's announced itself as the place to go to for ". . . Bibles, Prayer and Hymn Books,

PAGE

Books of every kind . . . every kind of Trinket, Toy, and Table Glass, Toasting Forks and Figures, Dolls, both of Dutch and Parian, also Wood and Waxlike Niggers, Wools and Vases, Phials and Whistles, Files and Horses, Chains and Crosses, Jewellery and Skittles, Fancy Goods from India, China, and Japan, from Paris, Venice, and Dutchland, in fact, from every spot of earth where'er you find a man." The photographer brought to the notice of the "Nobility, Clergy, Gentry, and Inhabitants generally of Camberwell and its surrounding neighbourhood, his Reduced Scale of Charges." (*Simpson's Clapham, Brixton & Camberwell Directory and Court Guide*, 1864.)

151 47 *Green's East Surrey Court Guide, Gazetteer, and County Blue Book* (1875). Jones & Higgins announced a Great Annual Sale in Jan. 1886, Holdron's in Feb. 1889, Messent's (tailors) in Jan. 1890 (Posters).

48 A. R. Bennett, *London and Londoners in the Eighteen-Fifties and Sixties* (1924), 34. The author lived in Camberwell between 1855 and 1860.

49 The following account is based on the various editions of Kelly's *P.O. London Directory* (*County Suburbs*) and *P.O. London Suburban Directory*, which appeared between 1868 and 1911.

152 50 *Census of England & Wales*, 1911. These figures may be compared with similar ones for other parts of London: the City, 6; Westminster, 30; Bethnal Green, 55; Southwark, 65; Battersea, 75; Bermondsey, 80.

153 51 SLP, 14 Aug. 1875; *Household Narrative*, Aug. 1854.

52 SLP, 20 Aug. 1870.

53 See James Greenwood, *Dining with Duke Humphrey; or, Curiosities of Life* [c. 1865], 109 *et seq.*

54 AP, 26-27 Sept. 1861, 21 Sept. 1863.

55 SLP, 1 Nov. 1884.

56 Handbill, 6 May 1889. The company which opened the Palace was The Oriental Palace of Varieties Ltd.: Prospectus, March 1896. There were also Godfrey's Castle Music Hall at 188 Camberwell Road and the Windsor Castle Music Hall at Coopers Road. See L.C.C., *Return of Theatres and Music Halls in the County of London*, 1892.

154 57 SLP, 30 Oct. 1894; W. C. Dendy, "Story of Ye Parish of Camberwell," *Surrey Mag.*, iv (1902), 4.

58 Biograph Theatres Ltd. opened at 121 High Street and 133 Rye Lane, Arthur Burgoyne at 213a Rye Lane; Palace Electrical Theatres Ltd. also had premises at 121 Lordship Lane: *Kelly's Post Office London Directory*, 1911.

PAGE

154 59 J. Hogg, *London as it is* (1837), 306, quoting Police Returns for 1833.

60 L.C.C., *Ret. Licensed Premises in Met. Boroughs*, 1904, 6-7.

155 61 SLP, 1 and 29 Aug. 1896; AP, 27 May 1872.

62 Blanch, 368, where much detail of old inns in the parish is available.

63 F. Willis, *Peace and Dripping Toast* (1950), 40.

64 SLP, 20 June 1874.

65 See H. W. Cole, *Our Commons and Open Spaces* (1866) and Lord Eversley [G. Shaw-Lefevre], *Commons, Forests and Footpaths* (1910). The principal source of information on the surviving open spaces in London is L.C.C., *Ret. of Parks, Open Spaces and Commons in the County of London*, 1892.

66 Eversley, Appdx. 1.

67 In 1849 it was nothing but "a vast deposit of slush and mud of all descriptions": B, vii (1849), 44. The cost of drainage, laying out, and planting was £227: *ibid.*, xvi (1858), 825.

156 68 B, xxvi (1868), 343.

69 SLP, 24 Feb. 1894. The cost was shared between Camberwell Vestry, £20,000, L.C.C., £18,000, Charity Commissioners, £12,000, Lambeth Vestry, £500, Newington Vestry, £250, St George's Vestry, £250.

70 South Grove Shrubbery, Dulwich Library Garden and Addington Square Garden (1897), Cox's Walk and Art Gallery Garden (1898), Sumner Road Recreation Ground (1900), Leyton Square Garden (1901): L.C.C., *Ret. of Open Spaces under 10 acres*, 1903.

71 L.C.C., *Rept. of Conference on Small Open Spaces*, 1899, 11.

72 James Greenwood, *The Wilds of London* (1874), 350.

157 73 *Census of Great Britain, 1851: Report on Religious Worship*, PP, 1852–3 [1690], lxxxix, *passim*. The figures for the rest of London, excluding the City, ranged between 17.9 per cent. for Shoreditch and 48.4 per cent. for Hampstead. The returns were partly invalidated by the churches making their own returns of attendances.

158 74 *S. Lond. Obs.*, 1 July 1876.

159 75 Information from Rev. A. G. Fagg.

76 See C. F. G. Masterman's penetrating commentary on the problems of the churches in South London in Mudie-Smith, 187-214.

77 Every Anglican church in the parish appears to have sustained some decline in congregation since the *British Weekly* census of 1886: *ibid.*, 285.

160 78 Most of the ministers of the Victorian churches and chapels which still survive have been kind enough to supply much

PAGE

detailed and helpful information from their archives or from the personal recollection of members of their congregations. This has provided the basis of the following paragraphs.

160 79 Rye Lane Chapel, *Member's Handbook*, 5.

80 W. R. Greenhalgh, *Camden Church: A Centenary Leaflet* (1944), 3. The chapel became a district church in 1844. It was badly damaged by bombing in Oct. 1940, closing service was held 23 Mar. 1952, and it was demolished in 1956.

81 For this and other information on St Chrysostom's I am indebted to Rev. L. F. Hopkins, Vicar, 1945–56.

82 See the informative little book by Joseph Lock, *The History of Grove Chapel, Camberwell* (1919).

161 83 W. J. A. Hahn (ed.), *A History of the Parish of St John the Evangelist, 1865–1951* (n.d.), 9.

84 [A. M. Robinson & H. G. Cryer], *History of the Parish Church of St Clement, East Dulwich* [1932], 9-11. This donor, who was a City merchant, agreed to pay for the whole of this church if nine others were built out of diocesan funds and other monies. He appears to have played a large part in financing in addition St Saviour's on Coplestone Road (Hahn, 22).

85 Information from Rev. V. Symons.

86 Anon., *Golden Jubilee, 1900–1950*, 4. The church was bombed in 1940.

162 87 *Green's East Surrey Court Guide* (1875), 122.

88 4,891: *Census*, 1871.

163 89 See Booth, 3rd Ser., vi, 20-36.

164 90 See J. W. Adamson, *A Short History of Education* (1919).

165 91 The building programme and the unexpected diversion of anticipated funds to the promotion of technical education caused the original Trustees to look for some corporate body to take over the future management of the school, and in 1894 it passed into the control of the Clothworkers' Company: this was in sole control until 1909, when the L.C.C. was represented on the governing body. From the 1880s the school took a few girls who had earned School Board scholarships; by 1914 these just outnumbered the fee-payers. See [F. E. Grimshaw *et als*], *The Story of the Mary Datchelor School, 1877–1957* (1957).

92 W. Young, *The History of Dulwich College* (1889), i, 277, 446-8.

93 Blanch, 263. All unattributed information in this section has been obtained from this source.

166 94 According to age and whether the pupil resided in one of four specified parishes.

PAGE

166 95 See D. H. Allport's excellent history, *A Short History of Wilson's Grammar School* (1951).

167 96 Blanch, 242-4. The Congregational Church school authorities took a census of children between 3 and 18 living around Camberwell Green in 1856, and discovered that out of a total of 403 children 181 were already attending school: *The Story of a Hundred Years* [1911], 22.

97 *Ragged Sch. Union Mag.*, iii (1851), 208; vi (1854), 100; x (1858), 184-8.

98 SLP, 19 Apr. 1877.

168 99 Hahn, 67-9.

100 SLP, 12 Apr. 1877.

101 See F. Willis, *Peace and Dripping Toast* (1950), 48 *et seq.* for a vivid recollection of one of these. For another, see William Margrie's diverting history, *Rosemary Street* (1923), reprinted with additional material in *Roses and Kippers* (1930). The School Log Books, almost all of which are now deposited in the Record Office at County Hall, provide very detailed information on staffing, enrolments, curricula, etc., and occasionally provide some oblique commentaries on the social complexion of the districts they served.

CHAPTER VII

169 1 For more details see Edward Walford's *The Southern Suburbs* in Walter Thornbury's six volume collection *Old and New London* [1873–8], vi, Chaps. XIX-XXII; and Sir Walter Besant's *South London* (1899) and *London South of the Thames* (1912), Chaps. VIII, XIII, XXIII: these have been used freely in writing this chapter. Recent topographies which contain useful references to the Victorian period are: S. P. Myers, *London South of the River* (1949), H. Williams, *South London* (1949), D. H. Allport, *Dulwich Village* (ed. 2, 1950)—which is very useful—N. Pevsner, *The Buildings of England: London except the Cities of London and Westminster* (1952), and O. M. Walker, *A Tour of Camberwell* (1954). There are also numerous books, like [W. S. Clarke], *The Suburban Homes of London* (1881), P. Fitzgerald, *London City Suburbs* (1893), and Mrs A. G. Bell's *The Skirts of the Great City* (1907), which contain information and illustrations not to be found elsewhere.

2 The best maps of all are the scrupulously prepared Tithe Redemption Plan (1842), based on a survey done in 1837–8 (kept at Tithe Redemption Commission, 33/37 Finsbury Sq., E.C.2), and the Ordnance Survey 1/1056 or 5 feet = 1

PAGE

mile, published in 1874–6 but based on surveys made in 1871 and soon after (sometimes known as the Ground Plan of London, 1870, and kept by the Valuer to the Council, County Hall, S.E.1). Other reliable maps, though inevitably containing some out-of-date information, are by Dewhirst (1842), Cruchley (1847), and Smith (1855); particularly useful is Stanford's Library Map of London and its Suburbs (1886). There are in addition many estate maps with auction particulars at the Minet Library, and maps for special purposes such as transport developments are contained in various parliamentary papers, especially the *R.C. on London Traffic*, PP, 1906, xli.

171 3 See J. Summerson, *Georgian London* (1945), 269-271.

172 4 Bombed in 1940.

175 5 R. S. R. Fitter, *London's Birds* (1949), 144. For a fascinating and beautifully illustrated account of the impact of the expanding suburbs on the existing wild life see also Mr Fitter's *London's Natural History* (1945).

180 6 It was founded in 1827, but was not completed until the North Wing was added in 1833; there were a number of subsequent additions and by 1880 consisted of 170 dwellings.

7 No population was assigned to it until 1872.

182 8 The social characteristics of particular districts in this period have been obtained from the contemporary survey of Booth, 1st Ser., ii, 50-53.

183 9 A. Amos & W. W. Hough, *The Cambridge Mission to South London* (1904), 54-5.

184 10 Destroyed by bombing in 1940.

11 Now bodily removed to Biggin Hill: see V. Symons, *The Moving Church* (1956).

12 SLP, 17 Jan. 1885.

189 13 See J. M. Richards, *Castles on the Ground* (1946) and W. Macqueen-Pope, *Back Numbers* (1954).

14 Badly damaged by bombing in 1940, but since restored.

15 Partially destroyed by bombing in 1940, but re-opened in 1957.

16 Bombed in 1940.

17 Bombed in 1944, but since restored.

18 The Pentecostal Sumner Road Chapel since 1921.

190 19 Bombed in 1940, but now reconstructed.

20 SLP, 1 Nov. 1884.

21 There is a vivid description of the village around 1900 in Richard Church's *Over the Bridge* (1955), 227. In it, too, he describes the experience of his family's removal and social advancement from a condition of semi-detachment in the

PAGE

marshes of Battersea to detached, double-fronted estate at "Gardencourt," Ruskin Walk.

190 22 See E. T. Cook, *Homes and Haunts of John Ruskin* (1912), 16-17.

191 23 B, xxvi (1868), 521 (for plans and front elevation see pp. 530-1).

24 B, xlvii (1884—II), 252.

25 B, xxxvi (1878), 547, 572.

26 H. D. Lowry & T. S. C. Crowther, "Suburban London: (1) The Life of Camberwell," *Windsor Mag.*, July 1895, 86.

192 27 "My Countrymen," *Cornhill Mag.*, Feb. 1866. I owe this reference to my colleague, Mr P. A. W. Collins.

28 The Watergate Classics edition (1947) contains a valuable introduction by William Plomer.

29 See "The Burden of London" in *In Peril of Change* [1905] and "The Suburbans" in *The Condition of England* (1909); also, C. & A. Williams-Ellis, *The Pleasures of Architecture* (Rev. ed., 1954), 31.

30 It is not possible to give a comparative account of suburban development by means of rateable values because the bases of assessment varied so much from time to time and place to place. For data for the period 1830 to 1857 see PP, 1857–8 (208), xlix, Pt. 1.

31 G. L. Gomme, "Local Taxation in London," JRSS, lxi (1898), 487. The highest proportions of all the suburbs were registered by Plumstead (52 per cent.) and Bromley (45 per cent.); the lowest by Kidbrook (1 per cent.) and Hampstead (2 per cent.).

32 T. A. Welton, *England's Recent Progress* (1911), 592.

LOCAL INDEX

GENERAL INDEX

Street Plan and Principal Estates

KEY TO ESTATES

1. Avondale Square
2. Bailey's
3. Barkworth Road
4. Blake's Road
5. Bowyer-Smijth
6. British Empire Mutual Life Assurance Company's
7. Brunswick Park (including Glebe)
8. Bushey Hill
9. de Crespigny
10. Denmark Park
11. Domville Grove
12. Dragon Road
13. Dulwich College
14. Dulwich House
15. Dulwich Manor House (Alleyn Park)
16. Edmond's (part)
17. Friern Manor Farm
18. Grenard Road
19. Minet
20. Newlands
21. Peckham Rye
22. Rolls'
23. Sandover Road
24. Selwyn (part)
25. Sultan Street
26. Talfourd Road
27. Trafalgar Avenue
28. Vicarage Grove
29. Waverley Park
30. Worlingham Road